D0723776

ADVANCE PRAISE FOR *NEW CALIFORNIA WRITING 2012*

"These stories and poems are as expansive as California itself, and every bit as surprising. They take us to hidden places, inner worlds, and other worlds. I love these authors for their audacity, for gripping and stunning and leaving me with new insights about the land and the beings—human and otherwise—that shape and reshape our boundaries. And I love Heyday for continuing to carry the vision."

—Darla Hillard, author of *Vanishing Tracks: Four Years Among the Snow Leopards of Nepal*

"Gayle Wattawa has compiled a wholly satisfying literary banquet: short stories, memoirs, poems, and lyric essays by writers exploring ties to the land, politics, and people of this enthralling state. These are bold California stories with universal appeal."

—Katherine A. Briccetti, author of *Blood Strangers: A Memoir*

"As this great anthology shows and re-shows in ways both subtle and unmistakable, the vitality and diversity of California's literature does the landscape proud."

—Bruce Patterson, author of *Turned Round in My Boots: A Memoir*

"This collection harvests the fresh and the local. For California readers, its publication each year is perhaps a bit like the annual release of Beaujolais, the drink-it-while-it's-young wine of the French countryside. The poetry and prose here is what's in the markets right now this year, produced in our neighborhood. Each poem or story or essay earns its place in this collection by its own manner of delighting or startling, informing, chastening, gladdening."

—Louis B. Jones, author of *Ordinary Money: A Novel*

"Here's our most populous, most unpredictable, and—let's face it—most important state in all its wondrous and cranky contradictions. It takes a lifetime to reckon with California. *New California Writing* is a perfect place to begin."

—Fred Setterberg, author of *Lunch Bucket Paradise: A True-Life Novel*

"Shiny red sports cars and flying Mexicans, a journalist who loves lemons and an actress who might do anything. Here are new stories about California, the promised land, the tawdry land, the land of contradictions, where anything is possible. The selections are eclectic and moving and artful—Gayle Wattawa has arranged a heady bouquet of new work."

—Beth Alvarado, author of *Anthropologies: A Family Memoir*

"*New California Writing 2012* bravely and powerfully digs beneath the smoking mirror of a faded California Dream and reveals, with grit, humor, tenderness, and rage, an astonishing cacophony of truths and lives of a California we never knew before."

—Ruth Nolan, editor of *No Place for a Puritan: The Literature of California's Deserts*

"This is a stunning collection of voices charged with humor and wit, desire and sorrow. With each piece, I found myself weeping, falling, and floating—as I rediscovered California, again and again."

—Burlee Vang, founder of the Hmong American Writers' Circle and author of *The Dead I Know: Incantation for Rebirth*

"*New California Writing 2012* offers a rewarding and panoramic vision of the Golden State that, like Puchner's affection for California's dreamers and pioneering spirit, 'makes me feel at home.'"

—Victoria Patterson, author of *This Vacant Paradise: A Novel*

"From her prehistoric desert tortoises to her collapsed dreams of Golden State fortune hunters, from the Coast Miwok's Sonoma Mountain to the furious highways of the Pacific's ghostly shores, this collection is an electric—and eclectic—origin song from the California that inhabits us all."

—Jennifer Elise Foerster, Wallace Stegner Fellow in Poetry

"California of faultlines, California of losses, California of apocalypses, California of dreams. California of broken dreams. California our national Rorschach, our continent's end, our western gateway. What a pleasure to see our geographically young and restless state captured in its contradictions and multitudes. New California Writing is a series whose installments I eagerly anticipate."

—Tess Taylor, author of *The Misremembered World*

NEW CALIFORNIA WRITING

2012

NEW CALIFORNIA WRITING

2012

Edited by Gayle Wattawa

Foreword by David Kipen

HEYDAY, BERKELEY, CALIFORNIA

Library of Congress Cataloging-in-Publication Data

New California writing 2012 / edited by Gayle Wattawa; foreword by David Kipen.

p. cm.

Includes index.

ISBN 978-1-59714-189-5 (pbk. : alk. paper)

1. California—Literary collections. I. Wattawa, Gayle.

PS571.C2N474 2012

810.8'09794—dc23 20110485199

Cover Photo: @ 2011 iStockphoto.com/jonathansloane
Cover Design: Lorraine Rath
Interior Design/Typesetting: Leigh McLellan Design
Printing and Binding: Thomson-Shore, Dexter, MI

Orders, inquiries, and correspondence should be addressed to:

Heyday
P.O. Box 9145, Berkeley, CA 94709
(510) 549-3564, Fax (510) 549-1889
www.heydaybooks.com

10 9 8 7 6 5 4 3 2 1

CONTENTS

FOREWORD

David Kipen

California
Tumbles into the sea
That'll be the day I go
Back to Annandale.

—"MY OLD SCHOOL,"
DONALD FAGEN AND WALTER BECKER

And if California slides into the ocean
Like the mystics and statistics say it will
I predict this motel will be standing
Until I pay my bill.

—"DESPERADOS UNDER THE EAVES,"
WARREN ZEVON

Under the paving-stones, the beach!

—PARIS GRAFFITO, 1968, EPIGRAPH TO
THOMAS PYNCHON'S *INHERENT VICE*

AS I WRITE these lines, the San Pedro neighborhood of Los Angeles is tumbling into the sea. Or not tumbling but wading, tentatively, a toe at a time, like a tenderfoot who'd much rather stay back on shore, where it's warm. Of course, the whole country feels like it's capsizing. California, as it always does, is just getting there first. For California writers, of course, the Great Depression is already back. Of the forty-three pretty sensational writers collected here, I count fewer than one in five who can be said to make a living at the trade. Partly that represents editor Gayle Wattawa's resourcefulness in beating the bushes, her disinclination to merely recycle the contributors' pages from *New California Writing 2011*. But even allowing for California's endlessly replenished reserves of new, un-sinecured, moonlighting talent, that's a lot of good writers spending a lot of time doing too much else besides writing.

Writers need life experience, yes. But they also need practice, and it's hard, though by no means impossible, to put in your desk time while busing tables or answering phones. It may be even harder while you're writing technical manuals or press releases, and especially while you're teaching others how to write. And because job-hunting is just another job—albeit without benefit of companionship or a paycheck—writing while unemployed is no picnic either. Mystified, shamed, I can only marvel at how the predominantly part-time writers gathered here manage to write so well.

How they would have kept body and soul together seventy-five years ago, during the first great depression, makes for less of a mystery: Their government would have found needful, useful work for them to do. I've gone on elsewhere about the glories and mercies of the original Federal Writers Project—most recently in last year's reissues of the WPA guides to Los Angeles and San Francisco—so I'll try not to overdo it here. Plenty of non-writers need work nowadays too, and with even fewer non-writing jobs per capita to go around. Too much bellyaching about poor writers starts sounding unseemly.

But I still can't help woolgathering about what a strong new WPA guide to California the contributors assembled here might put together. The WPA's original *California: A Guide to the Golden State* (unlike California's two longest city guides, still criminally out of print) fell roughly into three sections. The first focused on the history of California, and just the thought of turning some of these writers loose on our state's new true stories makes my mouth water like a Mojave mirage.

Manuel Muñoz, for instance, to go by his character study here from *What You See in the Dark*—an empathic conjuring of *Psycho*-era, Stockton-born Janet Leigh—is all but besotted by our shared past, its facts and its ghosts both. Can't you just imagine what he'd do with some of California's less storied heroes and villains? Or, for that matter, what he'd do with a contemporary enigma like Paul Thomas Anderson, who from *Boogie Nights* to *There Will Be Blood* hasn't made a movie yet that wasn't Californian down to its very sprocket-holes?

Or take T. C. Boyle, who long before the snatch here from *When the Killing's Done* was regularly demonstrating a wicked anthropologist's gift for nailing regional subcultures in collision—that, plus the true lore-maven's compulsion to trace any battleground back to its mistiest beginnings. Well, it so happens the whole middle section of *A Guide to the Golden State* brims with nothing but essays about cities, towns, and other places. Wouldn't you just love to read Boyle on Bolinas, or Bigfoot country, or Path 15, the mid-state electricity bottleneck that keeps Northern and Southern California literally incompatible?

And what about the guide's last section, cherishably devoted to California car trips from stem to stern? What Californiologist worth his road salt wouldn't want to read Caitlin Flanagan—so savvy in "The Madness of Cesar Chavez" about Route 99 and the broken promises of Golden State liberalism—write on the I-395 corridor, where this bluest of blue states blushes bright red? Or read Daniel Orozco ("The Bridge") on high-speed rail, or Michael Pollan ("The 36-Hour Dinner Party") on native plant nativism, or Mariah K. Young ("Masha'allah") on anything she pleases?

This is supposed to be a book introduction, I know, not a book prospectus. But the thought that more than half the talent so bountifully on display here is not just unsung but quite possibly uninsured is enough to make any civilized person crazy. Outrageously heartrending California stories are going untold at the precise hour that great California storytelling talent is going unemployed.

What will it take to wake up a state full of readers to the Great Writers' Depression around us? Does T. C. Boyle have to move back in with his parents? That may not happen right away. What will happen—is already happening—is that newspapers are gasping for breath. Established campus literary magazines are evaporating. Bookstores and libraries, the indicator species of a viable statewide literary culture, are eroding faster than the San Pedro bluff—where they're not somehow converging, that is, like in a little hybrid Boyle Heights shop I know of.

To help arrest this slide, I regretfully have to invite those of you not blessed with an extra half a million dollars or so to spare to skip ahead early to Eric Puchner's terrific curtain-raiser of an essay, and leave me here to talk a little turkey. There now, that aired the room out nicely, didn't it? For the rest of you still with me, I have a proposal. Read *New California Writing 2012* right now. If you don't care for it, fine. But if you do—if you agree that these writers are too good, and California today too unchronicled, to just hope they'll keep writing and not move out of state, or waste away from scurvy—come sit here a minute by the barrelhead with me.

The proposal is this: What if you fronted these scribblers just enough dough to spend a year or so writing a WPA guide to California today? Think about it. Most of 'em aren't exactly geezers, so the health costs might not break the bank. A few miraculously still have day jobs for the time being and could afford to say no. But the rest, working together, could hold a nonfiction mirror up to contemporary California that would make your head spin.

That's it. No hard sell. At the very least, such a book might help pass the time between now and the release of *New California Writing 2013,* for which I'm already greedy. And it might give Californians—readers and writers, in San Pedro or anywhere else—something better to do than just wait around for the horizon to go crooked.

David Kipen
Libros Schmibros
Boyle Heights, CA

Writer, editor, translator, and broadcaster **DAVID KIPEN**—founder of Libros Schmibros, a lending library/used book shop in the Boyle Heights neighborhood of Los Angeles—developed the nationwide Big Read program as the National Endowment for the Arts' director of literature. He worked for the *San Francisco Chronicle* for seven years as its book editor and critic and is also the author of *The Schreiber Theory: A Radical Rewrite of American Film History.*

ACKNOWLEDGMENTS

MY SINCERE THANKS go to everyone who offered their own work for consideration or nominated the work of others; once again, the selection process was an exhilarating, then agonizing affair. I am grateful to the contributors, their agents, and their publishers for kind permission to reproduce these selections—not to mention the magazines and book publishers who originally found and published such fine work. Thanks go to great Heyday friend David Kipen for writing the foreword to this edition. Early on, volunteer Karen Sorensen and intern Scott Rasmussen were helpful; thanks also to Cheryl Klein, Jeff Lustig, Michael McCone, and George Young for their eye-opening suggestions. NewPages.com is an amazing resource for new literature. Susan Straight pointed me toward several of the wonderfully promising young writers represented in these pages; she is, without doubt, our brightest and most generous literary star in California. Malcolm Margolin continuously challenged me to vary the collection's contents and to take risks; his influence is discernible throughout. I'm grateful to colleagues Lorraine Rath and Leigh McLellan for giving this collection its edgy but respectable look, to Lisa K. Marietta for her editorial eagle eye, and to Diane Lee, without whom I'd probably go crazy. I am, in fact, ridiculously in debt to everyone in my posse of family, friends, and coworkers: cheers to partners in crime, near and far.

SCHEMES OF MY FATHER

Eric Puchner

I WAS TWELVE THE first time I visited California, which as far as I was concerned was twelve years too late. I could barely sit still during the plane ride, thinking of all the girls I was going to have sex with once I became a Californian, the coolness that would drip from my every freckled pore. My father had recently moved to L.A. for the job of his dreams, and now my mom and I were flying out to visit him before returning to Baltimore to pack up the house and bid farewell to our lame eastern selves. I knew from my dad's tickled voice on the phone that something marvelous had happened to him and that it had to do with the money he was making or perhaps the warm ocean breeze ruffling his hair in the pictures he'd sent.

When he picked us up at the airport, I barely recognized him. He was wearing prescription sunglasses, some snazzy titanium numbers that said CARRERA on one lens, and his normally pink face was tanned from all the tennis he'd been playing. He had his shirt undone to the third button. Even his hair looked different: lighter and rakishly askew. He'd always been irresistible to me, but now I found him outright glamorous.

He drove us to the house he'd rented in Rolling Hills, a tony gated community perched above the cliffs of the Palos Verdes Peninsula. It was a beautiful summer day, and you could smell the salt air from the Pacific coming through the window. There was none of that Maryland mugginess that made you drip downstairs in the middle of the night and stick your head in the freezer. My siblings were all older than I was, getting ready to return to their boring eastern colleges, and I felt badly for them that they wouldn't be living out here with me in the land of endless summer.

I don't think I realized how rich we'd become until the moment we pulled up to the entrance of Rolling Hills and the man in the little guardhouse actually tipped his cap. The gate lifted, ushering us into someone's vision of paradise. By "someone's" I guess I mean my father's. There were horse trails and faux hacienda signs and old wagon wheels sitting in people's yards in islands of unmown grass, like the Hollywood back lot for some Waspy New England burg. And yet it was Californian through and through, the ranch-style homes as flat and gargantuan as UFOs. We slowed down to pass a group of horseback riders in skin-tight pants, and even the manure plopping from their horses seemed expensive to me, better smelling than the dogshit smearing our sidewalk in Baltimore.

Eventually we pulled into the driveway of our house. I got out of the car and was greeted by an enormous bird with a sapphire neck and a tail as long as a surfboard. It peered at me nonchalantly for a minute and then dragged itself into the bushes.

"Was that a peacock?" I asked.

"A wild one," my father said. "They're everywhere around here."

There was pride in his face, a touch of giddiness. He grinned, and I don't remember having seen my father look so happy before. My mom and I couldn't help grinning back. It was like he'd cooked this all up especially for us—the peacocks, the ocean breeze, the rolling-in-it hills. We were Californians now, a part of his dream.

People like my father will always think of California as a manifestation of their dreams, and in this respect he wasn't too different from the California dreamers of the past. Even the name itself—which first appeared in *Las Sergas de Esplandián,* a Spanish romance novel from the sixteenth century—was meant to make the mouth water with the promise of untold treasure. "California," as portrayed in the novel, was an island paradise populated only by women with "hardy bodies." Everything they owned was precious, because "in the whole island, there was no metal but gold." In other words, there were two girls for every boy, and the living was easy. From the gold rush to the dot-com boom, the myth of an earthly paradise welling over with riches and beautiful natives has proved remarkably durable.

These days, explorers to California will encounter a very different island. Twenty-five billion dollars of estimated debt and an unemployment rate topping 12 percent. An elementary-school system ranked forty-eighth in the nation. Subdivisions turned into ghost towns, and tens of thousands of families who've lost their homes. All this, if you believe the press, is proof of California's "implosion," as if we were victims of an overnight disaster. But the truth is, there've always been two Golden States: the one we yearn for and the one that most Californians wake up to every morning. As Woody Guthrie put it seventy years ago: *California is a Garden of Eden, a paradise to live in or see. / But believe it or not, you won't find it so hot / If you ain't got the do re mi.*

My father, who risked all our do re mi in pursuit of his own California dream, is a case in point. He'd been doing very well in Baltimore, earning six figures as the vice president of a bank, but he tossed his job out the window when some Reaganomics-drunk investor ("an admirer," my father called him) phoned him out of the blue to see if he wanted to direct a savings and loan out west. And for a while after we moved, he seemed to live up to the opulent vision he'd dazzled me with on my first visit. Unsatisfied with our first house in Rolling Hills, he leased us a big Mediterranean nearby for $5,000 a month, roughly $11,000 today. There was a swimming pool and a tennis court and a barn where my father put up a pen for his two hunting dogs. I didn't know what he was doing to make so much money, but I wholeheartedly endorsed it. In particular, I endorsed his expanding fleet of European sports cars, which he liked to bring to professional sporting events and rev over and over again in the parking lot to impress people, so loudly and relentlessly that he once ran out of gas.

One of these cars was a Lotus Esprit, the same kind that turns into a submarine in *The Spy Who Loved Me*. In 1983, I was susceptible to anything with four wheels and my father's esteem. One look at the Lotus and I was head over heels. Just the name itself—French and alliterative and sexy as a girl's—could send me into a swoon. When no one was home, I'd steal the spare set of keys from my parents' room and head out to the driveway in my Ray-Bans, revving the engine in neutral as I'd seen my father do, working the mahogany gearshift and pretending to screech around hairpin turns. The creamy smell of leather grew with the heat, and to this day I associate it with my father's California, the smell of sun and power and superfluous luxury.

Then there was my dad himself, who seemed as glamorous in many ways as his car. He wore driving gloves and those Porsche Carrera sunglasses and dressed impeccably in Brooks Brothers suits, a picture of blue-blooded dapperness. On the weekends, he traded in his tie for an ascot, which he tucked into his shirt like a scarf. He was the fastest driver I've ever seen, slaloming through freeway traffic or tailgating anyone in the left lane who wasn't doing a hundred. Once he terrified one of my friends so badly that she grabbed the parking brake and almost caused an accident. My dad blew up at her and made her cry. At the time, I thought his anger was entirely justified.

One morning—I must have been fourteen by then—I woke up and went outside for a spin, to captain the Lotus through my dreams, and discovered the car was gone. Vanished. My father never took it to work, never moved it from its allotted space behind the house except to impress people on the weekends. I glanced around, but nothing else seemed strange: The marine layer I'd grown accustomed to had begun to burn off, leaving a pondlike shimmer on the tennis court. My father's shorthaired pointers whimpered in their cage. From the canyon below our house, where the older kids in the neighborhood went to drink beer, came the lonely meows of a peacock. I peeked in the garage, but the Lotus wasn't there either. At lunch I asked my mom about it, and she said that my father had decided to sell the car. She fidgeted as she told me this, as if she could barely look me in the eye. My mom's face that day—her strange, antsy embarrassment—feels to me now like the beginning of the end.

My father didn't let on that anything was amiss. I knew nothing about the real estate crash, of course, or that savings and loans like my father's were going bankrupt all over the country, the calamitous tide of fraud and reckless lending that would become the S&L crisis. I didn't know that it would culminate in the failure of 1,043 S&L's or cost taxpayers over $120 billion to repair the damage. In Baltimore, at least, my dad had taken me to his office occasionally, a breathtakingly messy place that smelled like fast food and B.O. and Xerox ink, the floor carpeted with documents I wasn't allowed to step on. Strangely, though, after we moved, he never once brought me to his work. To this day, my own mother can't tell me a thing about what he was doing those years in California. As far as I was concerned, the secrecy added to his glamour. But even before more things began to disappear—the pool table and tennis lessons and Ferrari sedan he kept in the garage—the truth of my father's failure came out in subtler ways.

Not long after the Lotus vanished from the driveway, he took me to a barbecue at a colleague's beach club in Newport Beach. I was flattered. He rarely spent time with me one-on-one, too busy living out his fantasy to take much notice of me. What I wanted more than anything was for this dashing figure to tell me I was part of that fantasy—that he cared about me, in some precious way, as much as his cars. I knew he was capable of such adoration, because he mooned over my older brother, whose dark handsomeness and hard-drinking exploits were far more interesting to him than my good grades and admiration. He'd talk about how, *twice* in two years, my brother had crashed the Alfa Romeo he'd bought him, and my father couldn't help beaming with pride. I would have done just about anything to make his face look like that.

At the beach club, my father circled the parking lot a couple of times in the car he drove most often, a Porsche 928. I don't know why he wanted to impress the guests so badly, but I suspect it had something to do with the vision of Californian life arrayed so platonically before us: the mothers in bikinis, the *thwock* of Smashballs, the smell of sun lotion mixed with the briny breeze from the ocean, whose gentle waves seemed to frost the sand like a cake. Boys in Jams and rope bracelets slurped Cokes or played volleyball or skimboarded across the wash with sunglasses on. These of course were the effortlessly tan Californian kids

I so admired and feared, the ones who knew how to surf and skateboard and had managed to lose their virginities at preposterously young ages, generally to their older sisters' friends. They said "gnarly" with a straight face and spoke in a diabetic drawl that made each word seem like a message washed up on the beach. No matter how hard I tried, I couldn't get tan, and though I burned my face and arms every summer to a freckled variant of brown, my legs were hopelessly immune to the sun's rays. Somehow my father's legs were even whiter. In shorts he looked like a half-finished page in a coloring book. I'm guessing they were his secret shame, proof of the midwestern German heritage he longed to escape.

That afternoon he was wearing tennis shorts. As we were waiting for hamburgers from the grill, I overheard the host tell him he needed to get some color on his legs.

"No thanks," my dad said, grinning. "I try to keep them as far from colored as possible."

The man smiled but took a step backward, busying himself with the spatula. I had never heard my father say the word *colored* before; for some reason, the racism shocked me less than the antiquated weirdness of the term. But what really startled me was my dad's face, which, as we stood there waiting for our host to look up from the grill, turned pink as a grapefruit. The more the man ignored us, the pinker it became. When he finally served us our burgers, my dad mumbled out a thank you, avoiding his eyes.

Later, we sat in the sand as the other kids my age played a game of beach volleyball. My father must have seen an opening of some kind, because to my great embarrassment he stood up between matches and asked if I could join in. I tried to refuse, but there was no way to do so without seeming like even more of a loser. I was a decent athlete—I'd played lacrosse and hockey in Baltimore—but did not understand the most basic mechanics involved in keeping a ball up in the air with my forearms. While the other kids set and dug and belly flopped for shots, I stood in the corner of the court, praying that the ball would miraculously avoid my jurisdiction. Finally someone spiked the ball right at me, and I did something tragic. I caught it. I glanced at my father, still clutching the thing to my stomach. His eyes were squinched up, fixed somewhere near my feet, as if he couldn't stand to look me in the face. It took me a second to realize he was staring at my legs.

At the time, my father's shame was overshadowed by the disgrace I felt in front of my teammates. Now, though, when I'm watering the plants or jogging around the reservoir near my house, I'll think of my father's face that day and feel the punch of that ball in my stomach. I'll fantasize about all the things I might have done, like clock him in the teeth. Perhaps—at least I tell myself this, I insist on it, because the memory still hurts me deeply—he was really making the face at himself.

Before that, I'd often questioned whether I belonged in California, but that day at the beach was the first time I questioned whether my father belonged there as well. I began to question other things about him, too. Growing up, I'd more or less subscribed to his Gatsbyesque invention of himself as an aristocrat. There were the ascots, of course, usually paired with tweed. He liked to go bird hunting on the weekends, despite being a terrible shot. For a brief period he insisted we dress up for dinner every night, which for my brother and me meant coats and ties. He boarded horses in the country and prodded my oldest sister to take up polo. He refused to let us wear baseball caps indoors and liked to keep a Manwich-thick wad of cash in his billfold, flaunting it in front of cashiers. Even before the ascots and the polo, he'd saddled his children with increasingly absurd names meant to conjure riding breeches and hunt clubs: Alexander, Laurel, Pendleton, and his pièce de résistance, my own: Roderic. I didn't know that my dad had been one of the poorest kids at his wealthy private school in Milwaukee, and so I'd always accepted these affectations as part of my father's identity, as essential to who he was as his love of bratwurst.

Now, though, his blue-blooded habits began to seem absurd. For the first time I saw them in the same light as my own desperate attempts to fit in, which had begun to seem absurd to me as well. Despite an aggressive marketing campaign, I'd failed to become Californian in a way that would convince anyone but the drunkest tourist. I wore jungle-print Vans and shirts with wooden buttons and Wayfarers that were also made, inexplicably, of wood. I had a white Op poncho that I liked to wear with nothing underneath, thinking I looked like Jim Morrison on the cover of *Morrison Hotel.* My moment of reckoning came when I was at the mall with my best friend, Will, another East Coast transplant, and some surfers called me a "dingleberry." I had to ask Will what a dingleberry was, and his graphic description made such an impression on me that I went home and took off all my clothes and hid my jungle-print Vans at the back of the closet.

Soon after that, I bought my first punk record—*Los Angeles,* by X—and began to discover another California, one far removed from the beach bunnies and slack-eyed surfers who'd seemed to me like the epitome of West Coast cool. Minutemen, Black Flag, the Dream Syndicate: The songs coming out of my turntable were about as unsunny as could be, noisy and weird and full of anger at the well-tanned rich. And the singers, Californians themselves, weren't afraid to be smart. I started dressing like my old self again, slipping off to Hollywood clubs whenever I could, amazed at all the pale, black-booted kids pogoing in flannel. It was a culture as distant from my dad's beach-club ambitions as you can possibly imagine.

It's this real California—and not the one my father invented for us—that I still call home, one that's closer to my heart than any place on earth. There's something about my father's love for the state, no matter how misdirected it was, that seems to have seeped into my blood. Or perhaps it's the love itself that I love. Which is to say: Even if the dream isn't real, the dreamers are. There's something about the struggling actors and screenwriters and immigrants who live here, the pioneer spirit that despite everything still brings people to the edge of America in search of success, that makes me feel at home.

Sometimes, when I'm feeling stressed-out about my life in L.A. or my children's futures, I drive up to Griffith Observatory on a clear day and stand in the cool shadow of its dome, staring out at the enormous city below, from the snowcapped San Gabriels hovering like a mirage over the skyscrapers downtown to the Pacific in the distance. I used to get stoned here with my high school friends and watch the sun go down over the ocean, turning the city into a valley of lights, and the shiver of amazement I used to feel still slinks across my scalp, the wonder that one city could hold so much life in its pocket.

My father would never have driven to Griffith Park to check out the view; he didn't have any interest in peeling back the layers of myth and visiting the actual city. At the time, I had no idea how badly things were going for him—no idea that he was being sued by former partners or that his own board of directors had fired him. For a year or so, my dad was tied up in legal battles, sinking deeper and deeper into debt. As the California he adored began to betray him, he responded like a jilted lover, making himself as noticeable as possible. He invested in personalized license plates based on our last name, which he shortened to POOK. Between my mom and older siblings, we still had several cars, and for a brief period there were POOKs 1 through 5. Sometimes he'd show up at my soccer games or cross-country meets in POOK 1, his Porsche, which he would park on the grass for everyone to admire. He'd root for me as I played, yelling *Thataboy, Puchner!* until he was hoarse. I didn't want anything to do with him or his cars, as embarrassing to me now as jungle-print Vans. After the game, I'd run off the field without saying hello.

Our last Christmas in Rolling Hills, before we moved to a duplex near the shopping mall, my father decided that he wanted to buy me a road bike. By then he must have been close to broke, siphoning off the money my grandparents had left to me and my siblings. I don't know how he got the idea of cycling into his head, but I can imagine how iconically Californian the sport must have seemed to him. You couldn't drive down a street of Palos Verdes without seeing packs of men in Lycra outfits, hunched over their bikes in those itty-bitty caps. To me, whose California now consisted of *Repo Man* and John Fante and albums about working-class strife, the whole sport seemed as stupid as playing golf. Still, my father seemed to think this was the perfect gift, and I was loathe to break his heart. In truth, all I'd ever wanted from him was his pride and attention. Even when he was rooting for me on the soccer field or introducing me by citing my academic "accomplishments," it always seemed like another way of revving his engine.

We went to a fancy bike shop in Orange County, with rows of bicycles hanging from the ceiling. I couldn't tell a crank from a chain-wheel, but my dad insisted on describing me as "extremely athletic." The salesman steered us to a bike on the floor at the front of the shop.

"This is our entry-level model. A real nice bit of engineering for the price."

My dad looked at the price tag dangling from its seat. The bike seemed extravagant, more than I would ever need, but my dad was unimpressed. "Do you have anything else?" he asked.

The salesman looked at my father. For the first time, he seemed to take in my father's clothes, his eyes snagging on the ascot stuffed into his shirt. "I could sell you something you don't need, but I think for the novice rider, this is an ideal bike."

My father frowned. "Let's see what else you have."

The salesman glanced at me and raised his eyebrows. He did not understand that he'd thrown down the gauntlet. He showed us bike after bike, each one more beautiful than the last; my dad would listen intently to the salesman's spiel, to jargon he couldn't possibly have understood, and then insist on seeing something more expensive, "just to know what our options are." Eventually we arrived at a baby blue frame hanging by itself at the rear of the store. It looked like a chandelier, something you shouldn't touch. There was no price tag on it—only the name, Colnago, paired with a perfect white shamrock. I admit to feeling a twirl of longing. It was the same frame, the salesman explained, that somebody had ridden in the Tour de France. My dad inspected the bike with an expression that can only be described as proprietary.

He asked how much it was, but I could tell he'd already made up his mind. The salesman took him aside. My dad's face changed. He looked frightened, even a little sick.

"Dad, I don't need a bike like that," I told him when the salesman went to ring him up.

"No use getting a bike you'll outgrow."

"But this is for someone who, like, *races.*"

He looked at me angrily. "It's for anybody who wants it."

In the parking lot, trying to fit the bike into the back of his Porsche, my father seemed withdrawn. The sky was big and cloudless, the same heartbreaking blue as the bike he'd just bought. It was January; in Baltimore we would have been shoveling snow from the driveway. When I glanced back at the shop, the salesmen were smiling to themselves, watching my dad try to wedge the frame over the backseat.

Before leaving L.A., my father told my mom three things: "I'm divorcing you, we're $2 million in debt, and I'm marrying a woman who's pregnant with my child." He'd already tapped into my cousins' inheritance and was rapidly burning through all their money. One of the last times I saw him, he was living in the middle of the Utah desert, squeezed into a condo with a young son and a family of stepchildren, all his belongings auctioned off because he couldn't pay his storage bill. It was the first time I'd visited him in a couple of years. He wore ascots now only on special occasions, content to spend the day in sweats and Mephisto sneakers. By this time I'd worked up a powerful fury at him—for deserting me, for stealing my cousins' money, for failing to live up to the glamorous image I'd had of him—and could barely look him in the eye.

"How's San Francisco?" he asked. I'd moved there after grad school.

"Beautiful," I said.

"You're teaching at the state university?" he said, with genuine disappointment. "Aren't they all idiots?"

I ignored him.

"But you're on the coast, at least. The ocean. We'll be moving back as soon as I can get on my feet again."

I looked out the window at the empty scrubland stretching to the horizon. Even then, I knew he'd never be going back, that he'd most likely die in a place he felt little affection for. At the time, it seemed to me like just deserts. What I didn't know was how bad things would get—that my stepmother would end up moving to Beverly Hills to work as the personal assistant of an eighty-five-year-old tycoon, a man she would later marry, and sending money home to Utah to support the family. That was an irony I couldn't have imagined: that some nouveau aristocrat in California, living on the estate of my father's dreams, would end up supporting him.

That evening, my father decided he wanted to take me out to dinner. I expected him to change out of his sweatpants, but he sat on the stairs and slipped on his tennis shoes.

"Are you, um, ready?" I asked.

"I just need to find my wallet."

He had some grease stains on his T-shirt. For a moment something caught in my throat. I went into the bathroom to keep him from seeing my face. My dad's wallet was sitting next to the sink. After a minute, I left the bathroom and tried to hand him his wallet, but he dropped it on the stairs. Several driver's licenses spilled out, each with my father's picture on it. He scrambled to put them back, and I pretended not to look. I did not want to think about what sort of con he might be perpetrating, did not want to see how far he had fallen.

I have my own California dream now, much humbler in comparison. It's not a dream of gold-lined shores but a hope—foolhardy, perhaps—that the state will be able to look after my children's basic needs. Not long ago, my daughter's elementary school, one of the best in the city, was forced to squeeze its fourth and fifth graders into a single classroom. This is the new reality, they told us. Reality never really interested my father, or the California fortune hunters of the past, and I can't help blaming them—*him*—for the mess we're in. Read about the S&L crisis that spelled my father's ruin and you'll feel an uncomfortable prickle of déjà vu: unregulated bankers, reckless loans insured by the government, a federal bailout that cost taxpayers billions and spawned a nationwide recession. If one goes to Southern California to see the future, as Alison

Lurie once said, then it's a future that's been showing the same movie for some time.

For this reason, perhaps, I have a hard time thinking of my father, once such a golden boy, without immediately thinking of the once golden state where he met his ruin. After all, they have so much in common: Both disliked taxes, both had big dreams for themselves, both insisted on spending money they didn't have. They deserved each other in so many ways. If only they'd been less mercenary, more willing to invest in their futures, then things might be different.

When my father was dying from cancer, I flew out to help and found someone I barely recognized, about as far from the raffish figure in tweed as can be imagined. Those weeks before he died, there weren't any deathbed redemptions, no Hollywood hugs or teary confessions. He still ranted about idiots and tried to get me to sign on to a loan because his credit was shot. One night I drove him to dinner—in his Ford Taurus, indistinguishable from a zillion rentals—while he rested his head against the window. I'd seen him ride in the passenger seat only once in my life, when he'd taught me to drive. At the restaurant, he kept glancing up at me while he picked at his fish. I asked him what was wrong, and he took off the baseball cap he'd been wearing, as if remembering the rule he'd had when we were kids. The inside of his cap was lined with white hairs, like dandelion fluff. He told me, haltingly, that he wished he'd done something different with his life. His eyes were rheumy and tired, and he seemed real to me then—perhaps for the first time. I watched him return to his food. For a man who'd spent his entire life showing off to people, it was a brave thing to say.

This is not about forgiveness. I still think about that day at the beach, or the fact that my father abandoned me for so long—years with hardly a phone call—and my heart clenches with rage. We live in the age of forgiveness, of bailouts, of *doing our best to move on.* Too often these gestures have only to do with creating a nice tidy narrative, one we can wrap up and hide away somewhere and promise ourselves will never happen again. We choose the myth over reality every time. It's the Californian—which is to say, the American—way.

But it's just as tempting, I think, to see men like my father as two-dimensional villains. Strangely, when I think about who my dad longed to be all those years, I don't think about him out west, but rather as he was before we moved, when he seemed to me in some ways *more* Californian—at least in his goofy charisma and ability to dazzle. I remember one Halloween when I was six or seven: I'd gone trick-or-treating with a friend of mine, and we were coming home after a major haul when some teenagers sprinted by and stole our bags of candy. I ran home, bawling. My father listened to my tale of woe and then went out with me in the dark, hoisting me on his shoulders so that I had to duck under the oaks and chestnut trees lining the sidewalk. I was dressed, I think, as Dracula. From house to house we went, man and vampire, ringing people's doorbells until they came to the door in slippers or pajamas. Flushed with annoyance, their faces softened as my father recounted my story. They sighed and shook their heads and dumped the remains of their Halloween stash into the grocery bag I'd brought from home, a showering of goodies, piles of Smarties and Tootsie Pops and candy corn. In five minutes, we had more candy than I'd lost, but my father pressed on, stopping at every door in the neighborhood. It had to be embarrassing for him, to knock on these darkened houses, but he did it anyway. For once he was not trying to impress anyone, and yet I think the people—seeing how my father was spending his evening—believed me to be a lucky boy. Certainly I felt like one that night. By the end I had more loot than I could carry, and yet my father persisted, giving me for once what I wanted, collecting a bounty he didn't have to buy.

GONE, BABY

Suzanne Lummis

O BEST BELOVED, they're true, those tales
come down to us from Way
Then. In The Age of Money the money
vanished—overnight it did, as if
vacuumed through a funnel into deep space.
No one had it, the money. It didn't stew
in a bank or go forth and multiply.
Buried in the yard of the mad man it was not,
nor bent into wads and stuffed
in the robber's pocket. It had not burned,
had not melted; no guttering molecules slid
back to earth, their nuclei hot and
circling the memory of money.
O Best, it went Gone. It went Ain't. It went
as if it had not been, as if our lives
had been nothing but dreamt things
and we weren't even the primary dreamers.
Beloved, now dream again. It's late.
Close your eyes and think of that enchanted time
when money flowed from our palms like
blood through our veins. Then dream
of The Age Before That, when we had only
to point and golden fruit dropped
to our hands. And the most ancient
of all realms, imagine: The Era of Wands.

We waved them and, Lo, it appeared—
whatever we longed for.
And we never went hungry yet, somehow,
we always felt hunger, for there was always
more where that came from, and always
we wanted more.

HONEYMOON IN BEIRUT

Stacy Tintocalis

1

IN 1975, DURING the autumn of the Defense Industry, the Golden Age before Hughes Aircraft fell to General Motors, a Lebanese dressmaker by the name of Emile Saleem Haddad fell in love with a bolt of fabric. This happened in the City of Angels, where each Saturday before dawn a lively fashion bazaar spilled onto the streets of the Garment District. Merchants pushed dress racks out to the loading zones and draped gabardine slacks over cardboard drums. Inside the warehouses, shoppers mulled around towering bolts of textiles, a Parthenon of purple velvet pillars and toppled camel hair columns. In this wondrous place, this City of Angora and Acrylic, Emile lost his head over fine Oriental silk.

It was love, his wife Zahlah knew. Though married only nine months, she could see that Emile had gotten the lint in his eyes and could no longer see straight. Before their marriage, Emile was seduced by fine black wool that was heavy and soft, wool sweetly spiced with incense like an old widow's church clothes. Hundreds of *lira* were spent to design a spectacular coat with large custom glass buttons the size of *piasters*. Under each button, Emile placed an ancient photograph of a woman's face. Gold filigree clasps held down these photos of serious spook-eyed women, strange and unsmiling, the cutouts from wedding portraits depicting conjugal gloom—all of them the wives of arranged marriages. When Emile first presented the coat to Zahlah, cradling it with trembling pride, she received it with a sense of wonderment at its beauty, not recognizing those distant, unfamiliar faces in the buttons. These women were Zahlah's great-aunts and great-grandmothers, Emile explained to her, images he'd pleaded for late one night after Zahlah's mother had loosed her hair from its chignon, letting it fall long and dark over her nightdress. Zahlah could practically see the grimace on her mother's face as she knifed the yellowed photographs from the insides of lockets like the flesh from the shell of an oyster. Such destruction for a few photographs, such emotional expense.

The day Emile presented Zahlah with the coat, he'd said, "When we reach the American Promised Land, you will never be alone. See? You will have your whole family on your sleeve." When she arrived in California, however, Zahlah had no need for an overcoat. It never rained, never snowed, never even got cold in Los Angeles, so her ancestral coat remained boxed with mothballs in the bedroom closet, forgotten like the women knifed out of old lockets.

As they drove away from the Los Angeles Garment District that Saturday morning in 1975, Zahlah stared at the back of her husband's head. He and his friend Marouf sat in the front seat. She felt like a child sitting behind them. Only once did Emile swivel in his seat to look into the backseat at Zahlah and her brother Ramsey who'd moved to Los Angeles to finish medical school. The bolt of silk sat between Zahlah and Ramsey, propped upright like a silly giraffe. Emile then told Zahlah they would have to be more frugal for a while. "We'll have to eat *mujadarra* instead of meat," he said. "And there will be no honeymoon in Beirut. Not this summer. Not even this winter."

Zahlah tightened her kerchief around her chin and didn't reply. When they moved to the United States, Emile told her that America would be their honeymoon, an eternity of California sunshine, but she demanded a real honeymoon, a return home where they could stay at a Mediterranean resort.

Marouf raised his bushy eyebrows at her in the rearview mirror. "Don't worry Zahlah. Beirut will be there next year."

"But mother has been writing of civil unrest," she said. "Just last month, a Palestinian taxi driver was pulled from his car and killed in the streets."

"Things will get better," Emile assured her. "Such fighting cannot last."

"Can't it?" her brother Ramsey interrupted. He leaned forward so he could be heard. "Beirut has already been destroyed and rebuilt six times. What difference would a seventh time make?"

Zahlah remained silent. Since their move to the United States, fighting continued to break out in the streets of Beirut. Barricades had been put up in their old neighborhood. Garbage was not being collected. Zahlah's mother wrote her to say that mortar shots regularly rattled her apartment windows in Ashrafiyeh.

"Next year Beirut. This year Los Angeles," Emile said.

"Next year is so far off." Zahlah sat back. Her fingers clutched the scarf under her chin.

"And not long from now," Ramsey interjected, "mother and *sitta* will have received their emigration papers to live with us in America."

"Next year is not so far off. You'll see," Emile said. Then there it was—the touch; Emile gave Zahlah's hand a light pat, one of his moments of strategic affection—a kiss to quell a complaint, an embrace to upturn a frowned face.

Later that evening, after dinner, Emile touched Zahlah again—twice in one day!—and almost as intimately as he'd touched her on their wedding night. "With your permission," he now said and held out the yellow measuring tape.

She delightedly breathed in his musky hair pomade as he took her measurements. Around her waist. Over her hips. So close to touching her, yet not really touching, never once stepping out of professional decorum to have a moment of play with his wife—a pinch of her behind, a lingering hand on her hip. Instead he wound the tape behind her back and pulled it taut into a thin hug across her breasts.

"Why does it feel like you are measuring my body for a coffin?" she asked.

"Hush," he said, loosening the tape.

"Did you know ten people died in a mortar attack in Beirut yesterday?"

"I read it in *Al-Safir*."

"Did you know Abu Saleem, the coffin maker? He died in a recent bombing in Ashrafiyeh."

"Zahlah, quiet!" Emile said as he knelt to measure her waist.

Zahlah looked down at his sleek hair. "I remember Abu Saleem coming to our apartment when my father died. He came with his pet dog, a little terrier that lapped some spilled milk off the kitchen floor."

Emile let out a breath through his nose.

"He had webbed feet," she said.

Emile put down his measuring tape and looked up at her. "The dog?"

"No. The coffin maker. The coffin maker had webbed feet."

"Let me work," he said, then placed the tape measure around her hips.

When Zahlah introduced her family to Emile, when he sat in her mother's front room and sipped tea from a china cup, Zahlah wondered if even then he'd been thinking she'd make a good clothes rack. Her shy hips and long legs were ideal for modeling garments. She was taller than he by an inch, and Emile never mentioned it, not once.

The first time Emile met her mother and *sitta*, her grandmother, Emile spoke softly of his childhood in the hill country, where he and Marouf had grown up. Both moved to the city to attend the American University of Beirut. Emile studied art. Marouf studied engineering. It was only after Marouf took a ballistics engineering job in Los Angeles, designing bombs, that Emile began looking for a wife.

"Better to marry a dressmaker than a bomb maker," Zahlah's eighty-year-old *sitta* had interjected, crossing a traditional line of polite discourse and brazenly standing on the other side. There she was, a shrunken widow in black lacework, challenging Emile to cross the line with her. Such politics were not discussed publicly or privately, and Emile, in no position to silence her, listened to her prate about the Six-Day War of 1967, about how much she hated the Palestinian refugees who flooded into Beirut after the war, how she hated their dirty shanty towns.

"They wouldn't be so dirty if we helped them," Zahlah interrupted.

Zahlah's mother discreetly raised her eyebrows and continued to sip from her tea cup, saying nothing. *Sitta*, staring silently at her granddaughter, slowly freed her right arm from her lace shawl.

"And why," *sitta* asked, "why should we help them? Why when they don't belong here in the first place?" She spoke in a falsetto and punctuated every thought with a subtle hand gesture, an "O" formed by pinching her index finger to her thumb; between those pinched fingers she gently tugged an invisible thread. "The Palestinians—they are an eyesore with their slums and barefoot children selling flowers on the street," she said, tugging the thread. "It's a good thing the government built a high wall around their slum in Qarantina to hide them." She tugged twice, tightening a knot of silence.

Zahlah bit her tongue to conceal her irritation. She taught French at the *Dekwaneh* refugee camp for Christian Palestinians. These were people who had lost their homes and the ancestral property that had been in their families for centuries. Now they were displaced, homeless, forced to scatter among unsanitary dwellings with no home to return to.

Emile had been sitting there meekly, too shy to even glance Zahlah's way. Finally he sat up to straddle the line that divided polite and impolite discourse, saying, "Do you not think the walls of Qarantina are an oversimplified solution to a complex problem?"

"Walls or no walls," *sitta* retorted. "It's the Palestinians that remain the problem."

Emile merely gave a light shrug.

Zahlah could no longer remain silent and said, "Walls only cover up what the government does not want us to see, so we can pretend it's not there and go on with our lives. Those walls are the biggest problem of all."

At that, Zahlah's mother released a breathy laugh. "Enough... enough...perhaps you would like some more tea? Yes? Good!" she said, nodding. "More tea for everyone. Come help me with the tea," she said to Zahlah.

In the kitchen, her mother, tight-lipped, stroked back the freed strands of hair that had strayed from her chignon.

"Well?" Zahlah asked her mother.

"He's well-mannered," her mother said, then turned to look Zahlah in the eye. "Manners are good," she replied, nodding firmly.

Zahlah nodded back, eyes jeweled with delight, and her heart burst into a bouquet of *Yeses*. *Yes*, she would be permitted to court Emile. *Yes*, she would marry him. *Yes*, she would *yes* by his side.

But in America Zahlah felt so much anxiety that everything Emile said or did made her heart shake out a silent *No*. Emile himself was full of *Nos*.

"Don't you want to measure my neck?" she asked when he finished her measurements for the silk dress.

"No."

She touched her throat. "Last time you needed my neck."

"Last time I made you a coat, not a dress."

Emile unrolled several yards from the top of the bolt in the gesture of spinning a ballerina.

"Look at how it sways and moves. See how kinetic it is? Its vitality?" He lay several yards of fabric over a chivalrous arm and moved it to and fro in a dance. "It moves like a movie star," he said. Releasing it gently, sliding it from his arm, he let the silk pool on the rug, where it shimmered and rippled as though some elegant American actress from the '30s had melted on the floor.

It was on the plane to the United States that Emile confessed his passion for American cinema, telling Zahlah of the movie house in Beirut that showed old American films, a small theater with cheap wooden seats that squeaked whenever the patrons crossed or uncrossed their legs. There was no screen, only a naked wall. This was in Southern Beirut, on the Rue Ahmed Chaoqui, away from the resorts and the honey-sweet smell of bakeries, amidst the scrabble of high-rise apartment buildings where kids yelled down from their balconies and chased each other through alleys. Old men in fez hats came in from playing *sija* and smoked cigars while they watched films in English, flickering and bright, with the light from the projector perforating the darkness to reveal billows of smoke. This was the dream of America that Emile ingested before emigrating, a dream tangled up in Ginger Rogers and Jean Harlow and the syrupy taste of port wine that old men passed from seat to seat. This was the dream, born of celluloid, made possible with silk.

2

"I think I have married an impotent man," Zahlah confessed one day. She was lounging under the backyard's lemon tree beside the empty pool. A jagged crack ran through the pool's bottom. Leaves had gathered around the drain. Rotting lemons, brown and moldering, lay down there in a smelly huddle.

Geta, Zahlah's only friend in Los Angeles, lived in the adjoining duplex. She had taken Zahlah under her wing, teaching her how to read a bus schedule and navigate the enormous California supermarkets. Geta sat up in her lounge chair, squinting as she reaffixed the safety pin that closed the deep V of her cleavage. Her broad shoulders had grown pink from the sun. "Impotent?" she asked in French. Neither she nor Zahlah spoke English. Geta was Basque but spoke fluent French and Spanish.

Beyond a slatted dividing fence, a man turned on his garden hose. Geta chinned toward him. "That journalist is looking at you again," Geta said in French, calling him a journalist because she'd seen him photograph a car accident on Los Feliz Drive. "Yes," she joked. "I think he's taking notes."

The journalist watched them from afar, smiled, and removed his hat to wave, revealing his yellowish bald head. Once, when Emile was not home, he hollered at Geta and Zahlah over the fence posts, saying, "You got nice lemons. Nice lemons." The women had shrugged, pretending to be confused, though they knew perfectly well what he'd said.

"Forget him," Zahlah said. "Listen to me. My husband would rather make a dress than touch his wife."

Geta brushed a fly from her leg. "You are an American woman now. Speak up! Tell him exactly what you want."

That night Zahlah watched Emile spread the fabric over his sewing table in their bedroom. He took his dress shears and gently cut the silk, lovingly pressing it down with his free hand, stroking it smooth. The fabric fell away from the blade without a frayed edge. It was a delicate operation, and he stayed in the room all night, cutting and clipping.

Zahlah lay in bed listening to his sewing machine yammer on and on like a nervous debutante. Periodically, she'd hear the anxious sound of scissors, slicing, a metallic whisper.

Already the bodice of the gown was done, and he had placed it on his dress dummy, raising the stand to its full height so that it towered over their tiny twin beds. In the old country, especially the hill country where Emile was from, couples did not sleep in the same bed; sometimes they didn't even sleep in the same room. And Emile was so modest that she'd never seen him in his undergarments. When he wanted to change clothes, he went into the bathroom. That night, after Emile crawled between his covers and turned out the nightstand light, Zahlah dangled an arm over the side of her bed and into the cold cavern of space between them.

"Emile," she said, "what kind of feelings do you have for me?"

"What are you talking about?"

She heard him turning in his bed, the tight crunching of stiff cotton sheets. The ghostly dress woman watched beyond their beds, a decapitated white blur. In the old country, her mother claimed to have seen a beheaded female ghost standing in front of the stove. Such headless ghost women were common, most wearing black mourning dresses and walking vacantly from room to room.

"What do you feel for me?" she asked.

"Shush," he replied.

"I have needs," she said. "Have you forgotten me?"

"Zahlah, go to sleep."

Not since their wedding night had they made love; when they were finally alone in a small hotel room with twin beds, Emile refused to touch her, so Zahlah offered herself to him, flattening her spine against the cold sheet. "I don't know what to do," he said as he began to make love. "It doesn't matter," she replied. "You will learn." Zahlah tried not to wince with pain as he clumsily forced himself into her—no beauty to the act, only necessity. Emile kept his eyes upward, never once daring to look down at her breasts. "I am so sorry, Zahlah, so sorry," Emile repeated. "Tell me to stop," he begged. "Please tell me to stop." Tears fell from the corners of her eyes, but she let him continue. A good wife, she didn't get angry or complain. When he finished, Emile made her sleep alone on the blood-anointed sheets. "Forgive me," he said, sliding into the comfort of his clean bed.

3

Was this wrong? This silk obsession? Something that she should be worried about? Zahlah didn't know. Weeks passed and she said nothing, letting him love the fabric, letting him show it off to the men who picked up their fitted Italian suits. Sometimes he trotted out the entire bolt, leaning it up against the closet door beside the TV, and he was doing something in his head when he looked at it, designing something, reupholstering his mental world in silk.

No dress deals had been cut, not with the Lebanese and Syrian businessmen who shook church incense from their clothes. No wedding dresses had been ordered from the silk swatch he carried in his breast pocket. It was the pearly luster. That was the problem. No one wanted a creamy off-white but only the whitest of whites for virgin brides. The last time Emile brought out the bolt, eager to entice a customer, his banter was filled with desperation, as if pleading to save his precious silk's life.

For weeks on end, there was no good news. Not even good mail arrived, just bills, until finally Zahlah received a letter from her mother. "The emigration papers have arrived," Zahlah told her brother Ramsey over the phone. "Mother and *sitta* found a cheap boat to America, *very* cheap!"

"How cheap?" her brother grumbled suspiciously.

"I don't know. Mother sold everything in the apartment at a great loss. They will dock in New York in six weeks."

"Well, I, too, have good news." Ramsey then announced that he'd been accepted to the cosmetic surgery residency at UCLA. A celebration was in order.

That afternoon Zahlah sat on a lounge chair by the sun-warmed concrete of the pool, rereading her mother's letter, when the bald journalist across the fence called out to her from where he'd been watering his bushes. He came over, producing a paper bag from his pocket, and pointed to the lemon tree.

"Lemons," he said, pointing to the tree again. His bald head gave off an oily shine.

Pocketing her letter, Zahlah yanked a half-dozen ripe lemons from the tree. Leaves rained onto her head. Rotten lemons thudded to the ground. She filled his paper bag, handing it back to him as he bowed to thank her. It was then that he motioned for her to follow him, guiding her to a gap at the corner of the fence, urging her with his voice to come.

The way he smiled at her, so open, so full of *Yes*—how could she spurn such an invitation? He was a harmless man, after all. She turned sideways to squeeze through the fence stakes. Short juniper bushes and trumpet-faced flowers bordered his house. His grass was soft with tender thin blades. The journalist opened a sliding glass door, leaving Zahlah on a brick patio. Moments later he returned with a large black camera, then gestured that he wanted to take her picture, that he wanted her to come out of the sunlight, pointing up at the brightness of the sky. "Come inside," he motioned.

Zahlah looked behind her, over the fence, searching for Geta or Emile. There was no one to stop her, no one to say, "No."

Inside, her bare feet stepped onto a plastic entry mat. She stood stiffly beside his TV set. A convertible couch with the bed out, sheets rumpled as if someone had just left, sat unabashedly in full view.

The journalist picked up a magazine with photos of women in fancy clothes. He pointed at each picture, saying something she didn't understand. Finally he stepped back and held up the camera, motioning that he wanted her to pose. He adjusted the lens over one eye, his fingers twittery with excitement. Zahlah, breathing deeply to settle herself, placed her arms at her sides. When the flash went off, adrenaline raced through her chest.

"Sit. Sit," he said, patting the unmade bed, repeating it until she reluctantly sat on the edge, her thighs cold against the aluminum frame, her pose rigid, like a mannequin, with her hands in her lap.

The journalist motioned for her to wait, then walked outside to pull a cluster of white pear blossoms from a tree in his yard. Returning, he presented her with the flowers, taking a tiny white blossom and tucking it behind her ear. He lingered with her hair, sinking his fingers between the strands, down to her naked scalp. Her hair, always tightly bound into a bun, he suddenly loosed, gently finding the pins, freeing her long black tresses so that they fell to the base of her spine.

His voice gushed with pleasure. "*Bella bella,*" he said, speaking in what she thought must be Italian, not French, though she understood what he meant.

Standing back, he took one photograph, then another, each from different angles. He touched her chin to position her face, his eyes meeting hers affectionately. Sitting there, she felt a knot of repression in her soul begin to slacken, freeing her enough to smile easily, playfully almost, smiles that warmed her entire face. There was something between them—between Zahlah and this man—a kind of spark or electricity that gave her a jolt whenever they made eye contact.

When the picture taking was over, he put his hand in hers to help her stand, sending a rush of giddiness to her head. Ugly as he was, she wanted to kiss him, to thank him, to give him something in return. Instead, she backed out the door and raced to her side of the fence where Geta was now standing at the mouth of the drained pool, hands firmly on her hips, wearing a loose bathrobe that revealed a long line of cleavage.

"What were you doing over there with the journalist?" Geta asked in a chastising voice as Zahlah slid between the fence posts.

"He showed me pictures. In a book," Zahlah replied in French.

"What type of pictures?"

"Pictures of women. Lots of women."

Geta's eyes lit up. "That man is in lust with you," she said. "Never go back. You hear me?"

4

Later that evening, Marouf and Ramsey came to dinner, and each brought bottles of anisette and wine. At the dining room table, Ramsey described the contrary logic of rhinoplasty, how you break a nose to set it straight.

"I could get rid of that bump." Ramsey tapped the bridge of his nose, looking at Zahlah sitting across from him. "I could give you a Marilyn Monroe nose. How would you like that?"

Zahlah pushed away from the table. "Stay away from my nose," she said jokingly before retreating into the kitchen where the oven timer had gone off. Ramsey continued talking at her through the open doorway.

"You see Marouf? I'm going to make him look like Clark Gable. I'm going to sculpt away that excess flesh."

Marouf, at the head of the table, had opened a second bottle of wine and began to pour some into his glass. Ramsey pushed up the septum of his own nose for Marouf to see what he'd look like.

"Why do you look at me like I'm an ugly foreigner?" she asked her brother when she brought the leg of lamb out on a carving board and set it on the table.

"Zahlah! I'm not looking at you like anything at all. I just want you to be more attractive."

"You are a butcher," she said, teasing him. "Now stop talking and carve the lamb."

Ramsey stood, raising his wineglass in the air. "Hey, Clark Gable," he said to Marouf. "Why don't you drag my brother-in-law from his sewing machine and bring him to the table?"

Marouf walked across the room, holding the neck of the wine bottle he'd opened and tapped its base against Emile's bedroom door. "It's time to eat, you madman."

Emile came out, the strain of sewing crimping his brow. "I'm no madman," he said as he sat beside his wife.

Ramsey carved the leg of lamb and placed slices of meat onto a serving platter.

"Look at that knife work," Marouf said. He spooned yogurt mint sauce onto his plate. "You are an artist, Ramsey."

"Emile is the one with the hands of a surgeon." Ramsey sat down. "Look at his long fingers. With all that practice hand-stitching, he could suture without leaving scars."

Emile grabbed his napkin and put both hands below the table. He lowered his head and shyly reached up to twinch his mustache. "Stop teasing me," he said.

"It's true. Look at my hands," Ramsey held up his palms. "Fat fingers. I'm lucky I don't cut someone's nose off. But you, Emile, you have the hands of an artist. And to think," he said, "your wife could be a work of art if only she let me fix that nose bump."

"Why not cut off my head?" Zahlah said. "Wouldn't that solve everything?"

"Zahlah!" Emile protested. "There's no harm in wanting you to look nice."

"But I'm *already* beautiful!"

Marouf suddenly stood up and teetered on one leg. "You want to see beauty? You want to see a work of art?" he asked. "I'll show you something more beautiful than an American blonde." Marouf walked out the front door, still wearing his napkin tucked into his belt.

Outside Marouf slammed the trunk of his Cadillac. He came back into the house holding an unremarkable sphere of metal the size of a lime with two aerodynamic vanes. "You see this? You will never see anything more beautiful than this in the world!"

"It's a piece of junk," Ramsey said.

"It's a bomb," he replied. "A cluster bomb that I designed—me!" He poked himself in the chest then gave the bomb a twist. Inside was a spiral chamber where all the tiny bomblets would be held. Marouf explained how the force of spinning would split each bomb open right before hitting the ground so that a sunburst of bomblets sprayed into the enemy.

He dropped the bomb into Zahlah's hands, and she prized it open to look at the spirals, like the inside of a halved snail shell.

"Something this simple and elegant," Marouf said. "*This* is beautiful."

"Why does beauty have to be so destructive?" Zahlah asked. She placed the bomb beside Marouf's wineglass.

Marouf sat down again. "What have you got to be so upset about, eh? All you need to do is sit around looking pretty."

Zahlah squeezed lemon onto her rice. "My brother and my husband say I'm not pretty enough."

"Well," Ramsey said, pushing his glasses up his nose. "Let's forget about this. The first thing I am going to do when *sitta* arrives is lop off those warty moles on her face."

Zahlah put her fork down. "Ramsey, stop it!"

"Stop it?" Ramsey asked. "Just a minute ago we were talking about bloody bombs."

"That's completely different," Marouf protested.

Ramsey cut apart the lamb on his plate. "Don't be so naïve," he replied. "Your bombs are for ethnic cleansing."

Zahlah threw her napkin on the table. "Bombs? Scalpels? What's the difference? Tell me!"

Zahlah looked to her husband, who'd been sitting there quietly sipping his anisette, his face innocent and blank as if lost in his world of silk. When she was about to say more, Emile reached under the table and held her hand, his warm sweet pulse in her palm, and he sat there, holding her curled fingers down in his lap without letting go. Emile then looked to the men and said something in English that Zahlah didn't understand, something that made them laugh.

Later that night, after everyone had left, Emile tippled one more glass of anisette before stumbling into the bathroom that adjoined their bedroom.

"Why didn't you defend me?" Zahlah asked him through the door while he changed clothes.

"From what?"

"From my brother who wants to cut off my nose. And from your best friend who threw a bomb at me. You should have intervened."

"What for? It was your battle, not mine."

Emile came out in his Woolworth's pajamas and got into bed. Zahlah unfastened her dress right in front of him, watching his face, his averted eyes, as she freed each button and let the dress drop. Underneath she was wearing a black slip. She let the slip drop too, the underclothes, everything.

"Turn out the light," Emile said, then rolled to his side with one hand over his eyes. "I don't want to argue."

"This isn't an argument." Zahlah left the light on and quickly pulled back her husband's covers.

"What's the matter with you?" he asked.

"I'm getting into bed with you."

She squirmed next to him and held her husband close, feeling the fuzziness of static electricity between them.

"Get into your bed," he hissed.

"Biddi-yyaak," she said softly. "I want you—inch by inch."

Emile lay there, rectilinear beneath the sheet. Zahlah slid her hand between the buttons of his shirt and touched the sweaty skin beneath the cotton, the hairs standing on end, the rough outline of his nipple.

"Tell me you want me," she said.

He said nothing, so she lowered her hand to his private parts until she felt the flinch of his body rejecting her.

"If you don't want me, beg me to stop," she said, pulling herself on top of him, straddling him while his headless mistress watched. Emile's chest heaved up and down. He squeezed his eyes shut. His breath smelled heavily of licorice from the anisette. Zahlah pressed her breasts against him, waiting for his body to relax, for his arms to reach up and take her. Emile remained rigid, keeping his arms down at his sides, his face averted from hers.

"Don't you see how much power you have over me?" she asked.

His eyes would not open to see her face.

"I think you don't love me," she said.

"I do," he whispered. The corner of his eye tensed.

"Then what? You think I'm ugly? You're afraid of me?"

In the silence, his breathing trembled.

"It's true. Isn't it?" She exhaled a hot breath onto his wincing face. "You are the man with all the power, and look at you, you are afraid."

"I'm not afraid!" he said, eyes open now, looking at the wall.

"Oh no! Of course not," she taunted.

His face reddened with anger. "I love you," he said.

She pulled her torso up to look at him sternly, to see him cower beneath her. "No. You only love me in the quiet control of clothes," she said.

Zahlah quit the bed and saw her dark reflection in the full-length mirror, her body hard and ugly, her nipples righteously erect. An American woman. That's what she saw. Liberated and humiliated. She grabbed a dirty robe from the hamper and left the room to sleep by the empty pool.

5

The next morning Emile would not speak to Zahlah, wouldn't even look at her over the top of his *Los Angeles Times*. She walked from room to room, ignored, invisible to him, until he went out to the patio to finish reading his paper. By noon, she noticed that he'd vanished, leaving his newspaper on the lounge chair.

It was almost 2:00 p.m. when she heard Emile calling her name from the patio door, talking enthusiastically in English as he entered.

"There you are," Emile said in Arabic. The bald journalist appeared behind him, holding up his black camera and his sack for lemons.

What was this? Zahlah wondered. An invasion in her own living room? The two strolling in like grinning allies, the journalist waggling the camera at her.

"This man wants to see my clothing designs," Emile said. He explained in Arabic that he'd been talking to the journalist for an hour now, that the journalist knew fashion designers and boutique owners who could help him, people who wanted to see original work. "Go put on the wool coat," Emile told her, his voice full of authority. Zahlah waited for an enigmatic smile to relieve her from the room, but there was only the wave of his hand.

In the bedroom, she unboxed the ancestral coat. It seemed too precious to wear in public, too personal to be gazed upon by strangers. Her *sitta* was right there in the bottom button. Zahlah emerged from the bedroom, cradling the lapels close to her body, no longer warmed by the affection sewn into the sleeves or the loving squeeze of each stitch.

The journalist snapped two photos, then said, "No…no," He shook his bald head as he approached her. Without hesitating he reached up to her throat where she'd fastened the top button. He lingered there, and she thought that he'd come to liberate her, that their eyes would lock, and he'd pull her toward him to kiss her, right in front of Emile, placing his warm tongue into her mouth the way Americans kiss. Zahlah's lips parted, wanting the kiss, wanting it for herself alone, to ease her longing for love. No kiss came. He didn't even look into her eyes. Instead he placed his dirty thumb on her ancestor's face, smearing his fingerprint over the glass. His crabbed fingers went down to the next button, and the next, until the coat flapped open against her dress. Backing away from her, he shooed her out of the room with his voice.

The journalist spoke only to Emile now. They negotiated in English until Emile finally told her to put on the silk gown.

Zahlah, opening her mouth to protest, was stopped by Emile's hand, his finger pointing like a knife. "It is finished," he said. "Put it on,"

She retreated, outraged, her mouth soured by her own silence. In the bedroom, she stripped the despicable dress from the dummy and put it on, transforming into Emile's American mistress. The sleeveless bodice fit snugly. What had seemed so glamorous now looked fragile, about to rip at the seams, barely able to contain the body of a real woman. That's what she'd become. In Beirut she'd been a girl, but in America she'd gained weight and grown hips and breasts that filled out the dress. No longer the paper doll he'd married. No longer so easy to silence. And yet here she was, her head full of noise, and she could say nothing, not a sentence in English.

"So this is America," she thought, full of contempt, as if America couldn't get any worse, but in a few weeks she'd discover things *had* gotten worse. Her mother and *sitta* would disembark a boat cheering, "America! America!" Zahlah would be told that everyone was so happy until they realized they'd been deceived, arriving in Senegal, not America, swapping their homeland for a third-world country, and there was no legal recourse, no return ticket home, not even a safe home to return to. Civil war would break out, and bombs would explode in Beirut, destroying the seaside resorts.

When she came out from the bedroom, the journalist clapped his hands once, then said something to Emile, some word of praise for the gown. Emile responded by demonstrating the artistry of the skirt, the surgical precision of the line. He drew out the flounce of the gown and held it straight and proud, then let it drop in a lush wave that sent the skirt into a creamy swirl above Zahlah's feet.

The journalist snapped a picture of Zahlah standing alone. He stepped back, inspecting her. Not quite satisfied, he smoothed a hand along her waist, preening the gown. He acknowledged only the dress, not her, taking one picture after another. Finally, he posed Emile and Zahlah side by side, together but not touching. Zahlah could not smile. Shutting her mouth, she stared out at the camera to conceal the stone in her throat.

"Like a wedding portrait," Emile said quietly, in Arabic, before the camera's shutter released. "The only thing missing is the veil."

When it was all over, the journalist held out his empty sack to Zahlah, showing her the twiggy stems at the bottom of the bag, instructing her to go outside. "Lemons. Lemons," he said, the only English she understood.

THE RED COAT

Daisy Uyeda Satoda

THE EERIE WAIL of foghorns welcomed us as we disembarked from the ferry. We stepped into the soft, swirling fog of a typical summer evening in the City by the Bay: windy, bone-chilling, and misty. The strange foghorns intensified my loneliness and fear, and I buttoned up my bright red, all-wool overcoat, the fabric enveloping my body in a cocoon.

We had been released from the Topaz concentration camp—our home during World War II—two days earlier, on August 29, 1945. I had recently graduated from Topaz High School after having spent my entire three years of high school in this desert town in central Utah. Topaz was a self-contained and self-governed city where we had lived in isolation and had no contact with the world beyond the barbed wire fence that had imprisoned us.

When Topaz was going to close, my parents had to remain behind to clear out our barrack rooms. Papa asked me, "Can you please take Nancee and Elsie with you to San Francisco? That way they will be on time for you to register them for the fall semester." School was scheduled to start the following week, and I nodded "yes" as I continued with my packing. Inside my open suitcase, I folded my coat and placed it carefully over my other meager personal belongings—clothing, toilet kit, diary, album with photos of my schoolmates, the Topaz High Class of '45 yearbook, address book, and precious letters and postcards from friends who had left camp earlier. Then I closed my suitcase, both scared and excited about the prospect of freedom. Where would we live? Could I take care of my sisters?

Now hundreds of miles away from Topaz and frightened by the cacophony of myriad noises in this bustling city, my little sisters, Elsie and Nancee, ages eleven and thirteen, clung to my arms, their grip softened by the sleeves of my new coat. I pulled them along while feeling the weight of their shock: we had not had streets, sidewalks, cars, traffic, or outdoor lighting of any kind in Topaz. This chaos was uncomfortably new to us.

Elsie began to hyperventilate as she peered nervously into the street, hoping to catch a glimpse of my sister Kaye, who was scheduled to pick us up and deliver us to the hostel at the San Francisco Buddhist Church. The church was a temporary haven for those of us resettling in San Francisco after our incarceration in various camps. "Where is Kaye?" Elsie whimpered. Tears trickled down her face and she pleaded, "Can't we go back home to Topaz?"

To distract her younger sister, Nancee put her arm around Elsie and gently said, "Just look around you and take in the sights." We stood in awe at the passing parade of sleek automobiles, streetcars, buses, motorcycles, and taxicabs that whizzed by us at alarming speeds.

For the last three years, we had not seen any type of vehicle except for the army trucks that delivered food and coal to the mess halls in Topaz. Since we had no transportation of any kind, we had to walk to get anywhere within the one-mile-square boundary of our camp. We traveled on dirt roads past open ditches and nary a street sign. On our walks, we did not pass stores, movie theaters, hotels, or restaurants because Topaz had none.

It almost seemed surreal here in San Francisco: our footsteps on pavement, the bright lights of matinee shows on movie billboards, the vivid-colored dresses displayed on shining steel racks in shop windows, the smell of grease wafting from skillets where eggs and bacon were being fried in a nearby café.

As we took it all in, we grew more comfortable and forgot about our long wait for Kaye. Soon we were mesmerized by the electric traffic lights that alternately changed from green to amber to red. The towering heights of the skyscrapers overwhelmed us. Our necks swerved in huge arcs as the street lights turned on, almost blinding us with their brightness. We covered our ears with our hands to blunt the deafening noises of a bustling metropolis, the constant honking from seemingly every vehicle on the street.

We must have resembled displaced persons from a war-torn country, self-conscious as we fingered our unfashionable homemade dresses, gawking at every incredible sight: the towering office buildings, the variegated exotic flowers in storefront planters, the white boats in the bay.

In contrast, Topaz was one-dimensional: everything was flat, drab, dry, and colorless. There was very little greenery—no trees and only some scattered vegetable gardens. Our house was a bare army barrack shared by several other families, furnished only with cots and a cast-iron potbelly stove. Black tarpaper covered it all—the barracks, communal bathrooms, latrines, laundry rooms, and mess halls.

Our routine, like the landscape, was monotonous: get up, eat breakfast at the mess hall, go to school, return for lunch at the mess hall, back to school, play a bit, have dinner, and then go to bed. Details like what we wore ceased to matter as much because we all dressed the same—in G.I. (government-issued) black mackinaws, which were surplus items from World War I. These short, heavy coats weighed about five pounds and were distributed campwide. Since we had been uprooted from our homes in the moderate climates of the West Coast, we did not have warm clothing of our own to withstand the minus-zero degree winters of Utah. In our camp clothing, we couldn't fully express ourselves and our individuality. What we wore was extremely limited, and even when we tried to be unique, so many of us ordered similar clothing from the Montgomery Ward mail-order catalogs, which served as our fashion bibles. Placed under so many restrictions, we had become numbed by life in Topaz.

Here in San Francisco, the world stood in vivid contrast to Topaz. As we looked around the Ferry Building area, we noted that the majority population was no longer us but white people who were stylishly dressed in whatever they wanted: the men in suits and hats, carrying briefcases, and women who were so chic in dresses, suits, coats, hats, and gloves.

Suddenly, I wanted to look like them and be a part of the city's scene. I wanted to claim the streets as my own, without the stares or hushed whispers of each passerby who must have heard that we Japanese Americans had been released from the camps and were resettling in the western coastal states. Just then, I turned around and saw the enormous floor-to-ceiling windows of the Ferry Building; in the center of the middle window, I saw my full-length reflection. I was crestfallen. My beautiful red coat, the one I cherished as my most prized article of clothing, now looked like a bargain basement "hot sale item."

I don't think anyone had a floor-length mirror in Topaz. There, just a few months earlier, I had pored through the Montgomery Ward catalog to select this coat as my graduation present from Papa. I had proudly worn my red coat to the senior prom even though it was about 110 degrees that evening. I had felt so grown up and elegant. I treasured that coat, especially since it cost more than one-half of my father's monthly pay of sixteen dollars as a dishwasher in our mess hall.

I glanced at myself in the next window, and to my disappointment the mirror image remained the same. I unfastened the top button of my coat, turned up the collar around my ears, threw my head back, and struck a model-like pose. The sounds and sights of the city receded as I stared at myself in the window, my reflection blurred by passing cars and the lights at the foot of Market Street.

I was startled from my trance by Nancee excitedly shouting, "Look, look! Kaye is finally here!" Kaye was honking the horn and signaling for us to rush into the car since she was double-parked.

Only as we were pulling away from the curb did it dawn on me that my red coat really was not a fashion statement. No, it looked exactly like what it was: an inexpensive $8.98 coat from a mail-order catalog. Beautiful when I wore it in Topaz, here in San Francisco the coat looked like a cheaply made piece of clothing that no one even noticed.

HOW IT FEELS TO INHERIT CAMP

Tamiko Nimura

for my family

1.

YOU WEREN'T THERE. So what?

When someone mentions camp, you vibrate like a plucked string. You sit up straighter: heart beating faster, fight and flight. Your gut clenches into fists. You overflow with everything you know about camp, which is too much and not enough at the same time.

Yes, you know about "this shameful episode in American history."

Yes, you know about "the day that will live in infamy."

No, you can't finish this part of your family tree for your school project because this part of your family doesn't have any baby pictures. Your dad and your uncle had to burn these pictures, anything with Japanese writing on it, before they left for camp. Your grandfather, who loved to read, had to burn all of his books from Japan. Your grandmother burned her letters from her siblings in Japan.

Yes, you have read *Snow Falling on Cedars*. And yes, you have seen the movie. That wasn't what happened to your family, though. They didn't own land before they left. They came back to and restarted with even less.

No, camp was not "for their protection." The guns on the guards in their towers pointed inside the barbed wire.

And yes, this series of anticipated, practiced answers says something else: you are angry.

2.

And you are angry when people ask why you are angry, since it didn't happen to you.

And you are angry when some people praise your people for not being angry or bitter.

And you are angry when some people ask why you are not angrier.

And you are angry when you know that some people might like you better when you are angry.

Usually, you are not an angry person. Where does this anger come from?

Once you know that your family was in camp, you own history in your guts: it's written within the body.

Is there something ugly in the leap to ownership?—the desire to feel worthy of History's attention? The desire for pity? Maybe. Maybe. Maybe. Camp history, as much as any other history, is about the terrors and glories of the human heart.

But here's what your body knows: you are charged with history.

3.

And here's why you own it. Your family's story doesn't just "intersect" with History; your family's story is History.

Listen to the radio announcement of the attack on Pearl Harbor. Spy. Traitor. Jap.

Reread Executive Order 9066. Trace over FDR's signature. Read General DeWitt's Civilian Order 5. Walk up to the telephone pole where they have posted your orders. How much can you carry? What will you leave behind? What's your family number? Where will you attach the numbered tags to your clothes and your suitcases and your children?

Study the maps. Where did your family "assemble"? To which godforsaken strip of earth did the train eventually take them? Ohhhhhh. Tule Lake, eh? That's the one for disloyals and troublemakers. Where did your family "relocate"? How many White friends did they have, once they got out of camp? Did they know the words to the Pledge of Allegiance, to the Star-Spangled Banner?

Take the questionnaire. Combat duty? Forswear an allegiance that never existed? What's your brother going to answer? What will the wardens ask? What will they say?

Now, decades later, study the black-and-white photographs, even the famous ones from Dorothea Lange and Ansel Adams. Those young men playing baseball are now your community elders: the ones you see at the Obon festivals and the food bazaars, calling out a chicken teri order or fanning the sushi rice. If this woman is too old to be your aunt, maybe it's your grandmother standing in line for the latrine. Are those children your aunts? Sharp breath. They look like older versions of your daughters.

4.

Or, maybe you are possessed with history. You are possessive of this history, it's true. It's because you see your adolescent father through and behind barbed wire, trying to play in the desert by day, huddled under Army blankets in the horse stalls at night.

You want to make sure other people know about this history: why else would your family have endured? There's pride that swells the heart, and straightens the spine. "Right or wrong, yes or no," your family endured.

At a book club of older White women, you mention in passing that your father was interned. During a discussion break, their submerged histories swim through a river of guilt, and cross over to you unsolicited: "I was there. I remember." "It was in the news." "We had a woman we called Grandma, who cooked for us, and cleaned for us. We adored her." "We all knew what was going on. We went to school with them. We watched as they were taken away."

It's the knowing and the watching that chills you the most. At Days of Remembrance you hear: "It must never happen again." This mantra is the most important burden of your inheritance. You continue to ask yourself the harder questions: Who is being taken away now? And, are you watching?

What do you not want to know that, deep down, you already know?

5.

And so: how to explain that for you, the dominant note in the chord of internment sounds like loss? And how to explain that the opposite of loss is not gain, but redemption?

In your high school US history textbook, there's probably a paragraph about camp. Thousands of people fought for that paragraph, and over that paragraph. Thousands of people probably still want to leave it out. Read it. Study it. Read it. Study it. Read it. Study it. Is it enough?

To see yourself as a part of history also means that you can change it.

So you must make the textbook paragraph into a poem. Saturate history with meaning like water bleeds through paper. Infuse each word, each phrase, each date, each number, each comma, each space before and after the paragraph stops.

TORTURERS

Sean Bernard

I HAVE DREAMS ABOUT TORTURE. They're confusing as all hell. I'm in the middle of some desert, Dasht-e Kavir, Mojave, who knows. I'm sitting on a skateboard, hands tied behind my back, being dragged across the desert floor. I can't see who's pulling me, I can only look behind.

There's a lion following us, and his eyes glow yellow.

In the dream, I think, *What would Jack Bauer do?* And I remember how Jack Bauer always frees himself, and I rub my bindings against the skateboard. I feel my wrists warm and bloody, which is good for escape, and when I'm finally free I pull my hands loose and it turns out there's no rope at all, just a dead snake on the ground, no one's pulling me, I'm just sitting on a skateboard in the middle of the street, middle of the night, and I'm awake, not dreaming, and a car swerves past and someone shouts, *Get out of the street, lunatic!*

I watch my stepfather closely now.

He says that I'm sleepwalking, I'm disoriented from the big move. I doubt the theory.

He guards his Wheaties each day. He sits at the "Sausalito" coffee table assembled hastily with the other whitewashed particleboard furniture after our quick escape from the language school in Tehran. That's where our eyes widened as we realized, *These people are revolting!* At the table's center is a lurid red vase from whose mouth dangles a plastic yellow daisy. He sits bent forward, stooped, arm barricading the bowl. The hand at the end of his other arm holds a white plastic spoon, industriously scooping milky flakes.

Under the bathroom sink, past the Comet, we have fourteen boxes of Wheaties.

"Eat, eat, eat your Wheaties!" he sings, milk dribbling in his black beard.

No Wheaties in Iran. I prefer mango at breakfast, mashed in milk, bit of sugar, just so.

We bought the shoddy furniture at Target. It's basically glue and sawdust dipped in cheap paint, but the point is that I saw a beautiful Jansport backpack hanging from an endcap, emblazoned with my new school's team logo, a large cat sneering with yellow slit eyes, claws, fangs. I didn't say anything about the backpack, but my eyes lingered upon it a moment, and since my stepfather can see pretty much everything, I knew what I was doing. It was in the sporting goods section at Target. Target has great sales on family size boxes of Wheaties and shitty furniture. I'd stand near season packs of the television show *24* and gaze at the backpack. It had so many pockets, pockets in pockets in pockets. In Tehran I wore puffy shirts with pockets sewn into the sleeves, and in the sleeves I carried a pocket Bible, a pocket Koran, a Swiss army knife, and packets of artificial sugar to sweeten tea. Is the great appeal of pockets the ability to hide and to hide again? Like an unfolding mystery?

The first day of school, there on the white table it shone, a Jansport beacon, a gift.

My stepfather said, "Oh, everyone needs a little something-something at times."

I hummed my way to school sheathed in backpack, happily considering my many pocket options. We live in Topanga. It's mostly hot and dry, ready to burn. I found bottle tops and slid them into one pocket. Gum wrappers make for interesting conversation. Pocket. I walked into class bulging and excited, and what do you know, all the other students had leather briefcases slid in the wire baskets beneath their desk seats and not a single welcoming glance.

The teacher introduced me as the boy from Iran, which was a pretty awful way to begin. I fiddled with the straps and blushed. I heard snickers and felt embarrassed but defiant. I still wear my Jansport. During Current Events Hour I write tales of the Scandinavian hero Jan, a Christian backpack-wearing skier with big yellow goggles with which to better see, who skis the slopes of the Zagros mountains with Jack Bauer and together they fight Mahmoud Ahmadinejad in the high-stakes game of international intrigue. My stepfather has big yellow goggles he sports cutting onions, is where I got the idea. During Self-Exploration Hour today, the professor says all males have an instinctual biological impulse to kill the father, and this is apparent in many cultural productions, illuminating our human condition. "Homer," he says.

Homer, we all scribble.

"Arr sons must kirr the father," says the professor.

We jot this in poor script.

"Kirr the father!" he cries, jabbing chalkboard with chalk, which breaks off smaller pieces. His face is red with passion. The class smiles encouragingly. We're being patient. He's young. A first-year. Japanese. He says his l's as r's. We don't even laugh anymore.

When he says "Achires kirred Hector," we write "Achilles killed Hector." Etc.

The prettiest girl in class drops a scrunch of paper to the floor. Everyone knows how her parents tried to kill each other at her older sister's softball game (her sister is a star pitcher at UCLA). Her dad was drunk and shot a handgun at the mom, who was buying nachos at the snack booth. He ran out of ammo, and the mom took a bat to him. They're both in jail.

The prettiest girl in class, I don't know, does *things* now. Rumors abound.

I lean to valiantly rescue her slip, but she kicks it over to Harden. He's the nephew of the Fed Chairman. Harden drops his pencil, picks up the note, pencil, unfurls the note.

He whistles. "My lord, girl," he says aloud. "That is the filthiest shit I ever."

The professor says "Froyd, Froyd, Froyd," I write Floyd Floyd Floyd.

The prettiest girl sighs and the world sighs. Outside, olive branches sigh. Doves take flight. I want to press my nose against her various thingies, sighing, but never say so aloud.

It's Monday night, so my stepfather and I watch *24* in the dark with salty margarined popcorn, enjoying the exploits of former CTU agent Tony Almeida (a true friend) and of course Chloe, and most of all Jack Bauer. In this episode Jack needs information relating to the arrival of a chemical shipment of a powerful toxin that can destroy entire cities.

My stepfather says, "Information? What information? Information is inflated."

Jack begins to insert a ballpoint pen into a villain's eyeball (and the villain of course will now tell the secret, worried about a skewered eyeball, that's how it works with secrets, eyeballs). The villain screams. The commercial break comes. Jack in the Box mini-burgers.

My stepfather pulls me outside. "One day this will all be yours, just don't go poking your ballpoint pen into anyone's eyeballs, if you know what I mean." He's been acting funny lately. When I get home he throws thumbtacks at me, leftovers from the move, when we plastered the walls with maps of Antarctica. To cover the wood paneling, he said. Now he gestures generally at the yard and beyond and such, he smells richly of wine, grandly boozed, he means it all, orchards, mini-malls, the Getty Villa, breakfasts at Huckleberry, even Long Beach. Lately he's saying the world will be mine. *You'll run things someday, sooner rather than later.* "But what if I don't want it," is what I'd like to say, but he wants change, I get that, sure.

My stepfather says, "I know what you're thinking, but once you know desire is inconstant, you're in for unhappiness, them's the breaks. Jesus, would you look at that blimp?"

ESCAPE TO PECHANGA

BLACKJACK ONE HOUR AWAY

It's a new casino on one of the Indian reservations.

"Like India's anywhere close to here," I say grouchily.

My stepdad says, "Sarcasm leads to masturbation and loneliness."

My stepdad says, "Understand that humor always comes at someone's expense."

My stepdad says, "It's hard work, caring about every single soul in the world."

He puts an arm around me. "Let's go watch Jack fuck some more shit up."

As we sit, he pinches my arm. I barely flinch and he nods. "Good. Tolerance is key."

On weekends the other boys surf and make solid cash through corporate sponsorships, Speedo and Red Bull and Educational Testing Services. There's no surfing in Iran. Soccer's huge. I miss Tehran. There was a nice café on Grand Boulevard past the white-tiled mosque, and we'd sip espressos mornings before class. "You're too young for espressos," teased my stepfather, but he let me drink them anyway. I had to add a spoonful of raw sugar to cut the bitterness, and we'd watch the women in their wraps move lithely along like paisley tornados with flashing eyes, and the agents of the government followed us, Reza One and Reza Two, but we were friends with the two Rezas, and sometimes we four would share a croissant, and it felt, I don't know, maybe like we were at the center of things, like the people in that city and that country, that whole region of the world, cared about me and my stepfather, kept an eye on us, wanted to know what we thought of them, shop owners tugged our sleeves and said "What you think?" of their wares, ceramic ashtrays and woven sweaters, peach tobaccos, leather slippers, the students sent baskets of fruit home with my father and we'd eat soft melons for dessert, and he taught me how in England dessert is called pudding, and pudding can be cheese.

Now here we are like anyone else, school, work, home, dinner, *24*. Maybe I should surf like the other boys. Never in Tehran did it occur to me to be like the other boys.

The secret of this country is that it is a country of needing to belong.

My stepfather buys a mosquito zapper and is having way too much fun frying the bugs, so I walk down to the beach. The prettiest girl is reading on the shore wearing dark sunglasses, and I'm careful not to spray her with my feet splashing in the surf. She considers me. "Should I ask you if you like it here in LA? If you like our school? The professor? Freud? Have you noticed that many authorities don't consider female homicide regarding their mothers?"

"Do you like peaches?" I ask, and produce a blushing specimen from my pocket.

She sniffs it, rolls it into the ocean. "I mean, don't *we* get to kill someone?"

The peach rolls back, ushered on waves. I retrieve it and wipe it against my jeans.

"Perhaps," she says, pencil chew, book shut, holding place with slender finger on which to nibble and smell the bits of her, "the fundamental delineation between males and females is that women are not biologically impelled to command, but is this—"

"Bagel?" I offer. It's only half, and a little stale from being in my pocket. She declines.

"Is this a product of genetic evolution? Or was the first man driven to kill off Daddy and Woman One docile and kind?" She seems inside herself now, thinking and jotting notes against her forearm. Her hair is lovely, a bouncy blond foam. I offer a foil packet of tuna from my Jansport's deepest pocket. She squeezes fish into her mouth like toothpaste. Fairly gross.

Then she reads over what she's written.

"What do you think? Good stuff?" I ask warmly.

She shrugs. "No, but memories never have the flash of original thought." Her voice is strange, and I see that beneath her sunglasses she's crying. She rubs sand idly against the ink on her arm and says, "And do you, do you want to kill your daddy, too?"

"I just have a stepdaddy," I say.

She bites into the peach. “I like your backpack,” she whispers, leans close soft, soft, and I hear my stepfather calling, dinnertime, dinner, it’s enough to make me want to hit him.

Today during World Affairs Hour we watch the student protests in Tehran. I try not to seem too interested because it wouldn’t be cool. The other boys flick folded paper through upright fingers and ignore the professor. I pretend to be interested in their game and half-listen to the news. A reporter says that half the country is under the age of twenty-seven. They are young, they want to revolt, they want something new, it’s the privilege of youth. I wonder if in Iran all the twenty-eight-year-olds support the conservative mullahs. I wonder if twenty-seven-year-olds are driving the protests out of fear of a lost youth. It’s their last chance to matter.

Harden says, “You’re watching that news awfully close, we can all see so, you faggot.”

The boys laugh and say, “Faggot, faggot, faggot.”

The prettiest girl ignores me, ignores us all. She’s drawing babies on her thighs.

The professor says, “Revorution is the onry way to make rife better.”

After school I run home before the boys can catch me.

My stepfather used to have more say in things, but he doesn’t care so much these days.

I tell him I’m being bullied and ask for assistance.

“Life works itself out,” he explains, “whether or not we interfere.”

“Withdrawer in disgust is not the same as apathy,” I quote my professor.

“Actually, withdrawal due to understanding one’s meaninglessness within the grand scheme of things is common sense. *Not* withdrawing is vanity. Thinking we matter to other people who don’t know us? Vanity. Vanity, vanity, vanity.”

“Even you?”

“Even me.”

On TV, several soldiers hit a woman. Her tongue pokes out, pained, defiant.

Flames. Gunshots. Screams. A city is on fire.

"Recognize any of your students?" I ask quietly.

My stepfather shakes his head. "No, but that's Bill Buchanan, former head of CTU."

I look closer. It's not the news, it's *24*.

Does our government support the current dictator or the one waiting in the wings?

Wings, wings, wings, chants the lion in my dreams.

Harden and the other kids corner me outside a 7-11. "Nice backpack," they sneer.

"Thanks!" I say, trying to sound sincere though mostly I'm physically worried.

My sincerity discomfits them. "Yeah, well, you're welcome!" they say, still sneering.

Harden says, "So where'd you get it, tough guy?"

"Target," I say. "I like your briefcases, too."

"We got them at Nordstrom's!" he shouts, coming closer. "Got a problem with that?"

"Not at all!" I exclaim.

Harden sort of cuffs me on the neck, but maybe he means it as a friendly gesture to the new kid who "cares" about the world. We all skateboard to Pepperdine. On the sidewalks college kids sip coffee and chat on cell phones. No torture, no explosions, no protests. There's a farmer's market, and tiny women sell tiny carrots, tiny potatoes shaped like fingers.

"Midgets!" the boys shout happily. "Get 'em!"

The tiny women shriek and hide under the table. It's clear that this happens often.

The boys flip the table over. Spare change and miniature vegetables go flying. They put a midget on a bench and pour water up her nose. She writhes. The boys sing with glee. College kids film us on cell phones. I try to look regretful. A police car approaches. "Flee," they cry, and it's fun in a way, until I hear someone yelling, "It was the kid in the backpack!"

I want to confess my troubles to my stepfather, but he's on the phone, economical with worry: three steps, pivot, pause, pivot, three steps, repeat. "Yes. Do that. Long range to the Na Pali coast. In fact just leak it. Saying we're doing it is enough to put the fear into these people. There, I said it. Done." Pivot. Click. He looks at me. "The Chinese are always listening," he explains. "Koreans?" I ask. He laughs. "Sure, Koreans, like they know anything. Think," he says. "Kim Jong Il. Such an obvious pun." The phone rings. "Yes. Yes. No. Yes. But hold on a minute there. I never said I wanted onions." He looks at me again. "Why, do you suppose, you're standing in the kitchen, knife in hand, staring at me? Get out, play with kids your age."

At school the prettiest girl stops me in the hall.

"Someone told on you, on all of you, I have to go before I'm found out."

The boys come into the washroom while I'm peeing.

"There's a rat," Harden says. "Said you were responsible for all those things."

"All what things?" I ask, worried.

The boys laugh. "All *sorts* of crazy shit," Harden says, also laughing.

"Who's the rat?"

"Some kid you don't know," he says. "But we got him. We got him good."

Harden puts an arm over my shoulder and leads me to an unused classroom. They unlock the door and lock it behind us. There's a kid strapped to a chair with a hood over his head. I don't think I know him. He's peed himself and it smells like vinegar. And piss.

Someone knocks at the door. "I saw arr of you go in there! Get out! Arr get a key!"

The hooded shape sort of murmurs. The boys freak and run out a window.

The person at the door, probably the professor, goes away to get the room key.

So it's just me and the kid.

I think about torture. It can do many things. It can punish people and make them regret their actions, and that's good, right? Regret gives us character, depth of soul. And it can scare people into telling the truth. Truth is always a good thing. And, too, once my stepfather said that life is torture. He said if anything ever happened to him in Tehran, if the Rezas ever took him away, he would be okay, not to worry about any pain he might be in. He told me sooner or later that it would happen to me, that I had to be prepared, and maybe that's why he throws tacks at me all the time. He said that the secret to being in a dark place with bad people is to forgive them, pity them, love them. Best of all, get the hell out of there. Don't take it. Run.

I let the nervous kid go. He's blond and chubby. "But they'll know it was you!"

I shrug. I'm ready for it, anyway.

I get home, and my stepfather has popcorn ready and root beer, too, my favorite.

"Season finale!" he says, grinning.

We settle in to watch the exciting conclusion of *24*.

And you know what? I feel lucky not to have a real father.

Who do I feel compelled to kill? Exactly no one, which is fine by me.

But I'll tell you, it certainly doesn't make me want to have a son.

The girl who used to be the prettiest girl now is just the sad girl. All the boys wear Jansport backpacks. They sort of follow me, copying whatever I do. I don't do much, but they seem to think it's enough. Apparently being peaceful is "in" for whatever reason. The protests in Iran are over. The powerful remain in power. Everyone got the sugar out of their system.

Me and the girl who once was pretty stand in the lunch line with macaroni and cheese.

She says, "You think you're so special now, I thought you were different."

"I am," I assure her.

"Only in the way everyone's different," she says, clearly disappointed.

During Current Popular Television Hour we watch *24* even though we've all of us seen every season. We hoot when Jack tortures bad guys. It's ironic, in some ways. In others it isn't. During breaks everyone reaches into their deepest Jansport pocket and pulls out tuna packs. The room reeks. The sad girl stands and starts yelling during the scene where the African terrorists are storming the White House. She says, "Why do you watch this crap? Real life is all around us! The people of Iran rioted for change! Care! Care about the world!"

Someone says, "It is true that protest is important, that feeling attached to the suffering of our fellow men is a good thing. And often we *are* moved by a collective of voices shouting out from the void. But come on now. What are the Iranians really crying over? Oppression? Of *course* you protest oppression. We don't have oppression anymore. We're advanced. A *good* society. What could we possibly protest? Fast food? Too many entertainment options? Down with iPhones, down with baseball, down with Nintendo? Protesting a lack of protest is as much a luxury as fake boobs and Spanish ham. Enjoy life, honey, enjoy it, enjoy it, enjoy!"

Everyone cheers. They're all good points.

The sad girl has no response. I go to her and touch her wrist at the pulse. She says she can't see me anymore, I'm not the man I used to be.

That's when I decide to prove her wrong. I will care! Every day hence I'll make myself care! I'll lead the boys into battle. We'll drink too much wine and cut class. We'll start protests against nothing. We'll run away because if we're runaways we won't have to kill our fathers, and besides it's adventurous. At the next invasion we'll tape ourselves to our desks in protest, and the professor won't know what to do. We'll act out. We'll steal a donkey and ride it into town. I know it won't end well, probably with significant pain, but who cares, it'll be a good time, a memorable one, a rising action. Besides, donkeys are good pets. I learned that in Iran. My stepfather taught me. They awaken in the morning the same moment as you, even if you're inside your warm bed and they're out in the chill, before the sun has risen. They have the innate ability to sense that the consciousness of the thing they love, that strange form that scratches their ears, feeds them carrots, gives them meaning—it's back again. Glorious day!

I give the donkey a pat. It swings its tail.

We ride into town, the boys scattering petals from flowers I cannot name.

ON THE DAY OF THE DEAD

Hilda Johnston

CHILDREN, I KNOW you have nothing to say. Yet over and over again you'll be asked to say it. And I'm not asking you to turn your umbrella of silence inside out, the ribs poking into a five-paragraph essay; I am only asking you to write a few sentences. My head is heavy too. It's the season. We aren't farmers, yet we know the harvest is over—a few wisps of hay blowing over the bare fields, small birds pecking for grain. Even the dead are uneasy. That's why we have All Hallows Eve and, in Mexico, The Day of the Dead. But this is not a gloomy holiday, as you can see by this altar. In Mexico, skeletons ride bicycles, play the guitar, or dress up to be married. Children eat sugar skulls decorated with flowers.

For our altar I brought a photograph of my uncle when he was a boy with his horse, some tomatoes, green peppers and a beer bottle. My Uncle made Jambalaya—that's a shrimp dish—with beer, and it's the custom to put a favorite dish of the dead on the altar. No, they don't eat it; the aroma is enough. And every altar has marigolds, which, they say, smell like bone and attract the dead. Now you'd think the dead, being all bone, would long for something more sensuous and fleshy like rose or honeysuckle, but maybe marigolds are all they can bear.

We also have Indian corn because each kernel is a seed. I know it's not until you're teenagers that many of you will begin to marvel at the properties of seeds, but at the harvest it is most important to garner the seeds. If we lose the seeds, we lose the thread. See these dry stalks of fennel. Each stalk branches into umbels of licorice-flavored seeds.

You can come up to the altar when you've chosen your skeleton. Remember, each of you is the skeleton of someone who has died. You can pick someone you knew personally or someone from history. Yes, you can be a horse…or, yes, a dinosaur. I imagine you are more familiar with dinosaur skeletons than with the lumbering beasts themselves. At least we were in my day.

Whatever skeleton you choose, you should write about what your skeleton remembers. The dinosaur must miss the ferny marshes of the Mesozoic. But the horse has a harder time of it. His fields are still here, a blue-red in the autumn sunset. The horse is like the girl who dies in *Our Town*—that's a play. She comes back, invisibly, and watches life going on without her. She misses everything. Yes, even homework—her pencils and her copybooks. Death turns everything upside down. That's why we invite the dead back, not just to give them a day off, though god knows they deserve it, but to clear our own heavy heads. It's as though all summer we've been squirreling away nuts and seeds and now we can't remember where we've stored half of them, and anyway we have more than we need and we'd really like to go to sleep, but first we have to make sure we can get through the winter, and that's why we save these seeds. And why we welcome the dead. Now I want each of you to imagine what your skeleton would miss should he come back to visit.

The dinosaur is extinct. Yes I know, the seeds are lost. It must be a bit grim for a dinosaur to celebrate the cycle of life and death. But at least he has a skeleton. As they say on the day of the dead, he who was never born can never be a skeleton. Not *have* a skeleton but *be* a skeleton. It's an important distinction. A word can make a difference and so can a punctuation mark. Commas are important. Commas separate the essential from the nonessential. If I say my uncle who died last year made a delicious jambalaya, I don't use commas because that's how you know which uncle I'm talking about. But if I say John Smith, who died last year, was a good hockey player, I do use commas because who died last year is not essential to the sentence even if it is essential to John Smith. I'm afraid I'm confusing you. Why don't you write now from the point of view of your skeleton?

PREDATION

Janice Shapiro

WHAT WE THINK about a lot in our house is *extinction.* We think about the extinction of the dinosaurs. We think about the extinction of the ice age animals. We think about the extinction of my friend Larry.

"Say *cup,*" my son, Hank, shouts from his bedroom where he is looking for a tiny toy saddle. "Say *horse.*"

What I have found interesting about parenthood is how bad I am at it. This has come as a surprise. I always pegged myself as a natural and went through years of highly unnatural manipulations and unspeakable anguish to have Hank only to—in my opinion—completely fail in what is probably the most important role of my life.

This is not really surprising, and by *this,* I mean my complete miscalculation of what my true nature would be. That lack of self-awareness could, in fact, be the story of my life, which if it were just me going through this journey by myself would probably be pretty comedic, but throw a kid into the mix and, unfortunately, the dye of comedy quickly changes into something entirely different.

"Say *ooombabaooomba!*"

If Larry were still here, he would shake his head at all this. He was an optimist, sailing past bad tidings as if they were complete strangers, unseeable.

"You have to always look at the bright side, baby doll," he told me when I was pathetically crumpled on the pet groomer's floor, lost in the despair that can only come from another failed romance.

"Bright side?" I repeated incredulously.

"So, you made a mistake. He wasn't the right one for you. Now he's cleared the spot for someone better. In the end this fellow would've been more trouble than he was worth." Larry spoke in a calm and confident voice, carefully putting the blow-dryers (different sizes for different-size dogs) back on their hangers.

"Yeah. Yeah. Yeah," I mumbled, and picked the dog hairs off of the tile closest to me and held them above my head before releasing them so I could watch them float, almost invisible, back to the floor. Larry, who was considerably older than I was and so had certainly seen his share of sadness, never allowed himself to be pulled down by the weight of loss and disappointment. He had what is known as a buoyant personality. Larry was remarkably unsinkable.

"I'm laying my wager on you," Larry said soothingly, and reached out to lightly pet the top of my head as if I were one of his favorite dogs, a special one that he gave extra biscuits to and tied the prettiest ribbons on. "Take it to the bank, Maria. You're going to be fine."

And despite my better judgment, I would try to believe him. What choice did I have? I was a single mother; I had to keep soldiering on. The bed of utter despair was not mine to lie in for long. It was just so good to have Larry there to breathe hope into our lives when I was sure there was none.

So, of course, only the worst could happen to him.

"Say *bang, bang.*"

"Life's not fair," says the voice of Jeremy Irons as Scar, the evil uncle in *The Lion King,* a movie I've seen far too many times for anyone's good, let alone for a four-year-old who, if allowed, would probably watch it every day of his life. This is one of those parenting things that I am truly terrible at: *setting limits.* Actually, I have never been good with any sort of *limits*. I'm claustrophobic, for God's sake. Just the word, *limits,* does something to my lungs, makes it hard for me to breathe.

For about a month after Larry was killed, I let my son, Hank, watch *The Lion King, Beauty and the Beast*, and *Pocahontas* every day. In my despair, I rationalized that the almost constant rotation of Alan Menken lyrics could be a positive thing—something about how the healing power of overproduced, emotionally manipulative, relentlessly upbeat songs would get us through this most terrible of terrible times—and I most probably would still be telling myself this if Hank's actual (but never present) father, Tag, had not shown up unannounced one foggy Tuesday evening, only to step into the house and scream, "*Shut that shit off!*"

A word about extinction and how to explain it to a four-year-old: Well, what you say when you are inside the George C. Page La Brea Tar Pits Museum, gazing with your silent and scared son at the growling/howling animated mannequins of a saber-toothed tiger preparing to plunge its large canines into the neck of a blank-eyed ground sloth is "They all died off."

"They're dead?" the four year-old asks in the unnervingly quiet tone he's adopted since Larry's murder.

"Yes. All of them. For years and years and years," I say as cheerfully as possible.

"What do you mean, all of them?" he asks, nervously biting the inside of his cheeks.

"I mean, there's no such thing as saber-tooths or ground sloths or mastodons or wooly mammoths anymore, darling."

"Do you mean they aren't real?"

"Right. They aren't real."

"So, are they make-believe?"

And if the four-year-old's brown eyes had any magical power they would command me to nod my head, smile reassuringly, and give him the teeny-tiny thing he's asking for—the comfort of make-believe, the almost-but-not-quite realness of it. And I want to give it to him. I want to with all my heart, but for some reason I can't. No, sir. Not me.

Instead, I look away, lock eyes with that poor, screaming sloth—who is eternally trapped in that second that is worse than death, the one when you know with absolute certainty you're going to die, and if you have time to hope, you only hope it's not going to be as bad as you know it will be—before I take my child's hand, a small spot of warmth against my bigger, colder palm and say as gently as I can, "No, sweetie, they're not make-believe. They're nothing. Absolutely nothing."

Larry was not a young man when he died. He never told me how old he was but in their accounts of the murder the papers listed his age as sixty-four. Sixty-four is not young, but it's not really old, and if that unknown assailant hadn't come into the store just before closing on that unseasonably warm Monday, my day off, I believe Larry would've been by my side grooming dogs for many more years to come.

He really had a true talent for the work. I was good at nails, but that was more about speed than technique. The other part, the actual grooming, I could do a decent job of if the dog was real old or tranquilized (something I never did without the owner's consent), but Larry just had the natural touch. There was something about the way he whispered to the dogs and stroked their fur that seemed to make them feel instantly safe, certain of being well cared for.

"It's from all my years in show business," he once told me. "Believe me, a rabid Dobie is nothing next to Mitzi Gaynor on a bad night."

"Time to get ready for bed," I said, and picked Hank off the floor where he and Tag had been playing an elaborate game with his Fisher-Price toys.

"When will I see you again, Daddy?" Hank asked, delighted as always to see Tag, the man he calls *Daddy* (which is technically correct I guess but still bugs me).

Tag shrugged and said, "How 'bout tomorrow, kiddo?"

"You're coming back tomorrow?" Hank asked excitedly, and smiled first at Tag and then at me. I raised my eyebrows and gave Hank a surprised look and tried to smile in order to hide the fact that this surprise was far from a happy one for me.

"No, man. I ain't leaving," Tag said, and my faint smile instantly vanished, but before I could say a single word, Tag headed out of the room to get himself a beer.

"So, did the fag leave you any money?" Tag asked a little later that night after I had finally gotten Hank to sleep. He finished his beer in one long gulp and then sat down too close to me on the living room sofa. I just gave him a look of utter disgust.

"All right, all right, Maria. Allow me to rephrase the question," Tag said, and moved closer, forcing me to scoot further away. "So, did the *dude*—is that better?—your *friend,* the unfortunate bastard, leave you something?"

"Go!" was all I could bring myself to say. Utterly exhausted, I was no longer able to calculate the number of days that had passed since I had had a good night's sleep. "Just leave, Tag!"

I pointed toward the front door but Tag gently pushed my arm back down and looked at me with his "innocent" face, the same one he wore when he used to stumble into bed at five in the morning, claiming he lost track of time playing gin rummy with his mother.

"I have nowhere to go, Mar. I'm not going back to Melissa. Man, that chick just got too, too, too *emotional!"* Tag shook his head, and I thought Melissa must have started agitating for a commitment, something I could have told her was never going to happen and a bad move to play with Tag. Tag looked at me again and smiled slightly, saying something with his eyes that I both did and did not want to see, or hear.

I quickly stood up and walked across the room and turned off a light and then turned off another.

"What are you doing here, anyway, Tag? Surely, you have other places..."

I spoke quietly, because it was almost midnight and Hank had just fallen asleep, but I watched Tag closely, and the weird thing was that in the newly darkened living room, he suddenly looked ten years younger, like he did when we were both in our early thirties and I used to be so in love with him. I wished I had left the lights on.

"Just thought it was time I step up to my parental responsibilities," Tag said. Then he yawned and his forehead crinkled, making him instantly look his age again.

"You're not the parent, Tag. You're the sperm donor. There's a big difference," I was forced to remind him once again.

"Not to me," he said, before stretching out on the couch and firmly closing his eyes.

"Dinosaurs are extinct," Hank explained for about the fortieth time, as I pushed him around Trader Joe's in a shopping cart, a few days before Tag's sudden and unexpected reappearance in our lives. "All of them. The plant-eaters and the meat-eaters."

"I know," I said, and in an effort to change the subject, held up a bag of barbeque potato chips. "Are these the ones you like?"

"That means they're all dead," he continued as if I hadn't said a thing. "The plant-eaters *and* the meat-eaters."

"I know," I sighed, and checked the date on the tortillas—we'd been having a problem with moldy tortillas. "And you know what? The dinosaurs were all dead even before the ice age animals roamed the earth."

"But they're dead too," Hank said, grimly nodding his head.

"Oh, yeah. They are," I agreed.

"They're extinct."

"Right."

"Is Daddy extinct?" Hank asked, his brow now a small crease of confusion.

"No," I sighed.

"Where is he?"

"I don't know." I smiled and shrugged my shoulders to convey the absolutely false message that it's really no big deal not to know the whereabouts of one of your parents. No big deal. Misplaced toy. Misplaced shoe. Misplaced father.

"He could be extinct," Hank offered, helpfully.

"No. I don't think so," I said. "I think he's just busy somewhere else."

"Is Larry busy someplace else?"

"No. Larry's dead. You know that, honey," I said quietly, and lightly ran my fingers over the fine hairs on the top of his head in what I hoped was a comforting way.

"So maybe Daddy's dead," Hank said, and, in my own sick, perverted way, I wanted to give him this point, but I didn't.

"Daddy's not dead, sweetie," I said, and then muttered under my breath as I rummaged in the back of the shelf, hoping to find some fresher tortillas, "I'm just not that lucky."

The scene in Trader Joe's is an example of my failure as a parent. Meaning: Four-year-olds are not supposed to be thinking about death *all the time*. I'm sorry, but they're not. As a parent I should have protected him. I should've guarded my son's innocence with my life. Nothing as piercing as death, *death* we're talking about, should've come within five hundred feet of my child's soul. That night when I'd hung up the phone and Hank had looked at me and asked in a too, too quiet voice what was wrong, I should've said, *nothing*. That's what I should've said. *Nothing is wrong, everything's fine, sweetheart.* But what I said and I wish so much I hadn't was the truth.

Before becoming a groomer, Larry had a long successful career as a stage manager in Las Vegas.

"When I first got there, it was all Glamour with a capital *G!*" he told me one evening as I cleaned the grooming area, shaking out a thick coat of Clorox over all the white tiles while he counted the day's money. I noticed he often talked about his life in Vegas when he counted money. "I got to work with everyone! Sinatra, Lewis and Martin, Sammy Davis, Ann-Margret, Shecky Greene, Don Rickles, Joey Bishop..."

"What about Elvis?" I interrupted, something I knew Larry hated, but I couldn't stop myself. "Did you ever work with Elvis?"

Larry sighed, laid down the stack of tens, and gave me that look of his, the same one I got when I had to ask him to take over a too-jumpy dog: not exactly angry—Larry never got angry—just disappointed.

"Elvis was the beginning of the end," Larry spoke slowly, as if I were slightly mentally retarded. "He attracted a different kind of crowd, if you know what I mean, beauty."

"But did you ever work with him?" I persisted, mainly because I had seen that oddly silent black-and-white footage of Elvis at twenty-one, the black-haired beauty, all fire and nerves, dancing on some outdoor country fair stage, and lost a piece of my heart forever.

"Sweetie, I decided from the beginning never to work on something I didn't care about. There's never any point in doing that!"

I stared down at the dry turquoise powder that was slowly darkening on the damp counter and let him pinch the top of my arm lightly, which was what he did to show affection, all at once feeling so sad because I knew all the work I had ever done I hated, even the grooming—it was just hanging out with Larry that made it tolerable.

"You love doing this, don't you?" I asked.

"What? Talking to you?"

"No, grooming the dogs. You love it, don't you?"

"Honey, I wouldn't be here if I didn't. Because, believe me, life's too short, and Lord knows, I don't need the money!"

In the middle of the night, the bedroom door opened and Tag came in and sat down on the edge of the bed.

"Are you sleeping, Maria?" he whispered, and although I considered not answering, I somehow heard myself say, "No."

Tag lay down beside me in the dark. "You need a new couch."

"I know," I said, and turned on my side so my back was facing him. Since I hadn't been sleeping much anyway, I was secretly glad for the company during the long, quiet no-man's hour, even if the company was Tag.

"So, come on, just tell me, what's the money situation like around here these days?" Tag asked.

I didn't answer for a long time. It was a complicated question coming from Tag. A talented but lazy guitarist, he usually earned what money he had by being the lowest of middle men in tiny pot deals, but those deals tended to go bad, and I was worried he was going to ask to borrow some money, something I had specifically promised my parents I wouldn't do when they lent me the ten grand.

"I mean," he said, after a while, "if you need a hundred bucks..."

"No, that's okay," I said, quickly. "Dot and Herb actually came through this time."

"Well, stop the world," Tag said with true amazement. That had been a huge point of contention when we were together so many years ago. It drove him nuts that my rich parents would never spread the wealth my way. "They believe in survival of the fittest," I used to explain. "They're trying to make me fit."

"So, how is he?" Tag asked, shifting around beside me on the bed, rearranging pillows under his head.

"My dad?"

"No. The kid."

"I don't know. Not so good, I guess."

"He'll be all right."

"How do you know that?"

Tag thought for a minute. I could feel his breath lightly blowing the hairs on the back of my neck and the heat of his body filling up the small space between us under the covers.

"I guess I don't," he finally admitted, before his hand landed softly on the inside of my thigh, in the exact place I was hoping it would.

I often dream about Larry and in my dreams he is always happy but never says a word. It's not that he can't speak, but rather he doesn't want to. What he is usually doing is pushing my son on the swing at the park. In real life, Hank is a tireless swinger and Larry used to be a tireless pusher. Sometimes I would fall asleep on the grass under a tree watching them, and those were the sweetest rests of my life.

About a week after the murder, I finally got the nerve up to go back to the store. It was eerie walking into the place, mainly because it was almost exactly the way it was the last time I was there, the stacks of forty-pound bags of Science Diet in the corner, the shelves of neatly lined bottles of Mycodex flea shampoo, and the stubborn smell of wet dog hair still heavy in the air. All the same except for the two bloodstains, one on the white linoleum floor and the second on the far wall, directly behind the cash register.

I stood there for the longest time, unable to look away from the blood. Larry's blood. His blood. Something thick gathered in my throat making it increasingly hard for me to breathe, and even though it wasn't what I intended to do, I suddenly found myself filling a plastic bucket with warm tap water.

I started to scrub. I scrubbed and scrubbed and scrubbed. In case you have never done this, the interesting thing that happens is the dried blood that is brown actually turns red again when rehydrated, a bright, beautiful, shimmering red. And when I was done, when the wall was spotless and the tile floor gleaming white, I looked at the water in the bucket that was a gorgeous winelike color—so rich and delicious looking I knew I couldn't pour it down the drain. Instead, I carefully dipped my hands into the sweet-smelling mixture of water, cleansing solution, and Larry's blood and whispered a lot of words, most that probably made little or no sense, before turning and walking, dripping red, out of the store.

"Are you a plant-eater or a meat-eater?" I woke up early and heard Hank ask Tag this. I could feel Hank's small, perfect body wiggling beside me. He had wormed under the covers between me and his father, making the bed feel almost swampy with the three of us in it together.

"I eat both," Tag answered sleepily, and I opened my eyes to see Tag's heavily tattooed arm lazily snake around the child and pull him closer.

"That means you're an omnivore," Hank explained. "I'm an omnivore too. Mommy's an herbivore. She doesn't eat meat."

"Since when?" Tag asked, surprised, knowing my partiality towards rare, red meat.

"Since Larry died."

"It's a Hindi thing," I said, and both Hank and Tag looked at me, surprised I was there. "It's a way of honoring the dead."

"Larry's extinct," Hank said to Tag. "A bad man shot him in the head with his gun. The police didn't catch him. The bad man."

Tag looked at me with not a slight amount of disgust. "Do you two always start the day talking about this shit?"

"Yes," Hank answered before I could lie.

The theories are (1) a giant meteorite crashed into the earth, releasing poisonous gases and covering the land with an impenetrable cloud of dust that blocked the sun for years and years and killed off all of the dinosaurs; (2) man became a more sophisticated hunter and killed off all of the ice age plant-eating animals, leaving the meat-eating animals nothing to feed on, thus throwing off the balance of the ecosystem and causing all the large animals eventually to die off; (3) a high-on-crack, most probably gang member attempted to rob Larry, got scared, and shot him in the head before running out into the dark street, never to appear again—except in my child's nightmares, where he has landed himself an almost nightly starring role.

I love to stand on the observation platform and watch the gas bubbles explode through the thin sheet of water that covers the largest and most spectacular pit. The air smells deliciously like tar, although we've been told it isn't tar at all, but actually asphalt. On one side of the pit, a steady stream of traffic on Wilshire Boulevard heedlessly passes the statues of the mastodon family, the mother and child who stand on the bank with their trunks raised toward the father who has waded a couple of yards from shore and gotten inextricably stuck.

"Bad luck for him," Hank always says when we see it.

From where I stand, I watch Hank and Tag walk along one of the paths that winds through Rancho La Brea toward a *paleta* man. They are not holding hands but walk side by side, close enough to do so if they wanted to. I notice they have the same bouncy walk.

When I decided I wanted to have a child, I asked Tag to be my sperm donor even though we had been broken up for years. My logic in choosing him was that he was the one man I had ever been with who told me he loved me, and I thought even a technologically produced child should come out of love, even one that is no more.

And Tag really does have his winning side. When I asked him the other day what Elvis was singing in that silent piece of black-and-white film, he didn't hesitate. "Oh! You mean the one shot at the Alabama State Fair in 1956? Oh, it was 'Hound Dog.' You can tell by the way he's moving. It's definitely 'Hound Dog'!"

For the whole week he has been with us, Tag has been on his very best behavior. He washes all of the dishes. Goes out to his car to smoke dope. Reads Hank the endless Richard Scarry books that I long ago deemed too boring and has introduced the kid to T. Rex and Big Mama Thornton. And I can see a lightness returning to Hank's eyes. Just for moments, long moments when the grips of fear seem to loosen their hold and he can once again enter that almost weightless place of being a four-year-old, as light as a comic strip bubble without a word of dialogue inside.

There's a part of me that likes this, but then there's another part that thinks, *here I go again.* What *that* part thinks I really should do is try to keep Hank from getting too attached to this man—I guess, his father—because I know he will desert him. Tag said he loved me and I believe he *did* love me and he left. Tag may not even want to, but that's just who Tag is: a deserter. But days have gone by and I say and do nothing and I can't help but wonder why. Larry would, of course, know the answer. He would know what it is that makes us close our eyes to those things we just cannot face, the giant meteorite hurtling wildly through the cosmos, the bullet coming straight for our heads. Larry would know what it was that kept the mother and child mastodon planted on the edge of the tar pit, calling to the father to come back, please come back, as he sinks helplessly deeper into the thick, hot blackness below. Larry would know—but obviously, he's no longer talking.

from **THE SPLENDORS OF DEATH**

Aris Janigian

1.

MY BROTHER AND I loved to torture and kill things when we were kids. With a pair of scissors we'd snip off the wings of butterflies and moths until only their stubby bodies were left. With the same scissors, we'd bring the "praying mantis" to its knees, its little body flopping forward from the sudden loss of its big head. Someone told us that caterpillars and worms grew back the part you lopped off. We tested one after another until they lay scattered on the dirt like cigarette butts. Who would have guessed that with a sprinkle of salt a snail would bubble up and melt like the Wicked Witch of the West? In the summer, when you could cook an egg on the sidewalk from the heat, we'd take a magnifying glass and steady its pinpoint beam over ants. Smoke would rise as their little bodies shriveled up. Our backyard in Fresno, in old Armenian town, was chock full of fruit trees. Birds found it a good place for putting up their nests. We had Easter egg hunts all spring long.

2.

There is a Polaroid of us standing at the end of a walkway that stretches to the front porch of our house. We look just shy of school age, four and five years old. Shadows stretch from our feet, and on the curb in back of us a black Buick is parked. We wear tidy white shirts buttoned to the neck, roomy shorts, ankle length socks and shiny dress shoes. Our hair glistens as though a wet comb has just been run through it, and we are standing at attention with toy army rifles at our sides. My best guess is that we were on our way to church, and with a few minutes to spare our mother probably thought "how cute" and ran in to get the camera. We in turn fetched the rifles. Go ahead, mom—you shoot first.

3.

I felt sorry for the Jews, enslaved to the Egyptians that way, but I felt pretty bad for their enemies too. First, you had the flood; then the Tower of Babel. The people of Canaan and Bethel were all slaughtered, but worst of all is what happened to the citizens of Sodom: burned alive. When the Jews took a city, they even killed the animals, cows and goats and pigs, as though they had something to do with it. There were so many wars and killings I couldn't keep track of them. Our Sunday school teacher taught us "Thou shalt not kill," and then we sang songs about the people in Jericho getting buried alive.

I was happy when Jesus came around. He didn't kill anybody. Only himself, sort of.

4.

Why were people afraid to die if they were close to God? The bible said they were going to the bosom of God. How many people could fit in one bosom? Maybe they were scared they'd suffocate in there.

5.

On Thursday nights, we watched *Wild Kingdom*. Marlin Perkins was the fearless host of that show. He bravely stalked savage animals, all in order to give us a window onto their world. Sometimes he would show how beautiful the wild was; a field of flamingos, all on one leg; antelope coursing over the plains like a river; giraffe with necks long as palm trees loping into the horizon where the setting sun was colossal and turned the whole sky blazing pink. Mostly, though, these were backdrops for what we all wanted to see: one animal killing another. I remember the lion waiting in the grass, crouched. How, low to the ground and with stupendous patience it crept, and suddenly bolted. It pounced on the gazelle, went for its throat, and within minutes the bucking and kicking stopped, and all on the Serengeti was calm. Then it began feeding, remorselessly. The way it calmly stared at the camera, its muzzle all covered with blood, left no doubt: it had done what it had done, and it had the right.

6.

Murder: when someone bad kills someone good.

Capital Punishment: what they do to murderers where the president lives.

Massacre: when a whole bunch of people gets killed at the same time.

Genocide: what they did to the Armenians.

Slaughter: what they do to animals (or people who they think are animals).

Execute: when someone shocks you to death.

Suicide: when you kill yourself.

And now what happened to Robert Kennedy—assassination: killing someone important.

It was in the newspaper, a picture of a man cradling Kennedy's head in his arms. It reminded me of the way the Virgin cradled Jesus when he was pulled off the cross. A dark cloud descended over the whole school. The Mexican kids were so upset you'd think they were relatives of Kennedy. Some of the girls cried on their desks. Later, I learned that they like Kennedy were Catholic—all of them went to Catechism.

"The Kennedy family is cursed. I feel bad for Jackie," my mom said.

Dad said the Kennedy family, way back, made their money "bootlegging liquor." It had to do with how every bad thing you do eventually comes back to get you. Martin Luther King died the same year on a balcony. King was the one who told us "I have a dream." His face was childlike, but his voice was big as a river. Even my dad said, "He was a good man, King."

I'd barely heard of Robert Kennedy or King before they were assassinated. Now everybody talked about them. I was amazed at how important people became after they died. I thought it was unfair that they should become famous without being around to appreciate it. My dad said it always went that way.

"Not only that," he added, "but the meanest people live the longest."

He named a few of the meanest people he knew, and said that they had strong "constitutions."

Just like America, I thought.

7.

Our dog Pierre, a black French poodle, came to us from a wealthy acquaintance of my father (we learned a little later, Dad had also borrowed money from him). He was well behaved and groomed in the shape of an hourglass but after only a few months he resembled a bushy sheep. From empty fields we trekked through he got thistles and thorns and fleas. Every few months we'd dump some laundry detergent on him and hose him down for a shower. When we camped out in the backyard in the summer, Pierre slept between us, a kid brother. My brother and I would fight over who loved him best: He's my dog, I'd tell him; He's *my* dog, he'd tell me.

A year after we got Pierre, my dad told us that the owner wanted him back; "The bastard," my father muttered, "over a few lousy bucks." The next evening, the man rolled up in a big car. My dad slipped a finger beneath Pierre's collar and dragged him outside. I heard the two men exchange words. Then my dad walked back in the house with Pierre.

"He's yours for keeps."

We cheered, and jumped on Pierre: "Thanks Dad!"

My mom came out from the bedroom, where the shame of our family debt had sent her.

"What's happening?"

"I'll be frank with you all. The guy took one look and kinda choked; I guess ol' Pierre is so shabby looking he don't want no part of him anymore."

We must've had Pierre two three years before he got sick. His poop was the color of charcoal and the back porch was crisscrossed with bloody skid marks. His stopped eating his dog food. Lying there on his side he'd take us in with an eye and sigh. He seemed to be saying,

"Help." At night he howled. So that he wouldn't wake the neighbors, it got so that we had to shove him in the garage at night, what we'd nicknamed "the dungeon." Come morning we'd run out to fetch him from "the dungeon." *Pierre, Pierre,* we'd sadly sing. He'd meet us at the door, his tail barely wagging, shivering all over.

It was a Saturday morning when we found him dead in "the dungeon." My dad came out of the house to make sure. We cried—our world would never be the same without Pierre. We grabbed a couple of shovels, and start digging next to the fig tree. We planned to go six feet, but stopped at three, plenty deep, it seemed. Now we had to get Pierre, still in the dungeon, into the hole. My brother said he'd do it. I was relieved because I didn't know if I had what it took to carry his corpse. When he stepped out of the garage with dead Pierre in his arms, I was in awe of my brother's courage. He dropped Pierre in and we started shoveling. When the dirt reached our feet, we packed it all down with the shovel's flat side, and out of two sticks and twine, we made a cross and drove it into the ground.

I asked our Sunday school teacher, Mrs. Chamichian, where animals go after they die.

"Since they have no souls," she said; "nowhere."

"Even dogs?" I asked.

"Yes."

Did this mean that I'd never see Pierre again?

"No. But you *will* see your grandparents, and uncles and aunts."

When we got home, my brother and I yanked out the cross above Pierre's grave. Since he had no soul we were afraid it was a sin to leave it there. After the winter rain, I thought, after all the earth gets churned, there will be no spotting Pierre's grave. The seasons will erase his resting place. After we are gone, nobody will know he is there. All we'll be able to tell the next set of kids is, "Pierre, our dog, is buried beneath the fig tree." But who knows whether they'll believe us, no matter what we say, no matter what history we leave behind. Who knows whether they'll even care?

8.

Around age ten, we got real guns for Christmas; a revolutionary addition to our arsenal, which up until then was confined to slingshots. From a small cylindrical carton we'd pour BBs into the barrel's spout and with just a few ratchets of the handle the gun would get pregnant with enough pressure to kill. It's like we were sorcerers, the guns our magic wands, and the BBs our evil spells. We would strike things down from a world away.

Sparrows were all over the yard. From one branch to the next we'd watch them hop, their tidy little bodies turning this way, then that. The first one I shot fell from the tree and hit the ground like an overripe peach. We hardly found a mark on the bird; only a bead of blood swelled from its breast. I was disappointed: I expected something more dramatic. It hardly seemed worth it. Outside of its twiggy legs, politely folded up against its chest, it was unremarkable, common looking as the dirt upon which it lay. After turning it over and studying its every feature, we buried the sparrow. Above us, in the trees, dozens of its fellows were busy doing whatever it was that birds do. Strange how they hardly noticed when one of their own was gone.

9.

On TV, the Vietnam War was on. It was part of our lives, like the San Francisco Giants, except the war respected no season. They showed bodies lying in a field, or in a ditch. It was always raining, and looked very far away.

"What a shame," my Dad said.

When they posted that day's score, it was never close: we always killed twice as many as they killed. I kept waiting for the Americans to win. In any game I played, either time ran out or there were no more pieces on the board. How else did you decide when the game is over?

10.

Up from our house the miser Madame Hovanessian, who handed out walnuts for Halloween, lived. Her stockings, the color of rubber bands, gathered in rings round fat ankles, and she had several wiry whiskers sprouting from her chin. Three stubby palm trees where pigeons, plump as cantaloupes, roosted ran alongside her driveway, and even though you couldn't see them, the whole crown of the tree boiled with their voices. We'd gather rocks on our way home from school and from the alleyway we'd sling them into the fronds. After a week of trying, not only had we failed to kill a pigeon, not a single one even flew away in fright. Only their warbling suddenly stopped. One second the air was full of their voices, and the next second it was dead quiet, just like when a teacher suddenly hollers at a classroom of kids. After a while, we couldn't care less if we killed the pigeons. This was another kind of game. Silencing them.

BLUEBELLY

Greg Sarris

His name was Mr. Cortese, and with the way he peeked around the corner of the old barn when we went to see him, only his small dark face visible, his very long fingers clasped to the sideboards, he made us think of a lizard, or at least he made me think of a lizard, and now, many years later, I am there once more, seeing him for the first time. I am fourteen. I am holding the four-month-old fawn-colored goat that Mr. Cortese will kill. "There he is," one of the two brothers I have come with says. By this time, the man is coming toward us, and I can see that he is old and small, crouched it seems in his worn T-shirt and dirt-stiff jeans. His hands are huge, and already I imagine the butcher knife clenched in one hand, the wether's soft neck secured with the other. I don't want to watch—I didn't want to accompany Heralio and Isidro to this place where their father sent them with the goat he bought for tomorrow's Easter dinner. No, I didn't want to see a butchering but here I am braving myself through it because, after all, I am supposed to be brave. And then it's over; the two brothers are packing the newspaper-wrapped carcass back to the truck, and, somehow, I am following the old man past the barn to the far end of his property where there is a crumbling rock wall. "Help me get the ducks back to the barn," he commands over his shoulder.

At the rock wall, he stops. Dozens of bluebelly lizards are perched on the rocks watching us. The sun is shining brightly. It's warm, all at once it seems, as if spring in that instant had jumped over the rock wall and spread itself across the land. The old man points to a small lizard that scurries into a crevice. "I don't want the ducks to scare them," he says. "Sometimes they will try to eat the small ones." He glances down at a couple of large white ducks a few feet from us. I keep looking at the lizards, amazed: dozens of sets of eyes glinting in the sun. "Help me," he says, and we herd the ducks back to the barn.

Now, with rich late autumn light over the gravel walkway outside my window, and upon the rock wall farther on, I see lizards again everywhere, stationed at the edges of the walkway, perched on the rocks. Looking at me forty-some years later? I am an old man, or an older man. And, after thirty years of living elsewhere, I am home again in Sonoma County, where I was born and grew up.

I live now on Sonoma Mountain, a sacred landmark for my Coast Miwok and Southern Pomo ancestors. Not dramatic in shape, without the sharp peak of Mount Tamalpais or Mount Saint Helena, the mountain seems from a distance a mere assemblage of rolling hills rising out of the Santa Rosa plain. Where is "the mountain"? Yet its sheer size is astonishing, overseeing from its heights San Pablo Bay to the south and Mount Saint Helena to the north. And once you begin to explore the mountain, whether from its eastern side above Glen Ellen, or west from Petaluma, you will find unexpected oak and bay laurel groves, redwoods even, and hidden lakes and springs, surprise around a bend—a landscape as complex as any in Sonoma County, or as a Coast Miwok elder once said, "as beautiful as the designs in our baskets."

I did not grow up on the mountain, but in town, in Santa Rosa. Still, I heard the old folks talk of the mountain then, the place where the beginning stories were first told, when Coyote, along with the help of his nephew Chicken Hawk and several other animals, created the world as we know it today: this mountain; the Santa Rosa plain below, with its winding creeks and swath of meandering lagoon; the coastal hills directly west, and beyond them, the blue sea; and Mount Tamalpais, all the way south, whose peak rises out of the landscape like the pitched roof of a redwood bark house. Quail was the most beautiful woman then—at the time of Creation, when the animals were still people—which you will see if you look below her plume and find her black pearl eyes. There is a story from that ancient time that explains how Skunk got his stripes, why Woodpecker wears a red cap, and why Rattlesnake goes nowhere without his rattle. There's a reason warm winds dance with the fog on this mountain, and a reason too why the bay trees sing a lonesome young man's song. The sun is the oldest of us all—even older than Coyote. Bluebelly lizard knows this. No one knows the sun better.

The bluebelly lizard, formally known as the western fence lizard, is a staple of the rural Bay Area's long, hot summers, along with the dry grassy hillsides and the sharp smell of bay laurel trees. From light gray to black in color with multiple dark splotches, essentially the colors of the earth and rocks it inhabits, this lizard has a distinctive sky-colored belly, more pronounced in the males. Sentinel-like, the bluebelly perches atop rocks, tree branches, and fences, watchful for food—flies, small moths and spiders, fleas—as well as for predators: hawks, snakes, and larger species of lizards. The territorial males, known for their push-ups, will, during the mating season from late May through July, stage fierce wrestling matches during which one may lose his tail. But the bluebelly lizard, after losing its tail, will grow another. Perhaps the bluebelly's most distinctive feature for anyone living in or close to Bay Area rural landscapes is its ability to stem the spread of Lyme disease. According to countless studies, ticks that feed on its blood are much less likely to carry the disease.

My ancestors always knew the bluebelly was important. He knows the sun better than any of us, after all. According to the old stories, the sun gave Bluebelly a piece of its home—the sky—to wear as a sign of kinship. Sun said to Bluebelly, "With my home on your stomach the people will always know to remember me. When they see you each spring, again sitting atop the rocks, they will know too that I have returned. Your belly will match the sky where once again I'm looking down." That's why he's one of the first creatures to come out in the spring, and why he sits where the sun can see him. Have you noticed that wherever—and whenever—California poppies bloom, bluebellies abound? With their golden color, the poppies remind the lizards of the sun.

The bluebelly figures prominently in Native California lore. According to a story told among the Sierra Miwok of the western Sierra foothills, when Coyote made people, Lizard was the one who persuaded Coyote to give humans hands like Lizard's so we could use tools. Among the Chumash of coastal Southern California, Bluebelly was a person of great importance. There, in the Sierra foothills and along the Southern California coast, Bluebelly is no doubt an important character in the warp and woof of the storied landscapes.

But I don't know those landscapes.

Home is Sonoma County.

Santa Rosa was, forty years ago, still a relatively small town surrounded by agriculture, apple and prune orchards, dairies and chicken farms. Post–World War II sprawl had not yet claimed all the pastures and orchards from the town's edges. I remember once coming upon an abandoned dairy farm and seeing a developer's red flags crisscrossing the empty fields. The milking barn lay in ruins, a pile of heaped cinder blocks, as if the farmer, out of spite over the new zoning ordinance that forced him from his land, had blown up the building. There, in the rubble, were countless bluebelly lizards, vigilant, watchful, but trusting it seemed that nothing—no hawk or snake, nor imminent bulldozer—would destroy their kingdom.

One of the first things that appealed to me about my new home on Sonoma Mountain was its numerous rock walls. I moved into the house on a July day, when the mountain was warm, dry. There were plenty of lizards; the rock walls are a perfect habitat for bluebellies. But I didn't think much about them. There was the frenzy of moving, the unloading of boxes, then a water pump to repair, a broken window to replace. And then I experienced something I hadn't counted on: anxiety. Could I find my way here after having been gone for so long? Could I settle in? What of the mountain's silence, after my years of living in L.A.? Was there a door I could pass through and find myself home again, or might I find myself forever wandering in the dark, dissolved by the silence?

More and more my life on the mountain felt like a vacation that was lasting too long. Yes, I grew up in Sonoma County, but in town, never so far from neighbors; my home now is near the top of the mountain, at the end of a steep and winding dirt road. Not far from my property line, a large Coast Miwok community once thrived. But now? And what of those old stories I'd heard as a kid? The chasm between then and now felt impossible to cross. Was there ever a home here? Maybe I should have picked a house in town, I told myself. But, alas, even the town has changed, become unrecognizable: a huge mall where the movie theaters had been; the open fields and orchards I'd remembered now buried under housing tracts and strip malls advertising submarine sandwiches and all-year tans.

Then the land itself came out, pushed open the door I'd been looking for, and poured through. Or, say, Coyote, as tricky and surprising as the mountain he created, came out. Like this: I am driving home, up the mountain, with a bag of groceries alongside me in the front seat, and I spot a coyote as he trots past a fence post and disappears into the brush. Probably looking for a rabbit, I think. Maybe going back to its den someplace. Isn't that what coyotes do, hunt and live in hollowed tree trunks? And then there's a tickling sensation in my brain, and I'm laughing, laughing at my foolishness. Coyote hunt? Coyote live in a den? What was I thinking? Where had I been? No; Coyote created the world up on the mountain, along with his nephew Chicken Hawk; and, after he was disrespectful to his wife Frog Woman, she left him, living forever after in a lake, which is why to this day he howls at the moon. Quail, she doesn't just lay eggs in my lavender. She has the secret the lonesome young man from the bay laurel grove needed to seduce the woman he loved. And this lizard, the bluebelly on my rock wall, who else but the best friend of the sun? And now what's before me but trails of stories, one story leading to another, my known home, up the mountain and down. In town, on the Santa Rosa plain, voices rise up from below a cul-de-sac or a McDonald's: a heavy-set Pomo medicine man in suspenders and a top hat who walks with the grace of a hummingbird; a girl with a gold tooth who eats a raw egg to exorcise a demon; an old man with a butcher's knife and a million lizards.

I had presumed Mr. Cortese was Mexican. "No, he's Portuguese or something," said Heralio and Isidro, who were Mexican. Someone else said the old man was Indian, not Coast Miwok or Pomo, but Yurok or Hupa, from Humboldt County.

After my visit with Heralio and Isidro, I went again, one more time. His house was small; the yard was littered with box springs and rusted car parts. He raised goats and sheep and ducks, which he traded for staples—rice, flour, a crate of apples. I didn't understand then that, like many recently displaced farmers, Mr. Cortese no doubt rented his small farm for a pittance from a developer waiting to build houses on the land. His ducks were Muscovies, big white ducks with fleshy red faces, known to raise large batches of ducklings that grow fast. A cousin wanted to start raising Muscovies. "Feed them well. Do good to them. They'll give lots of babies," Mr. Cortese said, after placing a wooden crate containing ducks on the bed of my cousin's pickup.

"I'll help you get the ducks back to the barn," I offered.

I looked to the edge of Mr. Cortese's property, to the rock wall, but no ducks were there, and suddenly I felt stupid.

"Ain't no little lizards now. No lizards at all. Not until summer again." To make his point, he stomped his thick leather boot on the rain-soaked ground.

Looking out my window, beyond the rock wall with its sentinel bluebellies here and there, I see the curled dry leaves of a large oak scattered on the ground below the tree, and falling, one at a time it seems. Behind my house, clumps of poison oak have turned red. The old bay laurels drop their fruit—peppernuts my ancestors harvested for eons, along with acorns from the oaks. The birds are full-feathered. The deer's coats are long. In two weeks a first frost will cover the land, visible on the summer dry grass and thistle. Then rain. Short days. Lizards hibernate. No more atop the rocks walls. Not one.

Mabel McKay, the late Pomo medicine woman and renowned basket weaver, warned that we should only tell stories during the winter months, after the first frost and before the last. "You must pay attention in summer to where you are going," she said. "Don't be thinking about the stories then."

In the old days people had to pay attention in the summer, lest they step on a rattlesnake or scorpion. And they didn't need stories in summer; they could see where they were going, find their way in a world renewed by the sun. The winter nights, with hours of idle time, certainly provided the opportunity for storytelling, but wasn't it the long hours of darkness that prompted the need? Wouldn't one recall a washed-out hillside after a storm and worry about the changes to the landscape? Would the hill be recognizable? What of seeing the entire Santa Rosa plain under water? What of a memory in that long darkness of a broken path, long from the home village? Wouldn't one then welcome the stories, sing for the animals to chart again a known world?

I've been home five years, settled in. In the waning light outside my window, I see the cusp of winter. I know the long winter nights; I've known too the broken path. Winter? Darkness? Bluebelly, that fellow on my rock wall, hibernate? No. What I know, following him, now and again, is that there will be sun, that there will be a thousand more stories, some told with the pencil in my old man's hand, stories about Coyote and Frog Woman, stories about a medicine man who walks with the grace of a hummingbird, a gold-toothed girl who casts a demon from her body, and an old man with ducks and endless lizards, stories and more stories, until the sun returns to the mountain again, and there are new leaves on the trees I know, quail in the lavender and bluebelly lizards on my rock wall.

THE TORTOISE QUADRILLE
A FEW THOUGHTS ON SKIPPERDEE, MOJAVE MAX, AND MY FATHER

Deanne Stillman

OURS IS THE AGE of the grand gesture and outrage fatigue; it's hard to top planes flying into towers, and with every terrible story that has unfolded since 9/11, our attention spans have diminished. Yet now we are awash in images of the Gulf of Mexico in flames and sea creatures swimming in oil gushing from a deep wound in the planet. These images are difficult to look away from, and it seems as if this incident in the Gulf—the blowout deep under the sea that no one had prepared for—is so awful, so final in its consequences that nowadays, for the first time in many years, we are more fully engaged with matters beyond our immediate needs—at least for the moment.

The concern is both general and specific; many people with whom I've spoken about the oil spill have been following one very particular aspect of it—the geology of the sea floor or currents in the Gulf. Some are concerned with one animal, either because they always have been or are now drawn to it for a range of reasons. In my case, I find myself preoccupied with turtles. Unable to go down there and wash them, I ponder their fate all the time, dream about them, and was both thrilled and calmed at the news that their eggs are being rescued in a massive operation involving NASA and Federal Express. Because I live in the West and spend a lot of time in the wilderness drylands, my attention has turned to their earthbound kin, the desert tortoise, a prehistoric creature which crosses my path every now and then when I'm hiking in the Mojave.

When speaking of the natural world, for good reason we often turn to Native American myth. Turtle carries the world on its back is what many of these myths tell us; we are all citizens on turtle island. Yet we gringos often overlook our own stories in which various animals have served as totems and avatars (although sometimes that service has not necessarily been intended by the authors). Looking back on my early encounters with turtles, first literary and later real, I realize now that these turtles were among my first guides to the desert, long before I had physically ventured to my spiritual home. As I recall, I met my first turtle in *Eloise*, the classic book about the little girl who lived at the Plaza Hotel with only her nanny, her dog Weenie, and her turtle Skipperdee. "The Plaza is the only hotel that will allow you to have a turtle," Eloise said in her sophisticated and simple way.

Skipperdee ate raisins and wore sneakers. And he was sensitive; when Eloise went to Moscow, she had to send him back to the Plaza because of a nervous cough. I remember being quite taken with the hotel-bound turtle, perhaps because I, too, was a pampered little girl who lived in luxury until the day that it all ended. When we moved to lesser quarters, my mother bought me a turtle, perhaps as a bridge to paradise lost. But it wasn't grand hotels that I imagined, nor was it the marble and mahogany of the mansion we had left behind. Instead, the little reptile conjured the natural world, a sanctuary that would never vanish. I don't think I gave the turtle a name, or if I did, I don't remember. But it soon became a friend, a slow and steady companion who was always there, in the big glass dish with the plastic palm tree next to my bed. I remember coming home from school and going right to the dish to feed my turtle, fascinated by its slow lumber across the sand and the swirls on its back; somehow it spoke to my deeper streams, and it wasn't long before I started ordering desert botanicals from Kaktus Jack's through the mail (although this urge was also fueled by my father's frequent recitations of his favorite poem, "Eldorado" by Edgar Allan Poe).

As I now understand it, Skipperdee was preparing me for my next desert ambassador. This was the Mock Turtle in *Alice in Wonderland*—perhaps the most famous turtle in literary history. As many devotees of the Lewis Carroll classic will recall, Alice first learned of the reptile while she was playing croquet with the Queen, who asked if she knew how Mock Turtle soup was made. It was the first Alice had heard of such an animal, and the Queen commanded the Gryphon to take her to the turtle. When they met, he was sobbing, and explained that once upon a time he had gone to school in the sea and learned everything from an old turtle called Tortoise. Alice wondered why he was called Tortoise. "We called him Tortoise because he taught us," the Mock Turtle explained. Composing himself, he then said that he received a fine education, studying Ambition, Distraction, Uglification and Derision.

Alice pondered the information and then the Mock Turtle longingly recalled his earlier life, wiping tears from his eye with his paddle. "You may not have lived much under the sea," he said, "so you can have no idea what a delightful thing a Lobster Quadrille is." "What sort of a dance is it?" Alice asked. "Why, you first form into a long line along the seashore," the Gryphon said. "Two lines!" the Mock Turtle added. "Seals, turtles, salmon, and so on; then you've cleared all the jellyfish out of the way...." "It must be a very pretty dance," Alice said. "Would you like to see it?" responded the Mock Turtle, happy to demonstrate this part of his past. "Very much indeed!" Alice said, and the Gryphon and Mock Turtle went on to perform the Lobster Quadrille. And then the moment passed but the Gryphon wanted the show to go on. "Would you like the Mock Turtle to sing you a song?" the Gryphon asked Alice. "Oh, a song please, if the Mock Turtle would be so kind," Alice replied. "Sing her 'Turtle Soup,' will you, old fellow?" the Gryphon urged. And once again, the soulful turtle began to sob, belting out the tale of his own demise:

Beautiful Soup, so rich and green,
Waiting in a hot tureen!
Who for such dainties would not stoop?
Soup of the evening, beautiful Soup!
Soup of the evening, beautiful Soup!
Beau—ootiful Soo—oop!

Beau—ootiful Soo—oop!
Soo—oop of the e—e—evening,
Beautiful, beautiful Soup!

Years later, I was the one who was crying when, during a shamanic journey involving hundreds of people at an airport hotel, I had a vision of my maternal grandmother handing me a vial of tears—my own—as I stood under a Joshua tree in a trance. Along that subterranean path there was a giant desert tortoise; he had accompanied me to the rocky shrine where I received the gift that changed my life, and since then I have been comforted to know that even though I don't always see them, tortoises are in the Mojave when I am and, more important, when I'm not. Yet I sometimes feel the urge to be near them, and when I do, I drive north from Los Angeles, a latter-day Alice dropping through a freeway sinkhole and emerging at their home in the Desert Tortoise Natural Area near California City.

There's a famous old tortoise named Mojave Max at Red Rock Canyon in Nevada, and every year school kids bet on the moment when he will crawl out from his burrow after hibernating all winter. In the springtime and into the summer, I like to walk the paths of the California City preserve, hoping to get lucky; you can spot a tortoise burrow near the base of the creosote bush, and I sometimes plant myself near one and wait for the ancient critter to reappear. In the meantime, plenty of other desert entertainment abounds. If the rains have come, the preserve is a blaze of glory, with the violet Mojave aster popping on the desert floor, yellow seas of goldfield rippled by the winds, and purple and white profusions of flowers on the calyx bush. Red-tailed hawks and woodpeckers and cactus wrens frequent the tortoise habitat, and of course snakes and lizards and tarantulas also call it home, as do the ground squirrel and badger and coyote.

Once there were vast cities of tortoise in the Colorado and Mojave deserts of California. During the 1920s, there were a thousand of the creatures per square mile. By 1990, the state reptile had become officially endangered. Its habitat was degraded by decades of unchecked cattle grazing, and off-roaders had begun to take their toll. Today there is a profusion of ravens in the desert, because ravens follow what people throw away, and parts of the desert are strewn with leftovers. When they're finished, they turn to tortoise hatchlings. On the 40 square miles of the sanctuary outside California City, and elsewhere across the Mojave, the desert tortoise is making what may be its last stand. As it happens, this is no ordinary reptile fighting for its life (not that that makes its struggle any less compelling), but a reptile that may actually be like Skipperdee and the Mock Turtle. That is to say, it has a personality, according to a study made several years ago by U.S. Geological Survey biologist Kristin Berry. That critters have certain traits and feelings is not news to me, but if such "news" can stave off extinction, I'm all for it.

Berry studied the tortoise population at the Army base of Fort Irwin, before the animals were relocated to make way for expanded military maneuvers. After outfitting tortoises with transmitters, she learned that No. 43, for instance, a 10-pound alpha male, was actually a bully who turned to mush whenever he looked at a female. "But he was a heck of a fighter," she told a *Los Angeles Times* reporter. "And he patrols a huge territory. We've seen him make arduous journeys across a wash and halfway up a mountain just to beat up a smaller male." Then there was No. 41, an old, reclusive female with osteoporosis. She had four boyfriends, preferring them to the alpha males who occasionally visited her. No. 28 was an 80-year-old "cad" and "fearless kingpin." Soon 300 of the Fort Irwin tortoises would be moved to similar habitat. "There's so much we don't know about these creatures," Berry said.

But perhaps we know enough. According to Native American myth, the tortoise is responsible for our very existence. According to Kay Thompson, it kept a little girl company in her big empty suite at the Plaza Hotel. According to the old gringo Lewis Carroll, it remembered how to dance and made sure to pass the knowledge on, before it was made into soup. Recently, I was hiking in a part of the Mojave adjacent to Joshua Tree National Park. It was my father's birthday. He passed away 14 years ago, and as I walked across the sands on a spring day just after the first wildflowers had shot through, I heard a few lines from

"Eldorado" in my head—or maybe it was drifting on the wind—I do not know, but it was my father speaking them: "Gaily bedight, a gallant knight, in sunshine and in shadow, had traveled long, singing a song, in search of Eldorado..."

I walked on with my little hiking group, and the biologist among us spoke of different kinds of blossoms and how to tell the difference between male and female, and, as we walked, I found myself yearning for the sight of a tortoise. Turning to my right, a large one emerged from its burrow. I was stunned. I had not seen a tortoise in years, and I watched the old fellow paddle across an alluvial fan, making for some greens. In an instant, many things came together. A few years earlier, on the anniversary of my father's death, in a different part of the Mojave, a coyote appeared, running across some train tracks. My father in fact *was* a coyote—a trickster—and it seemed right. But a tortoise? At first the idea saddened me; had it come to this—the life of the party now represented by such an ancient, silent and gentle presence? But the more I thought about it, the more I knew the message to be true: His spirit was finally at rest—no more tricks and jokes and now you see me, now you don't kind of stuff—and he had come to reside in the land of escape that he had conjured for me long ago.

I watched the tortoise clamber on, from flower to flower, its mouth greening up as it devoured the desert buffet. Judging from its size, I guessed that he (or she) was about 75 or 80 years old—my father's age if he were still alive. It occurred to me that this tortoise could have been the last one in its range, or even the last one in the southern Mojave. Who will teach us the lessons of life and loss and rebirth if it vanishes? I thought as it headed back to its burrow under a creosote bush. Who will teach us the Mojave quadrille?

JOURNEYS

Lucille Lang Day

For my parents, Evelyn and Richard Lang

We do not live in our own time alone;
we carry our history within us.
—JOSTEIN GAARDER, *SOPHIE'S WORLD*

The past is never dead. It's not even past.
—WILLIAM FAULKNER, *REQUIEM FOR A NUN*

RIVERS GLITTER. A warm rain
spurs hunter-gatherers to migrate
out of Africa, past the Red Sea
toward unnamed fields and seasons.
Their descendants polish tools,
plant peas and wheat, which starts
the Neolithic Revolution. It says so
in all the rings my mother gave me
of mitochondrial DNA.

Glaciers take up so much water
that my ancestors can walk across
the Bering Strait. Through centuries
they walk without a map or compass
all the way to Massachusetts,
arriving thousands of years before
my Anglo-Saxon forebears take

their gods and goddesses to Sussex,
long before John and Peter
de Peckham join the Third Crusade.

In a heaving sea John Howland
is swept off the *Mayflower*. He grabs
a halyard. The crew snags
his clothes with a fishhook
to drag him back to the deck.
In my double helices he feasts
with Wampanoags on venison,
roast goose, wild turkey, pumpkins,
squash, plums and berries
under oaks with scarlet leaves.

John Peckham renounces his father,
Lord of the Manor in Sussex, wakes
on a ship, crowded with prisoners,
driven by the wind's stiff whip
toward Massachusetts Bay.

A German baron loses a battle
against King Wilhelm. His son
and daughter-in-law flee. Their son,
Bill Lang, finds his way to California,
proposes to Ada Peckham on a boat
bobbing in the middle of a lake.

With every breath I take, filling
the elegant, finely branched trees
of my lungs with oxygen, my mother's
mother dies again of pneumonia
in Massachusetts in the flu epidemic
of 1918, and my mother comes over
mountains, rivers and plains

to California, where she grows up
to marry Bill and Ada's son.

Over and over, in my round and spindly
cells where the past softly breathes,
my mother, who told no one
she was descended from the Pilgrims
and the People of the First Light,
who brought them corn and deer,
names me "Light." Over and over,
I ask myself, Where am I going?
How will I know when I'm there?

from *WHEN THE KILLING'S DONE*

T. Coraghessan Boyle

THOUGH ALMA IS trying her hardest to suppress it, the noise of the freeway is getting to her. She can't think to slice the cherry tomatoes and dice the baby carrots, can't clear her head, can barely hear Micah Stroud riding the tide of his emotions through the big speakers in the front room. Normally, aside from the odd siren or the late-night clank of the semitrucks fighting the drag of the atmosphere on the long run up the coast, the sound is continuous, white noise, as naturally occurring a phenomenon and no different in kind from the wind in the eucalyptus or the regular thump of the surf at Butterfly Beach, and she's learned to ignore it. Or at least live with it. But this is rush hour, when every sound is magnified and people accelerate randomly only to brake half a second later, making use of their horns an estimated eighty-seven percent more often than at any other time of day—a statistic she picked up from the morning paper and quoted to everybody at work in support of her conviction that mechanized society is riding its last four wheels to oblivion, not that anybody needed convincing. And her condo—over-priced and under-soundproofed—occupies the war zone between the freeway out front and the railroad tracks in back, a condition she's been able to tolerate for its access to the beach and the cool night air, and the option, which she almost always takes, even when it rains, of sleeping with the window open and a blanket wrapped tightly around her through all the seasons of the year.

Today, however—tonight, this evening—she's on edge, denying herself the solace of a glass of wine. Or *sake* on the rocks, which is what she really wants. *Sake* out of the bottle she keeps chilled in the refrigerator, poured crackling over the ice cubes in a cocktail glass, one of the six special glasses remaining from the set of eight she inherited from her grandmother, clear below, frosted above, with the proprietary capital *B* etched into its face. She swallows involuntarily at the thought of it, thinking *Just half a glass, a quarter*. The carrots—slick, peeled and clammily wet in the cellophane package—feel alive beneath her fingers as she steadies them against their natural inclination to roll out from under the blade of the knife. On goes the tap with a whoosh, the tomatoes tumbling under the spray in the perforated depths of the colander. A horn sounds out on the freeway, a sudden sharp buzz of irritation and rebuke, and then another answers and another. She pictures the drivers, voluntarily caged, one hand clamped to the wheel, the other to the cell phone. They want. All of them. They want things, space, resources, attention to their immediate needs, but they're getting none of it—or not enough. Never enough.

Of course, she's one of them, though her needs are more moderate, or at least she likes to think so. And no, the *sake* isn't a serious temptation—she can do without. Has to. Because if anything defines her it's self-control. And drive. And smarts. People look at her and think she's some sort of uptight science nerd—the people who want to tear her down anyway—but that's not who she is at all. She's just focused. Everything in its time and place. And the time for *sake*—in her grandmother's etched glass with the *B* for Boyd front and center—is after the lecture. Or information session. Or crucifixion. Or whatever the yahoos want to make it this time.

The anger starts in her shoulders, radiating down her arms to her fingers, the knife, the mute unyielding vegetables. Furious suddenly, she flings down the knife and stalks into the front room to crank up the stereo, staring angrily out the window at the off-ramp and the rigid column of invasives Caltrans planted there to mask the freeway from her—and her from the freeway, though she expects the pencil pushers in Sacramento didn't really have her welfare in mind when they ordered the hired help to plant oleander, in alternating bands of red, white and salmon pink, along both shoulders. If there's a bird or a lizard or a living creature other than *Homo sapiens* out there, she can't see it. All she can see, through the gaps in the bushes, is the discontinuous flash of light from the coruscating bumpers and chrome wheels and streaming rocker panels of the endless line of carbon-spewing vehicles inching by, thinking *Seven billion by 2011, seven billion and counting. And where are we going to put them all?*

While she's standing there, Micah Stroud cruising high on his Louisiana twang over a low-pressure system of furious strumming and dislocated bass, one of the cars detaches itself from the flow—or lack of flow—and rockets down the off-ramp right in front of her. It's a white Prius, humped, ugly, forgettable but salvatory, and unlike any of the other white Priuses on the road, this one contains her familiar—her boyfriend, that is, Tim Sickafoose—and he's staring right at her with a look of startled recognition, waving now, even as the car slides out of sight and into the drive.

By the time he comes through the door, she's back in the kitchen, keeping things simple: toast the pita, dice the carrots, slice the tomatoes, toss the salad. Hummus out of the plastic deli container, feta in a thick white slab so perfect the goat might have given birth to it. Somewhere on its farm. With all the other goats. *Naa, naa, naa.*

They are not the kind of lovers, she and Tim, who peck kisses when they enter rooms or hang from each other like shopping bags in public. They give each other space, time to adjust. Before she can breathe "Hey," the usual greeting, he's at the table, cracking a beer, his backpack splayed open on the floor beside him.

The view out the kitchen window is of raffia palms against a white stucco wall draped with bougainvillea, at the base of which a heavily mulched bed of clivia and maidenhair fern bows to an overwatered lawn of Bermuda grass so uniformly and unwaveringly green it pulls the color out of everything. Beyond the wall, a stand of eucalyptus that gives off a fierce mentholated funk in the rainy season so that everything smells of fermenting cough drops, and beyond the eucalyptus a gap for the railroad tracks, then the faded-to-pink roof tiles of the hotel that gives onto the ocean—the ocean she can't see from here and can just barely make out from the upstairs bedroom. This is a view that irritates her.

A view that's as wrong as it can be, and not simply because it's wasteful and cluttered and composed entirely of alien species, but because it defeats the whole point of living within sight of the ocean.

"Music's pretty loud," he observes.

She turns around now, her hands arrested in the act of halving tomatoes. "I left my iPod at work."

He has nothing to say to this, though she knows he hates Micah Stroud and Carmela Sexton-Jones and all the other new-wave folkies she plays in random shuffle through most of the day at her desk. When they'd first met, the first week they were together, she'd put on a CD she thought he might like and he'd waited through the better part of a sixteen-ounce can of Guinness before passing judgment. "I don't know how to say this without being too blunt or anything," he said, giving her his mildest look to show that he was only trying to be sincere, "but how can you listen to this...whatever you want to call it? I mean, give me rock and roll any day, the White Stripes, the Strokes, the Queens of the Stone Age." It was a challenge, a testing of the waters, and she didn't blame him for it—in fact, it was to his credit, because people didn't have to echo each other like twins to get along in a relationship—but still she stiffened. "At least they're committed," she said, "at least they sing about something other than sex and drugs." "What's wrong with sex?" he'd countered, too quickly, the faintest shadow of a grin creeping across his lips, and she knew she'd been had. He counted off a beat, letting the grin settle in. "Or, for that matter, drugs?"

"I was just looking in the paper," he says now, raising his voice to be heard over the music, "to see if there's an announcement about tonight."

Despite herself, despite her nerves, she can't help conjuring the name of the behavior he's just exhibited—the Lombard effect, which refers to the way people unconsciously elevate their voices to compete with ambient noise, the roar of the restaurant, any restaurant, serving as the most salient example—even as she moves away from the counter, crosses the kitchen and strides into the front room to kill the volume on the stereo. At which point the cars and trucks and honking horns rush back into her life as if there'd never been anything else. And why couldn't they put the freeways underground, deep down, and make a park out of all that recovered acreage on top? Or a walking path? A garden to feed the hungry? Trees, weeds, anything? If she had enough money—say, five hundred billion or so—she'd buy up all the property in town, raze the buildings, tear out the roads and reintroduce the grizzly bear.

"Here, here it is," he calls out.

The notice, a pinched little paragraph in the Upcoming Events section of the local paper, is squeezed between the announcement of a performance of selections from "Les Sylphides" by the Junior Dance Studio of Goleta and a lecture on Chumash ethnobotany at the Maritime Museum:

> *Lecture and Public Forum. Alma Boyd Takesue, Projects Coordinator and Director of Information Resources for the National Park Service, Channel Islands, will address concerns over the proposed aerial control of the black rat population on Anacapa Island. 7:00 p.m., Natural History Museum, 2559 Puesta del Sol, Santa Barbara.*

She's leaning over the table beside him, the print enlarging and receding because she's left her glasses on the counter, a trim pretty woman of thirty-three, with her mother's—and grandmother's—rinsed gray eyes and the muscular, ever-so-slightly-bowed legs and unalloyed black hair she inherited from her father. Which she wears long, down to her waist, and which slips loose now from where she's tucked it behind her ears to dangle across his forearm as he holds the paper up for her.

"Just the facts," he says. "I mean, that's all you can expect, right?"

It's somehow surprising to see it there in print, this thing she's been wrestling with privately for the past week made official, set down for the record in the staid familiar type she scans every morning for the news of things. Here is the fact of the news revealed: that she will appear at the place and time specified to make the Park Service's case for what to her seems the most reasonable and obvious course of action, given the consequences of inaction. And if that action requires the extirpation of an invasive and pernicious species—killing, that is, the killing of innocent animals, however regrettable—then she will show that there is no alternative because the health and welfare, the very existence of the island's ground-nesting birds, will depend on it. The entire breeding range of Xantus's murrelet lies between Baja and Point Conception. There are fewer than two thousand breeding pairs. Rats, on the other hand, are ubiquitous. And rats eat murrelet eggs.

"Not much of a come-on, though, is it?"

"No," she admits, straightening up and then stretching as if she's just rolled out of bed, and maybe she should have a cup of green tea, she's thinking, for that extra little jolt of caffeine. She stands there stationary a moment, gazing down at him, at the back of his head and the curiously fleshy lobes of his ears, at the way the hair, medium-length and mink-brown shading to rust at the tips, curls over the collar of his T-shirt and the ceramic beads he wears round his throat on a string of sixty-pound test fishing line. ("Why sixty pounds?" she'd asked him once. "So they won't break in the surf," he told her, matter-of-factly, as if he were stating the obvious. "They never come off?" "Never.") She lays a hand on his shoulder, the lightest touch, but contact all the same. "But then, when you think of what happened last week in Ventura"—she looks into his eyes now and then away again, her lips compressing over the memory, the wounds still fresh and oozing—"maybe we don't really want a crowd. Maybe we want, oh, I don't know, maybe thirty people who've read the literature—"

"Thirty ecologists."

Her smile is quick, grateful—he can always lighten the mood. "Yeah," she says, "I think that'd be about right."

He's smiling now too, suspended there above the perspective line of the table like a figure in the still-life painting she's composing behind her eyelids: the pita on the counter, the late sun breaking through to slant in through the window and inflame the stubble of his cheek, the freeway gone and vanished along with the mood of doom and gloom she'd brought with her into the front room. All is well. All is very, very well. "But I just wanted to be sure," he says, breaking the spell, "in case you want me out front for crowd control." He gives it a beat, reaching out to take her hand and run his thumb over her palm, to and fro, caressing her, bringing her back. "No rat lovers, though. Right? Are we agreed on that?"

On the second of December, 1853, the captain of the SS *Winfield Scott*, a sidewheel steamer that had left San Francisco the previous day for the two-week run to Panama, made an error in judgment. That error, whether it was the result of hubris, overzealousness or a simple mistake of long division, doomed her, and as the years spun out, doomed generations of seabirds too. She had been launched just three years earlier in New York for the run between that city and New Orleans, but in 1851 she was sold and pressed into service on the West Coast, where passenger demand had exploded after the discovery of gold in northern California. Built for heavy seas, some 225 feet long and 34½ feet abeam, with four decks and three masts, she was a formidable ship, named for Major General Winfield Scott, lion and savior of the Mexican War, a gilded bust of whom looked out over her foredeck with a fixed and tutelary gaze. On this particular trip, she carried some 465 passengers and $801,871 in gold and gold dust, as well as several tons of mail and a full crew. Where she picked up her rats, whether in New York or New Orleans or alongside the quay in San Francisco, no one could say. But they were there, just as they were present on any ship of size, then and now, and they must have found the *Winfield Scott* to their liking, what with its dining salon where up to a hundred people at a time could eat in comfort, with its galleys and larder, its cans of refuse waiting to be dumped over the side and all the damp sweating nooks and holes belowdecks and up into the superstructure where they could live in their own world, apart from the commensal species that provided them with all those fine and delicate morsels to eat. There might have been hundreds of them on a ship that size, might have been a thousand or more, for that matter—no one could say, and the ones that turned up in the traps set by the stewards were mute on the subject.

Captain Simon F. Blunt was a man of experience and decision. He was familiar with the waters of the channel, having been a key member of the team that had surveyed the California coast two years earlier, shortly after the territory was admitted to the union. Coming out of San Francisco the previous day, he'd encountered heavy seas and a stiff headwind, which not only put the ship off schedule but kept the majority of the passengers close to their bunks and out of the drawing room and dining salon. In order to make up time, he elected to enter the Santa Barbara Channel and take the Anacapa Passage between Santa Cruz and Anacapa, rather than steaming to the seaward of the islands, a considerably greater distance. Normally, this would have been an admirable—and expeditious—choice. Unfortunately, however, while dinner was being served that evening, fog began to set in, a frequent occurrence in the channel, resulting from the collision of the California current, which runs north to south, with the warmer waters of the southern California countercurrent, a condition that helps make the channel such a productive fishery but also disproportionately hazardous to shipping. As a result, Captain Blunt was forced to proceed by dead reckoning—in which distance is calculated according to speed in given intervals of time—rather than by taking sightings. Still, he was confident, nothing out of the routine and nothing he couldn't handle—had handled a dozen times and more—and by ten-thirty he was certain he'd passed the islands and ordered the ship to bear to the southeast, paralleling the coast.

Half an hour later, running at her full speed of ten knots, the *Winfield Scott* struck an outcropping of rock off the north shore of middle Anacapa, tearing a hole in the hull and igniting an instantaneous panic amongst the passengers. People were flung from their berths, baggage cascaded across the decks, lanterns flickered, shattered, died, and the unknowable darkness of the night and the fog took hold. No one could see a thing, but everyone could feel and hear what was happening to them, the water rushing in somewhere below and the ship exhaling in a series of long ratcheting groans to make room for it. As they struggled to their feet and made their way out into the mobbed corridors, terrified of being overtaken and trapped belowdecks—water sloshing underfoot, the hands of strangers grasping and clutching at them while they staggered forward over unseen legs and boots and the sprawl of luggage, spinning, falling, rising again, and always that grim hydraulic roar to spur them—there was an immense deep grinding and a protracted shudder as the hull settled against the rock. Curses and screams echoed in the darkness. A child shrieked for its mother. Somewhere a dog was barking.

The officer of the watch, his face a pale blanched bulb hanging in the intermediate distance, sent up the alarm, and the captain, badly shaken, ordered the ship astern in an attempt to back away from the obstruction and avoid further damage. The engines strained, an evil tarry smoke fanning out over the deck till it was all but impossible to breathe, the great paddle wheel churning in the murk as if it were trying to drain the ocean bucket by bucket, everything held in suspension—the captain riveted, the officers mouthing silent prayers, the mob thundering below—until finally the ship broke loose with a long bruising sigh of splintering wood. She was free. Trembling down the length of her, lurching backward, but free and afloat. It must have been a revivifying moment for passengers and crew alike, but it was short-lived, because in the next instant the ship's stern struck ground, shearing off the rudder and leaving her helpless. Almost immediately she began to list, everything that wasn't secured careening down-slope toward the invisible rocks and the dim white creaming of the breakers four decks below.

Captain Blunt, at war with himself—lives at stake, his career ruined, his hands quaking and his throat gone dry—gave the order to abandon ship. By the light of the remaining lanterns he mustered his officers and crew to see to an orderly evacuation, but this was complicated by the gangs of desperate men—prospectors who'd suffered months and in some cases years of thirst, hunger, exhaustion, lack of female company and the comforts of civilization to accumulate their hoards over the backs of sweat-stinking mules—swarming the upper deck, dragging their worn swollen bottom-heavy satchels behind them and fighting for the lifeboats without a thought for anything but getting their gold to ground. At this point, the captain was forced to draw his pistol to enforce order even as the stern plunged beneath the waves and ever more passengers emerged from belowdecks in a mad scrum, slashing figures in the dark propelled by their shouting mouths and grasping hands. He fired his pistol in the air. "Remain calm!" he roared over and over again till his voice went hoarse. "Women and children first. There's room for all. Don't panic!"

The boats were lowered and the people on deck could see, if dimly, that they were out of immediate danger, and that went a long way toward pacifying them. It was a matter of ferrying people to that jagged dark pinnacle of rock the boat had struck in the dark, a matter of patience, that was all. No one was going to drown. No one was going to lose his belongings. Stay calm. Be calm. Wait your turn. And so it went, the boats pushing off and returning over the space of the next two hours till everyone but the crew had been evacuated—and then the crew, and lastly the captain, came too. What they didn't realize, through the duration of a very damp and chilled night with the sea rising and the fog settling in to erase all proportion, was that the rock on which they'd landed was some two hundred yards offshore of the main island and that in the morning they'd have to be ferried through the breakers a second time.

It was a week before they were rescued. Provisions were salvaged from the ship before she went down, but they weren't nearly enough to go round. Fights broke out over the allotment of rations and over the gold too, so that finally Captain Blunt—in full view of the assembled passengers—was forced to pinion two of the malefactors, gold thieves, on the abrasive dark shingle and horsewhip them to the satisfaction of all and even a scattering of applause. A number of the men took it upon themselves to fish from shore in the hope of augmenting their provisions. Others gathered mussels and abalone, another shot a seal and roasted it over an open fire. When finally news of the wreck reached San Francisco, and three ships, the *Goliah*, the *Republic* and the *California*, steamed down the coast to evacuate the passengers, no one was sorry to see the black cliffs of Anacapa fade back into the mist. The ship was lost. The passengers had endured a night of terror and a week of boredom, sunburn and enforced dieting. But no one had died and the gold, or the greater share of it, had been preserved.

As for the rats, they are capable swimmers with deep reserves of endurance and a fierce will to survive. Experiments have shown that the average rat can tread water for some forty-eight hours before succumbing, can grip and climb vertical wires, ropes, cables and smooth-boled trees with the facility of a squirrel and is capable of compressing its body to fit through a hole no wider around than the circumference of a quarter. And too, rats have a superb sense of balance and most often come to shore adrift on floating debris, whether that debris consists of loose cushions, odd bits of wood planking, whiskey bottles, portmanteaux and other flotsam or rafts of vegetation washed down out of canyons during heavy rains. Certainly some of the rats aboard the *Winfield Scott*, trapped in the hold when the baggage shifted or inundated before they could scramble up onto the deck, were lost, but it's likely that the majority made it to shore. Of course, all it would have taken was a pair of them. Or even a single pregnant female.

In any case, as Alma is prepared to inform her audience, the black rats—*Rattus rattus*, properly—that survived the wreck of the *Winfield Scott* made their way, over the generations, from that naked rock to middle Anacapa and from there to the eastern islet, and finally, afloat on a stick of driftwood or propelled by their own industrious paws, to the westernmost. Only luck and the six miles of open water of the Anacapa Passage, with its boiling spume and savage currents, has kept them from expanding their range to Santa Cruz. And no one, not even the most inveterate rodent lover, would want that.

THE GUEST ROOM

Holly Myers

THE FIRST NIGHT she slept in the house in San Luis Obispo, she became aware of the breath of the previous owners filming all the floors and walls. It was thin and clear, like Vaseline; it pulsed slightly. She bought three gallons of bleach and spent the next four days scrubbing, beginning in the bedroom and working outward. Sounds arose as she dislodged the layers, faint and rippled, like the murmur of a restaurant heard from a distance. She plugged her ears with bits of toilet paper and tried to inhale as little as possible. She changed the water every six square feet.

Aiden's mother assured her that she would love San Luis Obispo. A college town. Lots of young people. It was a 1924 California bungalow with dark wood floors, a stone fireplace, stained glass in the dining room, a narrow kitchen with a door to the back, one bathroom, a linen closet, and two bedrooms. It was presented to her as a graduation gift, but came tangled in the same obscure legal netting that everything she had came tangled in—her father's signature on every page—and that left her always a little unsure of just how it was she could be said to exist. A good investment, he said, a good time to be buying, a charming little place, a steal.

The furniture came from the Palm Springs house, which her mother was currently redecorating. The bed was wide and heavy and took up most of the room, with a carved oak headboard and a comforter covered in salmon pink roses. When her arms tired, or the noise grew loud enough to penetrate the tissue, or she began to feel the residue of breath sticking to the skin of her face, neck, or shoulders, she showered and changed her clothes and lay on the bed to read. Reading calmed her. She lay and her body took on a different meaning, her thick flesh no longer a burden, a punishment, but a conduit, through which the sensations of her heroines rippled. She'd come to the house with five new books, two Joan Conways and three Caroline Lanaways, stowed at the bottom of the suitcase with her winter sweaters, where her mother wasn't likely to find them. She stacked them on the night stand in the order she intended to read them, with her inlaid butterfly jewelry box on top. The Conways were modern, but the Lanaways were historical, and she wanted to begin with the Lanaways.

When in her scrubbing she came to the front door—the outer reach of her expanding circle—she stepped outside. It was June. There were three houses across and one to either side and the proximity was vaguely confusing. There was a man in the driveway of the house to her right, loading boxes into the back of a pickup truck. He wore a T-shirt, shorts, and a baseball cap and looked like a man from a movie about something that happens in a neighborhood.

"You must be our new neighbor," he called, coming to the fence with one of his boxes. "I saw the truck the other day. I'm Chris Johanson. My wife is Carrie, and we've got a little one, Tyson, around here somewhere." He was handsome: slender and athletic, and there was a lightness to the way he moved. One imagined him running or climbing mountains. "And we've got a dog, Arnie, but he shouldn't bother you." He paused and grinned, and she knew she should say something. "Is it just you in there?" he asked.

She nodded.

"Are you from here?"

It took her a moment. She was aware of a moisture beneath her breasts, and the tug of her T-shirt across her belly. "Santa Barbara," she said.

"My wife is from Santa Barbara. Originally. We moved here from San Francisco. She teaches at the university."

Aiden nodded again.

"Well, I better get this stuff loaded. Tiles I'm taking over to a job site and heavy goddam things, let me tell you. You let us know if you need anything."

On the fifth day, she unpacked the boxes in the kitchen, then the boxes in the bathroom. Then she went to the grocery store. On the sixth day, she lay in the bedroom and read, drinking apple juice and eating saltines. The first book concerned a Civil War nurse who fell in love with a soldier. It was a dreary setting in Aiden's view, and she cringed at the thought of blood mixed with mud, which was something the author dwelt upon repeatedly. The second took place in Scotland, in a castle on a hill, which she preferred. The heroine was the daughter of a feudal lord, whose brother was killed in a war with the British. Though promised in marriage to a neighboring duke, she fell in love with the captain of her brother's regiment, who was a scoundrel in love but hero to the cause of Scottish liberty. When Aiden closed her eyes, she saw him crashing through the door of a dark, low-ceilinged room with a wide fireplace and stone walls, while the heroine—or someone, some woman—sat washing her feet in a tub of water, her nightdress slipping low down her shoulder.

On the evening of the sixth day, the ants appeared. There were three of them, black and tiny, across the counter beside the kitchen sink. She smashed them each with a paper towel, made sure they were dead and dropped the towel in the trash. She found two more circling near the coffeemaker. Something rattled within her at the sight of them: had the bleach been insufficient? She dispatched with the two, and then she went on with her evening.

The next morning, when she emerged there were ten times as many, moving in a trail from the lower edge of the cabinet, down the wall, across the counter, and up the side of her apple juice glass. It frightened her. She rinsed the glass, dropping it once when an ant made it onto her hand, then wet a paper towel and wiped up the others in their long configuration. She waited for more to emerge from the gap beneath the cabinet but the march had apparently ceased. She took out the bleach and scrubbed the counter again, then set about rushing to get herself together.

It was her first day of work. She made coffee and sat at the dining room table with the two cherry danishes she'd bought special, in her new lime green skirt and blazer. She was to be an accountant, like her father; she had a position at a firm several blocks away, run by a former employee of her father's. She told herself it was a bright new start, that the real world was filled with adults, not college students, and that she had every reason to succeed.

That evening, she found another trail, on the other side of the sink, onto the plate with the crumbs from the danishes. There were more of them this time. She smashed them with a handful of paper towels and tried to wipe the line toward the sink, knocking the plate so that it clattered and broke against the walls of the basin. There were so many; they scrambled out from under the paper towels and up the walls of the basin; they scrambled onto her hands and her wrists. She saw in their encroaching multitude that they were not themselves individual agents, but rather the few visible particles in a wave of contamination. With each tiny, tickling touch, she felt a dark haze creeping up her arms. She cursed as she shook them off, then pulled out the sprayer and flooded the counter, using wads of paper towels to steer them toward the sink. They curled into balls when the water hit them, like a hundred free floating decimal points gliding about the floor of the sink. When they were all swept away, she waited for more, but, again, the march had ceased. She pulled the bleach from beneath the sink and scrubbed the area once more.

She'd bought herself a frozen lasagna, special for the occasion, and two candles to go on the dining room table, but she couldn't bear to pull it out, with the kitchen contaminated as it was. She had her dinner at a Subway sandwich shop, watching a man through the window who was pacing the parking lot, talking on a cell phone and waving his arms. On the way home, she bought two bottles of ant spray.

The next day, there were no ants, neither morning or evening. In the evening, she baked her lasagna and ate it in the bedroom, cross-legged on the bed, while watching a program about Queen Elizabeth. She began the third book curled up in the bath, her body ballooned about her. This one was set during the American Revolution. The heroine, born an orphan, was raised by a Massachusetts landowner but cast out when he died by his jealous son and forced to work as a servant for the leader of a local army regiment.

On Thursday morning, Aiden opened the cabinet to find the ants swarming a box of cereal. Two days later, it was the sugar dish she used for her coffee, then a bag of oatmeal cookies, then an empty can of diet soda, then the trash can. The bustling spectacle revolted her; she sprayed each object of the creatures' devouring, sprayed the long, awful, wriggling trail, sprayed everything around, all cracks and crevices, then watched the ants curl and writhe in the poison. Once, in a fury, she sprayed everything in the cabinet—cereal, coffee, potato chips, spaghetti, ramen, cans of soup—and had to throw nearly everything out.

Having erased the stain of her human predecessors, Aiden was thus now sure of another intelligence, dark and inhuman, welling in the cabinets, the walls, the earth beneath the house. When she stood in the kitchen, she felt its motion beneath the stillness. The blindness of its determination appalled her, eliciting a kind of hysterical self-assertion. It sent its scouts, it sent its troops, it tried one angle, then another, then another, and she met each assault with a proprietary sense of injustice—the food was *hers* and the house was *hers*. But there was a hemming futility: it did not see her. She meant little more to its tactical perception did than a heavy rain storm or a tractor tire. It comprehended her existence from an ancient and amoral reservoir of consciousness, from which perspective her life, the lives of her predecessors, and the life of the house, for all its mass, all its charm, were merely temporary intrusions. She stood, then—but what did she stand on? She defended—but what did she defend? It was like standing alone in a very dark room.

After a while, the onslaught subsided, with she the apparent victor, having poisoned every inch of the kitchen and moved all that was permeable and perishable into the safe house of the refrigerator. Time went on. In the absence of the ants, her life took on a bland rhythm. She left for work at a quarter to nine. On Saturday, she cleaned; on Sunday, she rested. Her mother called every evening at seven. She finished the book about the American Revolution. When she imagined the hero, she saw Chris Johanson—only now a widower, his wife raped and killed by British forces, his little son drowned in a river. When she closed her eyes, she saw him bounding up a hillside, crashing through the doors of a barn, where she—the heroine—wavered on the brink of the very fate that befell his wife. She—the heroine, with her slender arms and narrow waist and breasts neat and modest and milky white—lay where she'd been thrown in the hay, her skirt hiked up above her knees. She—Aiden—read through the evenings, in the bath or the bed, and, when she finished the book, she read it again.

One Saturday morning when the sky was overcast, Carrie Johanson appeared on her doorstep with the child on her hip and a purple tin of chocolate chip cookies. She apologized for taking so long to introduce herself, said she'd been up to her ears in papers and exams and thank goodness it was summer and they were leaving the next day for Wisconsin to see Chris's family, but she wanted to leave these cookies as a housewarming gift. She had a capable air beneath the weight of her child and smiled with alarming sincerity.

"You're getting along O.K.? No problems? This is such a charming little place." She bounced the child and looked around. "The couple who was here before, they were sick to sell it, just sick. Dan and Jeremy. They were great people, so nice. But in this economy, you know. They ran a restaurant, but it went under, so they had to go back to L.A. But anyway. Chris said you're all alone over here. Is that true? You look so young. Well, if you ever need anything, he's quite the handyman. Or if you just want a chat. We'll be gone for three weeks, but after that—anytime. Come by for dinner, we'd love to have you."

The window in the bedroom looked out to a hillside behind the house, and Aiden lay with the tin of cookies, trying to discern the ants' dark essence spidering through the soil. They were somewhere, surely; they remained. They were everywhere but here. She looked at the hillside and imagined their trails weaving just above and below the surface of the ground, weaving a thin black lace that quivered as it lay, covering everything.

It was quiet with the Johansons gone. A girl came every couple of days to water the plants in the front and back yards; sometimes she went in and played music in the house. Hard music, with guitars. There was a boy with her once and they stayed with the music on for nearly four hours, in some invisible reach of the house, beyond the sight of the windows.

On a Saturday night, the ants returned. There were four cookies left—she'd been saving them special for Sunday—but she'd forgotten to return the tin to the refrigerator and left it on the counter, slightly ajar; by morning it was subsumed. She stood for a moment, shocked. She didn't know how she could have made such a slip, how she could have grown so complacent. She watched them in their slithering lines, blind in their triumph, smug and silent, and perceived in a flash and with fearful clarity the immensity of all that surrounded the house—soil, sky, city, continent—and the legions of forces she had to contend with, all driving ever at her and intertwining, though the things that she wanted were so few and simple. She wept as she drowned them: the ants, the cookies, the careful layers of yellow tissue paper. She wept as she sprayed, wept as she scrubbed, muttering and cursing. She wept as she folded herself into the bathtub, pulling her bathrobe over her head, and, when the weeping ceased, lay still there, bent and cramped in the quiet, through the afternoon.

The next day—Monday—she called in sick, and then again the next. On Wednesday, she rose, dressed, had her breakfast, and paused as she struggled with a buckle on her shoe before the door to the guest room. There was a hush about the room, with its matching bamboo furniture so familiar to her from the guest room—her room—in the Palm Springs house. There were palm trees on the bedspread, and matching lamps in the shape of giraffes, one on the dresser, one beside the bed. She adjusted the buckle and stood. There was a terrible vacancy. She went to the kitchen and took the sugar dish from the refrigerator, then returned to the room and poured a small pile of sugar onto the rug beside the bed. She watched it for a moment. She looked around. Then she left for work.

That evening, there was a single trail, slender and tentative, leading from somewhere beneath the bed. She brought the sugar dish and made three more piles, one in each corner save that with the door. When she went to bed, there were scouts around the pile that was closest to the window; by the time she woke the next morning, there were trails consuming all three. She lay down another half dozen piles, one foot in from the molding and two feet from one another. She sprayed a line of poison across the doorway, then shut the door and went to work. That evening, she lay down another ring, one foot in, under the furniture if necessary. Then she lay on her belly on the bed and watched the trails, weaving and rippling across the floor. She wondered if there was a central intelligence—an office somewhere, a cavern where the decisions were made. She wondered whether the ants had feelings. Over the next two days, she lay down several more circles, working toward the center, bending precariously around the edge of the mattress to spoon out piles under the bed. Then she lay back on the bed and imagined herself in a stone-walled room, high in a castle besieged by rebels. The sounds of battle thundered: cannon fire, rifles, the clanking of swords, the cries of men in fury and dying. There was a maidservant with her, clutching her waist and whimpering in terror. Footsteps thudded through the corridor, then shoulders pounded and splintered the door around its lock. There were five men; they approached in silence and surrounded the bed. They were bloodied and filthy and rank with sweat. The tallest nodded to one of the others and that one tore the girl from her arms, wailing and kicking, and carried her out of the room. The others approached, and she vowed not to scream or to make a sound, fierce in the dignity of her birthright. They cut her gown from her body with daggers and took her from above and from behind, one by one, pinning her arms and holding her hair in their fists.

Through all the next morning, she sat on the bed, watching the trails grow thicker and darker, like a network of tributaries swelling in the spring. There was a kind of peace in being thus suspended with this darkness roiling beneath her, consumed in the logic of its own motion and blind to the looming treacheries of scale. Strategic they are, she thought, but clearly not wise. She wondered which was more important in the end.

On Sunday, she filled the sugar bowl again and set about laying a smaller grid—half inch piles, two inches apart—across the surface of all the furniture: dresser, table, chair, bed. She did the bed last, careful to step only in the gaps between the trails and not let any of the ants touch her. Then she closed the door, sprayed the threshold again, and left it closed for a week.

Her mother called every night at seven; Aiden told her that she was happy in the house; that her co-workers liked her; that she was beginning to find her way around town. The Johansons returned, waving and grinning as they unpacked their car. She went to work every morning and came home every evening, changed into sweat pants, sometimes drew a bath, and had her dinner on the bed in front of the television. She bought three more Lanaways—a Regency, a Victorian, and another American Revolution—and finished all three in the course of that week, reading late into the night.

On Sunday morning, she showered and dressed and had her coffee on the back porch with a chocolate croissant. It was August now; the sun was hot and the greenery up the hillside had a dull, golden glow. She wondered if there were snakes up there. Chris Johanson and his son were romping about the lawn next door, the father groaning like a swamp creature, the son squealing and scampering. She washed her dishes and set them to dry, then put on her tennis shoes and a pair of gardening gloves and tied a dishtowel around her nose and mouth. She stood at the door for several minutes before opening it, telling herself she would need to work fast. There would be chaos, confusion. She imagined the darkness churning up like clouds of dust around a scuffle.

There were ants everywhere—thousands of them, millions. A twelve by twelve foot weave of blackness over floor, bed, dresser, chair. She didn't hesitate, but began at the door frame and worked methodically in long strokes, from one end to the other and back again, laying the poison like clear primer across the floor and all the furniture and up the lower reaches of the wall. It glistened in the light. The ants scurried around the edge of each stroke, but when the poison came upon them they slowed and curled and twitched and went still. A million decimal points, carpeting the room; life returned to a state of abstraction; one writhing branch of a massive strategy foiled.

When at last she'd covered every square foot of the room, she stopped and looked around. The bedspread was damp; the dresser glistened, and the stiff wooden flesh of the giraffe. There was a streak of moisture across the cream colored shade. She considered opening the window, but didn't. She left the two empty cans on the floor near the dresser. At the door, she paused and unlaced her shoes, leaving them just inside the threshold. She removed her gloves, then the dishtowel, and draped them over the shoes, then her socks and her sweat pants and her T-shirt and her underwear. She closed the door and stuffed a folded bath towel into the crack, then stood in the hall in her copious nakedness. She would shower, she told herself. She would dress. She would read. Perhaps that night she'd pull out a lasagna.

OCEAN BEACH AT TWILIGHT: 14

Dean Rader

WHO'S TO SAY the stars understand
their heavy labor, or the moon its
grunt work across the hard curve of absence?
Who's to say the gulls taut on their tiny strings

believe the air? Everything seems surprised
by the fat slab of pink strung up against the blue:
the dogs dark in night's water, the fishermen
buoyed to the beach's pillar of stillness.

Even the teenage boy playing in the spoor
of foam and backflow pauses longer
than expected, his father's voice dissolved

in the din-drop of surf and sea hush. Night
is no curtain. When he stares out across
the wave of waves, who's to say he looks inward?

THE BRIDGE

Daniel Orozco

IT WAS TRADITION on the bridge for each member of the paint crew to get a nickname. It was tradition that the name be pulled out of the air, and not really mean anything. It was just what you go by at work. But Baby's name was different. Baby's name was a special case.

Union Hall had sent him up when W.C. retired last summer. Although he'd been working high steel a few years, Baby was young, about twenty-five, but looked younger. He was long and skinny, with wide hands that dangled by thin wrists from his too-short sleeves. He had a buzz-top haircut that made his ears stick out. His face got blotchy and pink in the sun. He was the youngest in Bulldog's crew by twenty years. His first day, when Bulldog brought him to the crew shack inside the south tower and introduced him around, you could see this boy sizing up the old-timers, calculating the age difference in his head and grinning about it. He tossed his gear into W.C.'s old locker and flopped on the bench next to it. He pulled out a Walkman and started fiddling with the earphones. And while the crew was getting down to first things first, discussing a nickname for him, he let out a phlegmy little snort and muttered, Well, geez, just don't call me Kid. Then he turned on his Walkman, opened his mouth, and shut his eyes. Bulldog and the crew regarded him for a moment, this skinny, openmouthed boy stretched out on W.C.'s bench, his big, booted feet bouncing fitfully to the tinny scratching of music coming from his ears. The painters then returned to the matter at hand. They would not call him Kid. They would not call him Sonny or Junior, either. They would go one better. With little discussion, they decided to veer from tradition just this once, and Baby's name was born.

Being new to bridge painting, Baby is still getting the hang of things, with his partner, Whale, telling him to check his harness, to yank on it at least a hundred times a day to make sure it's fast; to check that his boots are laced up, because there's no tripping allowed, not up here, the first step is a killer; and to always attach his safety line, to clip it onto *any*thing and *every*thing. Baby listens, but under duress, rolling his eyes and muttering, Yeah, yeah, yeah, I got it, I got it, which sets Whale off. But Bulldog and the rest of them tell him to take it easy. They are old hands at this, they remind him. They are cautious and patient men, and Baby's just young, that's all. He'll learn to slow down, as each of them learned; he'll learn to get used to the steady and deliberate pace of their work, what Bulldog calls the Art of Painting a Bridge: degreasing a section of steel first; sandblasting and inspecting for corrosion; and after the iron crew's done replacing the corroded plates or rivets or whatever, blasting again; sealing the steel with primer one, and primer two the next day; then top coat one the day after that, and top coat two the day after that.

Whale doesn't like working with Baby, but he's partnered with him. So the two of them are under the roadbed, up inside the latticework. They go from the joists down, moving east to west along a row of crossbeams on the San Francisco side of the south tower. Whale is blasting rust out of a tight spot behind a tie brace, and Baby moves in to spray primer one, when suddenly his paint gun sputters and dies. He yanks off his noise helmet, shouts at Whale over the wind, and unclips his safety line to go look for the kink in his paint hose. Pissed off, Whale yells, Goddammit, but it's muffled under his helmet. Baby clunks down the platform in his big spattered boots. His line trails behind him, the steel carabiner clip skittering along the platform grating.

He spots the trouble right away, at the east end, just over his head—a section of hose hung up between the power line and the scaffold cable. He reaches up, stands on his toes, and leans out a little, his hips high against the railing. He grasps the hose, snaps it once, twice, three times until it clears. And just as he's turning around to give Whale the thumbs-up, a woman appears before him, inches from his face. She passes into and out of his view in less than two seconds. But in Baby's memory, she would be a woman floating, suspended in the flat light and the gray, swirling mist.

The witnesses said she dived off the bridge headfirst. They said she was walking along when she suddenly dropped her book bag and scrambled onto the guardrail, balancing on the top rail for a moment, arms over her head, then bouncing once from bended knees and disappearing over the side. It happened so fast, according to one witness. It was a perfect dive, according to another.

But her trajectory was poor. Too close to the bridge, her foot smashed against a beam, spinning her around and pointing her feet and legs downward. She was looking at Baby as she went past him, apparently just as surprised to see him as he was to see her. She was looking into his face, into his eyes, her arms upstretched, drawing him to her as she dropped away.

And wondering how you decide to remember what you remember, wondering why you retain the memory of one detail and not another, Baby would remember, running those two seconds over and over in his head, her hands reaching toward him, fingers splayed, and her left hand balling into a fist just before the fog swallowed her. He would remember a thick, dark green pullover sweater, and the rush of her fall bunching the green under her breasts, revealing a thin, pale waist and a fluttering white shirttail. He would remember bleached blue jeans with rips flapping at both knees, and basketball shoes—those red high-tops that kids wear—and the redness of them arcing around, her legs and torso following as she twisted at the hips and straightened out, knifing into the bed of fog below. But what he could not remember was her face. Although he got a good look at her—at one point just about nose to nose, no more than six inches away—it was not a clear, sustained image of her face that stayed with him, but a flashing one, shutter-clicking on and off, on and off in his head. He could not remember a single detail. Her eyes locked on his as she went past and down, and Baby could not—for the life of him, and however hard he tried—remember what color they were.

But he would remember hearing, in spite of the wind whistling in his ears, in spite of the roar of traffic, the locomotive clatter of tires over the expansion gaps in the roadbed above, in spite of the hysterical thunking of the air compressor in the machine shed directly over him—Baby would remember hearing, as she went past, a tiny sound, an *oof* or an *oops,* probably her reaction to her ankle shattering against the beam above less than a second before. It was a small, muted grunt, a sound of minor exertion, of a small effort completed, the kind of sound that Baby had associated—before today—with plopping a heavy bag of groceries on the kitchen table or getting up, woozy, after having squatted on his knees to zip up his boy's jacket.

Whale drops his gun and goes clomping down the platform after Baby, who stands frozen, leaning out and staring down, saying, Man oh man, man oh man oh man. He gets to him just as Baby's knees buckle and hooks his safety line first thing. He pulls him to his feet, pries his gloved fingers from around the railing, and walks him to the other end of the platform. He hangs on to Baby as he reels the scaffold back under the tower, too fast. The wet cables slip and squeal through their pulleys, and the platform jolts and shudders until it slams finally into the deck with a reassuring clang. He unhooks their safety lines—Baby's first, then his own—and reaches out to clip them onto the ladder. He grabs a fistful of Baby's harness, and eases him—limp and obedient—over the eighteen-inch gap between the scaffold gate and the ladder platform. He puts Baby's hands on the first rung. They brace themselves as they swing out, the gusts always meaner on the west side of the bridge. The shifting winds grab at their parkas and yank at their safety lines, the yellow cords billowing out in twin arcs, then whipping at their backs and legs. They go one rung at a time, turtling up the ladder in an intimate embrace—Whale on top of Baby, belly to back, his mouth warm in Baby's ear, whispering, Nice and easy, Baby, over and over. That's it,

Baby, nice and easy, nice and easy. Halfway up, they can hear the Coast Guard cutter below them, its engines revving and churning as it goes past, following the current out to sea.

They knock off a little early. In the parking lot, Baby leans against his car, smoking another cigarette, telling Whale and Bulldog and Gomer that he's okay, that he'll be driving home in a minute, just let him finish his cigarette, all right? Whale looks over at Gomer, then takes Baby's car keys and drives him home. Gomer follows in his car and gives Whale a ride back to the lot.

Suiting up in the crew shack the next morning, they ask him how he's doing, did he get any sleep, and he says Yeah, he's okay. So they take this time, before morning shift starts, to talk about it a little bit, all of them needing to talk it out for a few minutes, each of them having encountered jumpers, with C.B. seeing two in one day—just hours apart—from his bosun's platform halfway up the north tower, first one speck, then another, going over the side and into the water, and C.B. not being able to do anything about it. And Whale taking hours to talk one out of it once, and her calling him a week later to thank him, then jumping a week after that. And Bulldog having rescued four different jumpers from up on the pedestrian walkway, but also losing three up there, one of them an old guy who stood shivering on the five-inch-wide ledge just outside the rail and seven feet below the walkway, shivering there all afternoon in his bathrobe and slippers, looking like he'd taken a wrong turn on a midnight run to the toilet; and after standing there thinking about it, changing his mind, and reaching through the guardrail for Bulldog's outstretched arm, and brushing the tips of Bulldog's fingers before losing his footing.

Nobody says anything. Then Bulldog slaps his thighs and stands up. But that's how it goes, he says, and he tells everybody to get a move on, it's time to paint a bridge.

At lunch, Baby is looking through the paper. He tells Gomer and C.B. and the rest of them how he hates the way they keep numbering jumpers. She was the 995th, and he wished they'd stop doing that. And when they're reeling in the scaffold for afternoon break, he turns to Whale and tells him—without Whale's asking—that the worst thing about it was that he was the last person, the last living human being she saw before she died, and he couldn't even remember what she looked like, and he didn't need that, he really didn't.

And that's when Baby loses his noise helmet. It slips out from the crook of his arm, hits the scaffold railing, and lobs over the side. It being a clear day, they both follow the helmet all the way down, not saying anything, just leaning out and watching it, squinting their eyes from the sun reflecting off the surface of the bay, and hearing it fall, the cowl fluttering and snapping behind the headpiece, until the helmet hits with a loud, sharp crack, like a gunshot. Not the sound of something hitting water at all.

At break, Baby's pretty upset. But Bulldog tells him not to sweat it, the first helmet's free. Yeah, Red says, but after that it costs you, and Red should know, having lost three helmets in his nineteen years. But Baby can't shut up about it. He goes on about the sound it made when it hit the water, about how amazing it is that from 220 feet up you can single out one fucking sound. He's worked up now. His voice is cracking, his face is redder than usual. They all look at him, then at each other, and Bulldog sits him down while the rest of them go out to work. Baby tells him he's sorry about the helmet, he really is, and that it won't happen again. And that's when Bulldog tells him to go on home. Go home, he says, and kiss your wife. Take the rest of the day, Bulldog says, I'll clear it with the Bridge Captain, no sweat.

Everybody's suiting up for morning shift. It's a cold one today, with the only heat coming from the work lights strung across a low beam overhead. They climb quickly into long johns and wool shirts and sweaters and parkas. They drink their coffee, fingers of steam rising from open thermoses, curling up past the lights. They wolf down doughnuts that Red brought. Whale is picking through the box, looking for an old-fashioned glazed, and C.B. is complaining to Red why he never gets those frosted sprinkled ones anymore, when Baby, who hasn't said a word since coming back, asks nobody in particular if he could maybe get a new nickname.

The painters all look at each other. Tradition says you don't change the nickname of a painter on the bridge. You just never do that. But on the other hand, it seems important to the boy, and sometimes you have to accommodate the members of your crew because that's what keeps a paint crew together. They watch him sitting there, concentrating on re-lacing his boots, tying and untying them, saying, It's no big deal, really, it's just that I never liked the name you gave me, and I was just wondering.

So they take these few minutes before the morning shift to weigh this decision. Whale chews slowly on the last old-fashioned glazed. Bulldog pours himself another half cup, and C.B. and Red both sit hunched over, coiling and uncoiling safety line. Gomer tips his chair back, dances it on its rear legs, and stares up past the work lights. The boy clears his throat, then falls silent. He watches Gomer rocking back and forth. He follows his gaze upward. Squinting past the lights, peering into the dark, he listens to the gusts outside whistling through the tower above them.

APPROACHING SAN FRANCISCO

Soul Choj Vang

A FULL MOON SHINES
Over a city of embers.

A lighted bridge floats
Like a silver ribbon

Over the ink-dark bay.
Planes descend and lift off

Like a scattering
Of fireflies.

from *RISE OF THE RANGES OF LIGHT*

David Scott Gilligan

If you were to walk a straight line from the central coast of California to the Nevada border, you could boast of having seen six, and arguably seven, of the eight terrestrial biomes of the world. There is no place else in North America where you could make such a boast, and few places in the world. Pick just about any spot on the globe and you will find one, maybe two, rarely three of these eight biomes represented there. Alaska has Arctic tundra, boreal forest, and arguably some temperate forest in the southeast. Equatorial Africa has tropical savanna and tropical rainforest. Siberia has only boreal forest. Australia, an entire continent, is predominantly desert, with smaller areas of temperate forest and grassland on the eastern seaboard, and tropical rainforest along the north coast. To find the place where the most of the world's biomes are represented in the smallest area, you need to either pick a long, skinny piece of land with a vast latitudinal span, such as Chile, or find somewhere where a wide latitudinal range is simulated by a wide range of elevation. To do that you need mountains.

It had long been known that going up a mountain was like traveling north, but it was not until the late nineteenth century that the naturalist C. Hart Merriam consolidated and published his lifezone concept to explain it. Merriam had traveled widely in the far north of Canada and spent time amongst the spire-like spruces of the great boreal forests and the wide tundra to the north. While surveying on the Colorado Plateau of Northern Arizona, Merriam was struck by the readily apparent bands of vegetation along the flanks of San Francisco Mountain. Only fifty miles away, at the bottom of the Grand Canyon, Merriam had stood amongst the cacti and dusty shrubs indicative of the warm lower Sonoran Desert. Climbing out of the canyon, he passed through the blackbrush and scattered junipers of the colder upper Sonoran Desert. Approaching the San Francisco Peaks, the open woodland of juniper and pinyon thickened to a forest of ponderosa pine and oak. Up on the slopes, the pines and oaks gave way to glowing stands of aspen and thick, dark firs. Further up, past 9,000 feet these trees, reminiscent of what might be seen in Canada, gave way to Engelmann spruces and bristlecone pines, analogous to the boreal forests of the Hudson Bay region. Above 11,500 feet, even the stalwart trees of the north bent down to the prostrate mats and shrubs of the tundra, reaching past 12,600 feet, the summit of Humphreys Peak. He named his lifezones accordingly: Lower Sonoran, Upper Sonoran, Transition, Canadian, Hudsonian, Arctic-Alpine.

What Merriam encountered in that small cross-section of Northern Arizona was nothing new. It is because he wrote it down that he is so remembered, and thus Merriam's lifezone theory has become a cornerstone in our modern understanding of the natural world. The short version is that temperature decreases with elevation, now quantified at a rate of three to five and a half degrees Fahrenheit for every thousand feet, depending on the relative humidity of the air mass. Not by mere coincidence, precipitation rates increase with elevation. The upshot: mountains are colder and wetter than the surrounding lowlands, thus simulating more northerly climes. Going up the mountain a thousand feet is like going north two hundred miles.

Merriam's idea was a simple one, yet profound. Modern scientists have been quick to criticize his lack of attention to details and apt not to recognize that the only reason there are details is because Merriam got the basics down for all who follow to footnote. Further observations have shown that slope aspect greatly affects lifezones. In the Northern Hemisphere the sun is in the southern sky, and slopes with southerly exposure are warmer and drier than those facing north. Accordingly, north-facing slopes host lifezone communities at a far lower elevation than their southerly counterparts. Engelmann spruce, the quintessential Hudsonian species on San Francisco Mountain, may occur just above eight thousand feet on north-facing slopes, while on the south-facing slopes it is rare below ten thousand feet. West-facing slopes are also warmer and drier, as the afternoon sun is more intense than that of the morning, and more heating of the earth's surface has occurred by that time of day. Southwest-facing slopes, then, tend to be the warmest, and northeast-facing slopes the coolest. Another detail of great importance is the drainage effect. Just as hot air rises during the day as the earth's surface is heated, cold air sinks at night as things cool down. This sinking air takes the path of least resistance downslope, moving much like water, and follows natural drainages, creating a temperature inversion relative to the area around it. Thus drainages are cool and moist relative to the land surrounding them, and they may host vegetation typically found thousands of feet higher. Subsequent analysis of Merriam's life-zone theory found that distinct plant associations were not quantifiable, and that each species responded to its own set of ecological conditions independent of other species. What Merriam saw as distinct bands of vegetation was actually a spectrum of species, each with its own unique ecological niche, a seamless continuum. Yet somehow we still see what we see. Merriam's terms are still in use, and the basic idea that elevation simulates latitude is still at the forefront of our consciousness as we journey up the mountain.

Perhaps nowhere else on the continent is this idea more drastic, more stunning, more overstated than in the canyon of the Kings River, the deepest canyon in North America. Here, the waters of the south-central Sierra Nevada gather from the highest snow-encrusted peaks and ridges and cut down through the landscape in an incessant quest for the sea. Nine thousand feet of elevation are spanned by the walls of the canyon, from the chilling alpine heights at fourteen thousand feet to the warm pine woodlands and chaparral of the canyon bottom, at five thousand feet. The Kings is deeper than the Grand Canyon, and in contrast to its southwestern counterpart, to look in you must climb up to its rims, to the skyscraping granite tops of innumerable mountains.

From an ecological perspective, walking the nine thousand vertical feet from the canyon floor to the surrounding summits is like walking eighteen hundred miles north. On such a lengthy northerly sojourn, you would pass through semi-arid conifer woodlands laced with lush riparian gallery forests, interspersed with open grassland and temperate savanna, shrubby chaparral, cold sagebrush desert, sweet-smelling pine forests, well-ordered boreal forests, and finally, the windswept expanse of the Arctic tundra. You would end your journey after months, if not years of traveling to tell the tale that going north it gets colder, the weather changes, and the plants and the soils they grow upon change correspondingly. You would be standing on the permanently frozen soils of the Yukon Plateau, perhaps looking up at a shimmering display of aurora borealis and settling in for a night of subpolar slumber as the mercury dropped to fifty degrees below zero. You could spend just a few days walking in Kings Canyon and see things much the same.

I leave Road's End with six students to simulate the journey to the Arctic. My students have long since heard of the idea that going up the mountain is like going north. Now is their chance to prove it. We have been out in the backcountry together for over two weeks already, as part of a ten-week field quarter studying natural history and ecology in the mountains of California. Thus, our bodies are becoming accustomed to the rigors of life in the field and the strain of carrying on our backs everything we need for eleven days in the mountains. Our noses are burnt and peeled, calves taut, we know what each other likes to eat, who stays up late and who sleeps in, what each other smells like, and who is the turtle and who the hare on the trail. Laden with necessities and strengthened by some experience, we set out across the hot, dusty, pine-scented flats of the canyon. Thoughts of cool alpine meadows and crunchy snowfields give meaning to the sweat that soaks our packs as they press into our backs; we knew well the toll that nine thousand vertical feet would exact on our legs before we would ever reach such high places.

We ascend steeply up the Bubbs Creek drainage, trudging up switchbacks on a slope that cruelly faces southwest. It is a textbook ecological situation. Here, along the hot and dry southwest slope, are woodland and chaparral species, species that Merriam would have called Upper

Sonoran, growing higher than the lower montane Transition zone species of the valley floor, where cold air pools regularly every night. We pass canyon live oaks, bush chinquapin, manzanita, whitethorn, and even a stray pinyon, leaving drops of sweat on their parched leaf surfaces as we walk by. When we reach the top of the slope, we tuck into the valley of Bubbs Creek, thankfully noticing gigantic sugar pine cones littering the ground as the forest trees of the Transition zone close in around us.

Continuing upward, we find ourselves once again pounded by the midday sun as we plod up the rocky switchbacks along Sphinx Creek. The terrain is typical of the Sierra Nevada: flat treads of valley walking characterized by meandering or rushing streams and placid lakes, interspersed with huge, steep risers of bare granite and plummeting waterfalls. This is the glacial staircase, an undulating stair-step topography fit for the most giant of giants, which we will follow up to its uttermost summit. The switchbacks seem endless, each hopefully the last but leading inevitably to yet more. The valley of the Kings gapes large and far away, now three thousand feet below us, with its forest dark green and thick. Eventually the riser bends into another tread, and we follow a less hurried Sphinx Creek into its sheltered drainage. Tucked away from the sun, huge trees grow here, and the massive trunks of red firs and western white pines grow up to thick branches and green scented boughs. Beneath the canopy, numerous small streams intersect flowering red mountain heather and pinemat manzanita, cascading down the slope towards Sphinx Creek. Paralleling Sphinx Creek, we cross these tributaries, one after the other, each decorated with vibrant seep-spring monkeyflowers, largeleaf lupines, big red paintbrushes, cinquefoils, and secretive bog orchids. This forest is decidedly more northern than the one below. At the Sphinx Creek crossing, we rest. We lean comfortably against rocks and logs, and spontaneously and simultaneously fall asleep.

We awaken an hour later to the high wail of thousands of mosquitoes. Surely we must be in Canada now.

With another thousand feet up to go that day, we hoist our ten days' worth of food, clothing, shelter, notebooks, textbooks, ice axes, and helmets and set out off-trail. We follow Sphinx Creek more closely this time, ascending yet another riser towards where we hope to find some slabs to camp on. Passing through forest-line wet meadows abloom with goldenrod, rose-smelling Kelly's tiger lilies, and Jeffrey's shooting stars, we emerge into an extensive stand of quaking aspen, leaves aflutter in the up-valley afternoon breeze. Here we pause and listen to the sound of the wind in the trees, green leaves all shaking against each other. As in all places where they grow, the aspens here are pioneering a recently disturbed area, in this case an area where a combination of rockslides and avalanches falling from the steep valley walls above has scraped off any pre-existing vegetation and scoured the underlying soil. If there was any doubt we were in a mid-montane Canadian-type forest, this sight dispels it. Not only is this forest similar to those of the north in terms of its climatic conditions, structure, and organism functions, but actual species are the same. This is the very same *Populus tremuloides* found in the Canadian-type forests of Alaska, all the way across Canada to the North Woods of Maine. Biogeographers appropriately call this northern forest the boreal forest, after Borealis, the Greek god of the north wind. This is the largest and most contiguous terrestrial biome in the world, covering much of Alaska and Canada and patches of the lower forty-eight, as well as most of northern Europe and all of Siberia. Here in the Sierra Nevada we are in a southern extension of the boreal forest, a finger of northern forest that extends conspicuously far south, following the cold, wet spines of the mountains. Here, because it is elevation rather than northerly latitude that creates the ecological conditions conducive to this type of forest, biogeographers refer to the forest as montane boreal.

The last stretch is a grunt up the steep riser and through the trees. Soaked with sweat and covered in dirt and debris from bushwhacking, we let our packs drop and roll across blessed flat slabs of granite. We have made it to camp.

For three days we study the ecology of pollination while watching rufous hummingbirds draw nectar from *Penstemon newberryi*. We discuss and debate the ecological causes and potential value of the diversity of life on earth while keying out innumerable species of wildflowers, turning our heads upside-down to peek into the corollas of crimson columbines. We study the evolutionary characteristics of mammals while fending off *Ursus americana*, the ubiquitous black bear of the Sierra Nevada. Eventually it is time to ascend another three thousand feet, through the uppermost montane forest and into the land above the trees. With our packs three days lighter and the wide expanse of the alpine Sierra Nevada on our minds, we rise to the task at hand.

As we ascend the glacial staircase from our camp at 9,000 feet, we strain our legs once again and wind our way up the steep granite slabs and through the trees. As the riser we camped against rounds out to the next tread, we come to the marshy shore of a shallow lake, nestled like a babe in cradling arms of granite. Here, the undulating glacial ice of the Pleistocene had carved out a small basin, the way a waterfall does when it falls with force down a steep slope and abruptly meets a flat bed. Since the ice pulled back, the lake has slowly but surely been filling in with sediments washed down from the heights above. The banks of the lake are lined with willows, tolerant of the fluctuating lake levels and prolonged periods of inundation. Further in from the shore, rooted aquatic plants grow, their foliage floating on the water's surface. Over time, as sediments have washed into it, this lake has grown increasingly shallow, and its waters have spilled outward into the surrounding forest. We peer down into the lake at dozens of submerged logs, trees that once lined the shoreline and collapsed into the lake as its waters widened. Mosquitoes whir around us by the thousands, urging us to keep going, up, up, above the trees and into the wind. Judging by the scene before us, we might be in Alaska, or deep in the lake country of Ontario, Manitoba, or Quebec. We could be in Scotland, on the shore of some haunted loch, or chasing reindeer herds across northern Scandinavia. But this is the Sierra Nevada, and one look above the lodgepole pines that line the lake reveals walls of glinting granite mountains. The glacier that carved this basin was no sprawling gargantuan continental ice sheet, but a steep and undulating alpine glacier. We are not in the boreal forests of the north, but rather the montane boreal forest of the Sierra Nevada of California!

Two more risers and another lake later, we emerge from the trees and into the wide-open sunlit space of the High Sierra. At just below 11,000 feet, this is an unusually low elevation for treeline, and sure enough, as we traverse the shores of Sphinx Lakes, sporadic trees continue to make appearances all the way up to 12,000 feet, hugging warm south- and west-facing slopes. We cross granite slabs glistening in the sun, worn and polished by the undersides of long-past glaciers, striations etched into their shining surfaces by the rocks and sand that were once pressed between the bedrock and the overbearing ice. We crunch our way across extensive gravel flats, where drought-resistant pussy-paws and wild buckwheats eke out a living. Bright green ribbons of dense vegetation burst forth from the ground just a few feet away, where snowmelt water gurgles in countless threaded streams and delivers moisture to wet meadows all summer long. Flowers grow here in lavish abundance and uncountable numbers, and the buzz of flying insects fills the air. In between are dry and moist meadows, rich with sedges and early flowering dwarf bilberries and kalmias. Snowfields persist in nooks and crannies and cover the north- and east-facing slopes, melting in the heat of summer and watering the ground. Here is the tundra, where small is beautiful and a closer look reveals entire miniature worlds.

Tucked into a rock crevice at 11,000 feet, just up from the lower Sphinx Lakes, a cluster of columbines catches our attention. Unlike the crimson columbine, whose bright red nodding flowers are so common along streamsides in the montane forest, this plant bears larger, paler flowers, creamy whitish-yellow with rosy streaks. The flowers face sideways, with a horizontal orientation, rather than down, and have only half the nod of their montane counterparts. The place where they are growing is different as well. This is no streamside, but a rock cranny. Leaving the matter for speculation, we continue to ascend.

We keep climbing, from treads filled with sparkling lakes to steep risers of big granite. At 11,500 feet, we begin our final climb across old glacial moraine and huge chunks of angular talus, picking our way carefully, slowly but surely, to an obscure pass at over 12,000 feet. Our journey north is complete, and if not for the serrated peaks surrounding us on all sides, we might be in the Arctic, the midnight sun just coming down from its midsummer apex, spiraling around the polar skies. Merriam's lifezones, just a concept before, become as solid in our experience of the world as eating and breathing. Elevation really does simulate latitude, and the truth is written across every feature of the snow-crusted, tundra-graced alpine zone of the Sierra Nevada.

from *I LOVE A BROAD MARGIN TO MY LIFE*

Maxine Hong Kingston

I'M STANDING ON top of a hill;
I can see everywhichway—
the long way that I came, and the few
places I have yet to go. Treat
my whole life as formally a day.
I used to be able, in hours, to relive,
to refeel my life from its baby beginnings
all the way to the present. 3 times
I slipped into lives before this one.
I have been a man in China, and a woman
in China, and a woman in the Wild West.
(My college roommate called; she'd met
Earll and me in Atlantis, but I don't
remember that.) I've been married
to Earll for 3 lifetimes, counting
this one. From time to time, we lose each other,
but can't divorce until we get it right.
Love, that is. Get love right. Get
marriage right. Earll won't believe
in reincarnation, and makes fun of it.
The Dalai Lama in *How to Expand Love*
says to try "the possibility that past
and future rebirth over a continuum
of lives may take place." We have forever.
Find me, love me, again.

I find you, I love you, again.
I've tried but could not see
my *next* life. All was immense black
space, no stars. After a while,
no more trying to *pro*gress, I returned—
was returned—to an ordinary scene that happened
yesterday, and every sunny day: Earll and I
are having a glass of wine with supper—bruschetta
from our own tomatoes and basil—under the trellis
of bougainvillea, periwinkly clematis,
and roses. Shadows and sunlight are moving at Indian
summer's pace. The Big Fire burned
the grove of Monterey pines. We planted
purple rain birches, Australian tea
trees, dogwood, the elm, locust, catalpa,
3 redwoods from seed, 4 pepper
willows, and 7 kinds of fruit trees.
The katsura and the yucca are volunteers.
That Texas privet and the bamboo, survivors. Here,
I feel as I felt in Hawai'i, as I felt in Eden.
A joy in place. Adam and Eve were never
thrown out; they grew old in the garden.
They returned after travels. So, I,
like the 14th Dalai Lama, have arrived
at my last incarnation? I don't feel a good
enough person to be allowed off the wheel.
I am guilty for leaving my mother. For leaving
many mothers—nations, my race, the ghetto.
For enjoying unconsciousness and dreams, wanting
sleep like thirst for water. I left MaMa
for Berkeley, then 17 years in Hawai'i.
Couldn't come home winter and spring breaks,
nor summers. She asked, "How can I bear
your leaving?" No, I'm not translating right.

"Can I seh doc your leaving?" Seh doc
tells the pain of losing something valuable.
How can she *afford* my leaving?
Seh doc sounds like *can write.*
Sounds almost like my father's name.
Father who left her behind in China for 15
years. I too left her.
"Lucky," she bade and blessed, in English. "Lucky."
She and Father stood at the gate, looking
after me. Looking after each child as
we left for college, left for Viet Nam.
Her eyes were large and all-holding.
No tears. She only cried when laughing.
Me too. I'm in tears laughing.
From the demimonde, Colette wrote, lying
to her mother, All's well, I'm happy.
Our only son did not leave us;
we left him in Hawai'i.
Generations. Karma. Ah Goong
walked my mother to the end of Tail End
Village. Whenever she looked back, he was still
standing there weeping and looking after her.

from *WHAT YOU SEE IN THE DARK*

Manuel Muñoz

THE ACTRESS WAS set to arrive in Bakersfield in the morning. She would be driven from Los Angeles, picked up from the studio at 6 a.m. sharp in a black sedan, and carried over the mountains into the city of Bakersfield to meet with the Director. She was a dedicated actress, script in hand as the sedan wound its way out of the quiet Los Angeles morning, a croissant and a carton of juice to sate her appetite. The driver respected her need for silence, her head bent over the script. She fought the nausea of reading against the car's steady thrum.

The Director had told her explicitly not to worry much about the entire script: they were shooting only two exterior shots, coming quietly into Bakersfield without a lot of fanfare, and the rest would be filmed at a Los Angeles studio. The Actress already knew her lines, but it never hurt to read again or to review scenes that had nothing to do with her. The exteriors were to be shot on the outskirts of the city, somewhere along Highway 99: A woman is driving a car on a road, all alone. The woman has no one to talk to, hence the Actress had no real lines to rehearse. But the Actress knew, at the very least, that her facial expressions would have to match the mood of the final edit, would have to match what she saw in the parentheticals scattered all over the script: there would be voice-overs, something else telling the story besides her own face.

She put down the script and watched the slope of the hills roll by in the October morning light. Excursions like these—trips to actual locations, away from the studio lot, all in the name of authenticity—made her wonder about the fuss, whether it was much of a role at all. The Actress had two children and a husband at home. Luckily, most of this film was scheduled to shoot in Los Angeles; it was becoming too difficult to get away from the city for work. The roles had to be studio-shot for her to be able to accept them, but these days that meant only the smaller pictures or television. Color was splashing across enormous screens and that meant directors wanted to go out to the Painted Desert, to the skyscrapers of New York City, even Japan—the real thing, not a backdrop, had to appear on the screen. At first, she believed it to be nothing more than the directors and the studios wanting to show off their enormous budgets, but the films coming over from Europe flashed with a bold realism that signaled a readiness to deepen the craft. Even the actresses appeared as if they were hauled in from the street, frighteningly believable and fully invested in their roles, not a hint of studio training in their performances. Maybe they were not even actresses at all, but authentics: a housewife, a drunk, a gold digger, a prostitute.

She had her own doubts about her ability. Sometimes she wondered if she hadn't been born twenty years too late, the way she'd been ushered in, discovered when she was up north in the Valley, way past Bakersfield, at the little college where she had modeled. Ushered in: a little star on a string, handshakes with the right people, a contract to sign, scripts to read, and her cooperation at every turn. In exchange, a whole bevy of people hovered around her: hair stylists and publicists, women who led her to Los Angeles department stores for personal fittings, awards ceremony appearances. A whole other life that had nothing to do with acting, nothing to do with any realism, nothing on the level of those European actresses, who came from places rising up out of the rubble of the war and knew a thing or two about stories.

Her scene today would be a woman driving a car, not a word said to anyone. Tomorrow, a character actor would arrive for a scene to be shot somewhere to the east of this very road she was traveling, maybe out by Lancaster. In the scene, the woman has pulled over to the side of the road to sleep for the night, only to be awakened in the morning by a policeman, who knocks on her window and questions her. At most, a three-minute scene, but there was a crucial signpost for Gorman, California, the Director had told them, some signal to the audience that this woman was headed north. Did it matter that no one knew Gorman? She knew it, the little stop-off point for the traffic snaking through the Grapevine from the Valley on through to the Los Angeles area. Almost anyone in Los Angeles would probably know that. But would an audience member in New York City know, or even care?

The Actress wasn't supposed to ask those questions, and she smirked at herself dismissively, looking out the window. It wasn't her place to ask. She had a task at hand and nothing more. A silent scene of nervousness just this side of panic. Yes, she thought. That was exactly how she would play it.

It was easy, she knew, and maybe even halfway logical, for an audience to think a film was shot scene by ordered scene. That's how life worked, after all, one thing happening after another. But this picture was being done piecemeal, a haphazard schedule. She had to think hard about the story. She found it difficult to follow the script sometimes, forgetting where the scene was placed in the story's arc, what her character did or did not know. But she held her tongue and chided herself: she knew exactly what the Director would tell her. *You hold in your hands a script. It tells you everything you need to know. If it's not there, you don't need to know it.*

She looked up at the October sky over the hills, completely and unsurprisingly blue. Would the weather hold? No rain was expected, not even cloud cover, no worries for tomorrow. Just the technicalities of a short location shoot, away from the city itself and no onlookers: the equipment, the crew, the two actors. All for a scene that wouldn't take place until well into the movie's first act. But that was the beauty of editing, the layered splices after so many takes, a story without a seam. Such was her responsibility, to suggest continuity without effort, every scene making its crucial contribution, even though she had little to say. She looked at the script again and pictured how the shooting would go. First, the scene shot with a camera near the driver's side window. Then the scene shot again with the camera crowding into her by the passenger seat. Then the shots again for line delivery, for lighting, for the position of the actor playing the policeman, for the microphones, for the position of her hands on the steering wheel, for the lighting director to adjust his reflective screens as the sun slowly made its way through morning. Again and again and again.

For such a small role. She wasn't going to be in the picture after the first third. When the Actress had first read the script, she stopped on the character's fate, then flipped back to the first page and the cast of characters. She was going to disappear. Violently. She tried to pay no mind to how the Director might have to stage this particular scene, focused only on the end of her character, the bulk of the script's pages still gripped in the fingers of her right hand.

A supporting role. Nothing more. In the Director's previous picture, that one actress had appeared playing two roles. She hadn't done a particularly stellar job, some in the industry had said, but the Actress thought the performance more than adequate. She had sat in the theater with mild envy, the role too rich for words: A distraught wife is trailed silently throughout San Francisco by a police detective, from flower shop to museum to the foot of the glorious Golden Gate Bridge, where she finally tries to hurl herself into the bay. The detective rescues her and later falls in love, only to lose her again to a successful suicide attempt. It played, the Actress thought, like an odd type of silent movie, and she felt maybe she had fooled herself into believing she could have fit perfectly into the part. Was it really requiring much beyond posing, or was there something about silent-movie acting that she didn't know? She wondered what the script must have looked like, that other actress—who couldn't have been professionally trained—skimming the pages until she found her first line.

No matter how small the role was going to be, it would have been foolish to say no to the Director. He was in the midst of doing something extraordinary and uncanny with some actresses, finessing their star wattage and burnishing it into a singular, almost iconic image. That was the way the Actress saw it anyway, mesmerized by how he was stripping out all the trappings of the industry and pushing these women toward something beyond even acting, something nakedly cinematic—postures, poses, gestures, as if the women were in magazine ads come to life for just split seconds at a time, just enough motion for the public to remember them as images and not characters. It was like opening up a jewelry box she had had many year ago as a young girl, fascinated by the tiny plastic ballerina in the center and its brief circle of motion. She had closed and opened that box endlessly, even though the ballerina did nothing differently. But even now, in a black sedan carrying her over the Grapevine back toward the Valley, where she had grown up, the Actress could close her eyes and remember the golden lace of the ballerina's costume, the full circle of her deliciously patient twirl, her perfect timing with the delicate chime of the music box's single tune. And that was the way the screen worked, too, she had discovered. Every actress's trajectory carried a moment like that, and the Director was staging them effortlessly.

She could feel the car's engine release a little—the upward climb was ending, and the road was leveling out briefly before the inevitable decline. She peered over the bench seat to get a look out the front window, but so far they hadn't reached a place where she could see the horizon of the Valley stretching out before them.

"We're almost there, ma'am," the driver said. "Probably another hour or so."

"Oh, I hope I didn't look impatient," she said. "There's a point in the road where you can see for miles across. I thought I had missed it."

"You've been on this road before, ma'am?"

"Absolutely. Does that surprise you?"

"Well, mostly it's people going the other way," the driver said. "Getting away from Bakersfield, Fresno, all those little towns in between. Everyone wants to go to Los Angeles. I don't see any reason why anybody would be going into the Valley."

"Fruit buyers. Cotton. Oilmen, too. There's money to be made down there."

"You're a smart lady. I'm from the Valley, you know, and most people don't think of this place that way."

She said nothing in response for a moment, not wanting to reveal much about herself. She had learned to be careful over the years. She studied the back of the driver's head, his careful concentration on the road. "I was born here," she finally offered, "over past Fresno."

"Is that right?" he said, meeting her eyes in the rearview mirror. "I'm from Stockton myself, born and raised."

"Do you still have family there?"

"Yes, ma'am. My parents are still there, but they're getting on in years."

She smiled at him when he glanced at her in the mirror, but did not respond. But the silence wasn't awkward. He went back to the task at hand; she knew how the studios laid down the law on drivers, on crew, even on extras. She studied the back of his head, a handsome square with a clean line from a fresh haircut. Ever so slightly now, the sedan was beginning to pick up speed, the road taking a gradual slope downward, but she resisted leaning forward again to catch a view.

"I hope you won't think I'm being nosy," said the driver, "but I hardly think you're on your way to do a musical."

She laughed a little and shook her head. "No, nothing like that. Not in Bakersfield."

"Well, it is a big music city, you know. Lots of country. I'm sure there's a good story in there somehow. With a country music star and all."

"Maybe," she replied. "But you couldn't see me as a cowgirl, could you?"

"I sure could!" He was beginning to take his eyes off the road just a bit much for her comfort, but there wasn't going to be a way to return to the silence of before without seeming rude. She could feel the pull of the road downward. "I tell you what—you'd make a prettier cowgirl than that Elizabeth Taylor."

"That's very kind of you to say," she said, then leaned up to look at the road. They were most definitely on the way down the slope of the Grapevine, but the road curved here and there and the full, unobstructed view of the Valley had yet to come. They went silent again, and she looked once more at the driver's clean hairline, the square rigidity, and then let her eyes travel briefly down the slope of his shoulder.

This girl is in love with a divorced man and will do anything for him, she'd been told, but the direction had ended right there during the read-through. *This girl.* A read-through, not a rehearsal. Silently, she had sat at the table with the Director and the other actors and asked herself if she knew what it would be like to love another woman's ex-husband, but the script said nothing about shame, about moral obligations, nothing about right or wrong. And the Director had long ago put his foot down on any shenanigans about character, about Method, about needing quiet spaces before a scene started: this was a job, not a psychiatric couch.

She pictured running her finger along the edge of the driver's shoulder and wondered if his eyes would register complicity when they looked up to meet hers in the rearview mirror.

Is that how the European actresses did it, how they lost themselves in their scripted terrors?

You have beautiful eyes, said the woman who had discovered her years ago, a silent-film star. *It's all in the eyes.*

"I'm not exaggerating, ma'am. My wife and I both admire you very much, especially in the movies where you sing and dance. You're an absolutely talented lady. First class! We think you're just wonderful!"

"Thank you," the Actress replied, and the moment she said it, she wished she could have given the words more than the note of resignation underneath. She wondered if she had betrayed what she had been thinking just by speaking aloud, and this worried and thrilled her at the same time: it was a private knowledge she wanted to hone, to use during the filming, in order to practice at being a real actress, to use every available tool. Her voice, her eyes, her fluttering tone. That would be all she could control. Everything else, she was beginning to suspect, would be modeled for her.

The driver went quiet again, his eyes back on the road, and she felt sorry for not taking in his pleasure, his willingness to give her praise, even though she had long ago discarded the need for adulation, that small bird singing inside. It was one thing to enter this business for that very reason—she could be honest with herself about that—but it was quite another to let that feeling guide her well-being. She had come from this very Valley to Hollywood as a starlet—a dancer and singer with enough talent not to embarrass anyone—but that was over ten years ago now, and somewhere along the line, she had realized the adoration would not last very long. She should drink it in, every chance she had.

You have beautiful eyes, the silent-film star had told her, as if there were an urgency in using them, as if the silent-film star herself had never noticed anyone taking an indiscreet glance at her lazy eye, drooping a little when she had too much champagne.

"Look," said the driver. "There's your view."

The Actress leaned forward and there it was: the long green Valley flanked on the west by the low coastal hills, over on the east by the towering Sierra, the place she had been born in, had come from, maybe was destined to return to. "Majestic, isn't it?" she said. "Gorgeous, really."

"Yes, ma'am. From the Lord's point of view, everything looks beautiful."

The road was level, but she could feel the sedan picking up speed. The descent would start soon, and with it the curving roads. She felt her stomach drop heavy for a moment even before they began going down, the Valley beckoning below.

Are you willing to wear only a brassiere for the opening scene? The Director had asked her. *It's important for the atmosphere.*

Fruit. Cotton. Oil. The land spread out as far as she could see. The story of the woman would take place in the Valley, but there was no landmark to let the audience know. No leaning tower, no red bridge, no streets of stark white monuments. It was a terrible story to tell.

Ma'am, I know where I can have you fitted for some black brassieres, a wardrobe mistress assured her. *Very elegant, very discreet.*

The script made no claim on morals, on shame, on right or wrong. But there were white brassieres and black ones, a black purse matched by a white one. What for, if only to signal the audience? Were things ever so dear in real life?

In the story, there was a sister. She kept her clothes on. The Actress wondered about that role, if maybe it wasn't the one she should be playing.

The road started down, and just as she suspected, her stomach sank. She wanted to lean back into her seat and not look ahead, where the view of the majestic Valley dipped away from their sight, obscured by the hills as the road dove down their descent. The curves began making her feel nauseated and regretful of the orange juice and croissant she'd had for breakfast, but the Actress remained leaning forward, one hand on the bench seat, feeling a little proud of her bravery as the driver negotiated the turns.

The girl will do anything. She steals the money and runs.

She could not ask the Director. She only asked herself, silently. What is it like to love a man who left his wife, who is still angry at her? What is it like to steal money? What is it like to run? What is it like to know you've made an error, to know you've acted in complete haste? What is it like to have a police officer arrest you? What is it like to know there might not be a turning back?

Would she do anything?

In my opinion, the girl should bare her breasts in the opening scene. It would tell the audience everything about how tawdry and put-upon this girl is. But we're behind the times. Oh, now, I can see by that look on your face that you wouldn't have done a nude scene. Rest assured that I would never have asked you to do so. But in ten years' time, I do believe it will be fairly common practice, don't you agree? Don't you think the European girls will show us their bare breasts before the Americans?

The feeling in her stomach lightened. The road had only a few curves left, but already she could see that the hills were giving way, as if they were gates of some kind, and the Valley opened up before them, Bakersfield now a straight shot along the flat, dry road.

"Thank you," the Actress said, and she put her hand on the driver's shoulder. She could feel his strength through her fingertips. "I appreciate getting here safely."

THE MADNESS OF CESAR CHAVEZ

Caitlin Flanagan

ONCE A YEAR, in the San Joaquin Valley in Central California, something spectacular happens. It lasts only a couple of weeks, and it's hard to catch, because the timing depends on so many variables. But if you're patient, and if you check the weather reports from Fresno and Tulare counties obsessively during the late winter and early spring, and if you are also willing, on very little notice, to drop everything and make the unglamorous drive up (or down) to that part of the state, you will see something unforgettable. During a couple of otherworldly weeks, the tens of thousands of fruit trees planted there burst into blossom, and your eye can see nothing, on either side of those rutted farm roads, but clouds of pink and white and yellow. Harvest time is months away, the brutal summer heat is still unimaginable, and in those cool, deserted orchards, you find only the buzzing of bees, the perfumed air, and the endless canopy of color.

I have spent the past year thinking a lot about the San Joaquin Valley, because I have been trying to come to terms with the life and legacy of Cesar Chavez, whose United Farm Workers movement—born in a hard little valley town called Delano—played a large role in my California childhood. I spent the year trying, with increasing frustration, to square my vision of him, and of his movement, with one writer's thorough and unflinching reassessment of them. Beginning five years ago, with a series of shocking articles in the *Los Angeles Times*, and culminating now in one of the most important recent books on California history, Miriam Pawel has undertaken a thankless task: telling a complicated and in many ways shattering truth. That her book has been so quietly received is not owing to a waning interest in the remarkable man at its center. Streets and schools and libraries are still being named for Chavez in California; his long-ago rallying cry of "*Sí, se puede*" remains so evocative of ideas about justice and the collective power of the down-trodden that Barack Obama adopted it for his presidential campaign. No, the silence greeting the first book to come to terms with Chavez's legacy arises from the human tendency to be stubborn and romantic and (if the case requires it) willfully ignorant in defending the heroes we've chosen for ourselves. That silence also attests to the way Chavez touched those of us who had any involvement with him, because the full legacy has to include his singular and almost mystical way of eliciting not just fealty but a kind of awe. Something cultlike always clung to the Chavez operation, and so while I was pained to learn in Pawel's book of Chavez's enthrallment with an actual cult—with all the attendant paranoia and madness—that development makes sense.

In the face of Pawel's book, I felt compelled to visit the places where Chavez lived and worked, although it's hard to tempt anyone to join you on a road trip to somewhere as bereft of tourist attractions as the San Joaquin Valley. But one night in late February, I got a break: someone who'd just driven down from Fresno told me that the trees were almost in bloom, and that was all I needed. I took my thirteen-year-old son, Conor, out of school for a couple of days so we could drive up the 99 and have a look. I was thinking of some things I wanted to show him, and some I wanted to see for myself. It would be "experiential learning"; it would be a sentimental journey. At times it would be a covert operation.

One Saturday night, when I was nine or ten years old, my parents left the dishes in the sink and dashed out the driveway for their weekend treat: movie night. But not half an hour later—just enough time for the round trip from our house in the Berkeley Hills to the United Artists theater down on Shattuck—they were right back home again, my mother hanging up her coat with a sigh, and my father slamming himself angrily into a chair in front of *The Bob Newhart Show*.

What happened?

"Strike," he said bitterly.

One of the absolute rules of our household, so essential to our identity that it was never even explained in words, was that a picket line didn't mean "maybe." A picket line meant "closed." This rule wasn't a point of honor or a means of forging solidarity with the common man, someone my father hoped to encounter only in literature. It came from a way of understanding the world, from the fierce belief that the world was divided between workers and owners. The latter group was always, always trying to exploit the former, which—however improbably, given my professor father's position in life—was who we were.

In the history of human enterprise, there can have been no more benevolent employer than the University of California in the 1960s and '70s, yet to hear my father and his English-department pals talk about the place, you would have thought they were working at the Triangle shirtwaist factory. Not buying a movie ticket if the ushers were striking meant that if the shit really came down, and the regents tried to make full professors teach *Middlemarch* seminars over summer vacation, the ushers would be there for you. As a child, I burned brightly with the justice of these concepts, and while other children were watching *Speed Racer* or learning Chinese jump rope, I spent a lot of my free time working for the United Farm Workers.

Everything about the UFW and its struggle was right-sized for a girl: it involved fruits and vegetables, it concerned the most elementary concepts of right and wrong, it was something you could do with your mom, and most of your organizing could be conducted just outside the grocery store, which meant you could always duck inside for a Tootsie Pop. The cement apron outside a grocery store, where one is often accosted—in a manner both winsome and bullying—by teams of Brownies pressing their cookies on you, was once my barricade and my bully pulpit.

Of course, it had all started with Mom. Somewhere along the way, she had met Cesar Chavez, or at least attended a rally where he had spoken, and that was it. Like almost everyone else who ever encountered him, she was spellbound. "This wonderful, wonderful man," she would call him, and off we went to collect clothes for the farmworkers' children, and to sell red-and-black UFW buttons and collect signatures. It was our thing: we loved each other, we loved doing little projects, we had oceans of free time (has anyone in the history of the world had more free time than mid-century housewives and their children?), and we were both constitutionally suited to causes that required grudge-holding and troublemaking and making things better for people in need. Most of all, though, we loved Cesar.

In those heady, early days of the United Farm Workers, in the time of the great five-year grape strike that started in 1965, no reporter, not even the most ironic among them, failed to remark upon, if not come under, Chavez's sway. "The Messianic quality about him," observed John Gregory Dunne in his brilliant 1967 book, *Delano*, "is suggested by his voice, which is mesmerizing—soft, perfectly modulated, pleasantly accented." Peter Matthiessen's book-length profile of Chavez, which consumed two issues of *The New Yorker* in the summer of 1969, reported: "He is the least boastful man I have ever met." Yet within this self-conscious and mannered presentation of inarticulate deference was an ability to shape both a romantic vision and a strategic plan. Never since then has so great a gift been used for so small a cause. In six months, he took a distinctly regional movement and blasted it into national, and then international, fame.

"The ranchers underestimated Chavez," a stunned local observer of the historic Delano grape strike told Dunne; "they thought he was just another dumb Mex." Such a sentiment fueled opinions of Chavez, not just among the valley's grape growers—hardworking men, none of them rich by any means—but among many of his most powerful admirers, although they spoke in very different terms. Chavez's followers—among them mainline Protestants, socially conscious Jews, Berkeley kids, white radicals who were increasingly rootless as the civil-rights movement transformed into the black-power movement—saw him as a profoundly good man. But they also understood him as a kind of idiot savant, a noble peasant who had risen from the agony of stoop labor and was mysteriously instilled with the principles and tactics of union organizing. In fact he'd been a passionate and tireless student of labor relations for a decade before founding the UFW, handpicked to organize Mexican Americans for the Community Service Organization, a local outfit under the auspices of no less a personage than Saul Alinsky, who knew Chavez well and would advise him during the grape strike. From Alinsky, and from Fred Ross, the CSO founder, Chavez learned the essential tactic of organizing: the person-by-person, block-by-block building of a coalition, no matter how long it took, sitting with one worker at a time, hour after hour, until the tide of solidarity is so high, no employer can defeat it.

Chavez, like all the great '60s figures, was a man of immense personal style. For a hundred reasons—some cynical, some not—he and Robert Kennedy were drawn to each other. The Kennedy name had immense appeal to the workers Chavez was trying to cultivate; countless Mexican households displayed photographs of JFK, whose assassination they understood as a Catholic martyrdom rather than an act of political gun violence. In turn, Chavez's cause offered Robert Kennedy a chance to stand with oppressed workers in a way that would not immediately inflame his family's core constituency, among them working-class Irish Americans who felt no enchantment with the civil-rights causes that RFK increasingly embraced. The Hispanic situation was different. At the time of the grape strike, Mexican American immigration was not on anyone's political radar. The overwhelming majority of California's population was white, and the idea that Mexican workers would compete for anyone's good job was unheard-of. The San Joaquin Valley farms—and the worker exploitation they had historically engendered—were associated more closely with the mistreatment of white Okies during the Great Depression than with the plight of any immigrant population.

Kennedy—his mind, like Chavez's, always on the political promise of a great photograph—flew up to Delano in March 1968, when Chavez broke his twenty-five-day fast, which he had undertaken not as a hunger strike, but as penance for some incidents of UFW violence. In a Mass held outside the union gas station where Chavez had fasted, the two were photographed, sitting next to Chavez's wife and his mantilla-wearing mother, taking Communion together ("Senator, this is probably the most ridiculous request I ever made in my life," said a desperate cameraman who'd missed the shot; "but would you mind giving him a piece of bread?"). Three months later, RFK was shot in Los Angeles, and a second hagiographic photograph was taken of the leader with a Mexican American. A young busboy named Juan Romero cradled the dying senator in his arms, his white kitchen jacket and dark, pleading eyes lending the picture an urgency at once tragic and political: *The* Third of May recast in a hotel kitchen. The United Farm Workers began to seem like Kennedy's great unfinished business. The family firm might have preferred that grieving for Bobby take the form of reconsidering Teddy's political possibilities, but in fact much of it was channeled, instead, into boycotting grapes.

That historic grape boycott eventually ended with a rousing success: three-year union contracts binding the Delano growers and the farmworkers. After that, the movement drifted out of my life and consciousness, as it did—I now realize—for millions of other people. I remember clearly the night my mother remarked (in a guarded way) to my father that the union had now switched its boycott from grapes to...lettuce. "*Lettuce?*" he squawked, and then burst out in mean laughter. I got the joke. What was Chavez going to do now, boycott each of California's agricultural products, one at a time for five years each? We'd be way into the twenty-first century by the time they got around to zucchini. And besides, things were changing—in the world, in Berkeley, and (in particular, I thought) at the Flanagans'. Things that had appeared revolutionary and appealing in the '60s were becoming weird or ugly in the '70s. People began turning inward. My father, stalwart Vietnam War protester and tear-gasee, turned his concern to writing an endless historical novel about 18th-century Ireland. My mother stopped worrying so much about the liberation of other people and cut herself into the deal: she left her card table outside the Berkeley Co-op and went back to work. I too found other pursuits. Sitting in my room with the cat and listening over and over to Carly Simon's *No Secrets* album—while staring with Talmudic concentration at its braless cover picture—was at least as absorbing as shaking the *Huelga* can and fretting about Mexican children's vaccination schedules had once been. Everyone sort of moved on.

I didn't really give any thought to the UFW again until the night of my mother's death. At the end of that terrible day, when my sister and I returned from the hospital to our parents' house, we looked through the papers on my mother's kitchen desk, and there among the envelopes from the many, many charities she supported (she sent each an immediate albeit very small check) was one bearing a logo I hadn't seen in years: the familiar black-and-red *Huelga* eagle. I smiled and took it home with me. I wrote a letter to the UFW, telling about my mom and enclosing a check, and suddenly I was back.

Re-upping with the twenty-first-century United Farm Workers was fantastic. The scope of my efforts was so much larger than before (they encouraged me to e-blast their regular updates to everyone in my address book, which of course I did) and the work so, so much less arduous—no sitting around in parking lots haranguing people about grapes. I never got off my keister. Plus, every time a new UFW e-mail arrived—the logo blinking, in a very new-millennium way, "Donate now!"—and I saw the pictures of farmworkers doing stoop labor in the fields, and the stirring photographs of Cesar Chavez, I felt close to my lost mother and connected to her: here I am, Mom, still doing our bit for the union.

And then one morning a few years later, I stepped out onto the front porch in my bathrobe, picked up the *Los Angeles Times*, and saw a headline: "Farmworkers Reap Little as Union Strays From Its Roots." It was the first article in a four-part series by a *Times* reporter named Miriam Pawel, and from the opening paragraph, I was horrified.

I learned that while the UFW brand still carried a lot of weight in people's minds—enough to have built a pension plan of $100 million in assets but with only a few thousand retirees who qualified—the union had very few contracts with California growers, the organization was rife with Chavez nepotism, and the many UFW-funded business ventures even included an apartment complex in California built with non-union labor. I took this news personally. I felt ashamed that I had forwarded so many e-mails to so many friends, all in the service, somehow, of keeping my mother's memory and good works alive, and all to the ultimate benefit—as it turned out—not of the workers in the fields (whose lives were in some ways worse than they had been in the '60s), but rather of a large, shadowy, and now morally questionable organization. But at least, I told myself, none of this has in any way impugned Cesar himself: he'd been dead more than a decade before the series was published. His own legacy was unblighted.

Or so it seemed, until my editor sent me a copy of *The Union of Their Dreams*, Pawel's exhaustively researched, by turns sympathetic and deeply shocking, investigation of Chavez and his movement, and in particular of eight of the people who worked most closely with him. Through her in-depth interviews with these figures—among them a prominent attorney who led the UFW legal department, a minister who was one of Chavez's closest advisers, and a young farmworker who had dedicated his life to the cause—Pawel describes the reality of the movement, not just during the well-studied and victorious period that made it famous, but during its long, painful transformation to what it is today. Her story of one man and his movement is a story of how the '60s became the '70s.

To understand Chavez, you have to understand that he was grafting together two life philosophies that were, at best, an idiosyncratic pairing. One was grounded in union-organizing techniques that go back to the Wobblies; the other emanated directly from the mystical Roman Catholicism that flourishes in Mexico and Central America and that Chavez ardently followed. He didn't conduct "hunger strikes"; he fasted penitentially. He didn't lead "protest marches"; he organized peregrinations in which his followers—some crawling on their knees—arrayed themselves behind the crucifix and effigies of the Virgin of Guadalupe. His desire was not to lift workers into the middle class, but to bind them to one another in the decency of sacrificial poverty. He envisioned the little patch of dirt in Delano—the "Forty Acres" that the UFW had acquired in 1966 and that is now a National Historic Landmark—as a place where workers could build shrines, pray, and rest in the shade of the saplings they had tended together while singing. Like most '60s radicals—of whatever stripe—he vastly overestimated the appeal of hard times and simple living; he was not the only Californian of the time to promote the idea of a Poor People's Union, but as everyone from the Symbionese Liberation Army to the Black Panthers would discover, nobody actually wants to be poor. With this Christ-like and infinitely suffering approach to some worldly matters, Chavez also practiced the take-no-prisoners, balls-out tactics of a Chicago organizer. One of his strategies during the lettuce strike was causing deportations: he would alert the immigration authorities to the presence of undocumented (and therefore scab) workers and get them sent back to Mexico. As the '70s wore on, all of this—the fevered Catholicism and the brutal union tactics—coalesced into a gospel with fewer and fewer believers. He moved his central command from the Forty Acres, where he was in constant contact with workers and their families—and thus with the realities and needs of their lives—and took up residence in a weird new headquarters.

Located in the remote foothills of the Tehachapi Mountains, the compound Chavez would call La Paz centered on a moldering and abandoned tuberculosis hospital and its equally ravaged outbuildings. In the best tradition of charismatic leaders left alone with their hand-picked top command, he became unhinged. This little-known turn of events provides the compelling final third of Pawel's book. She describes how Chavez, the master spellbinder, himself fell under the spell of a sinister cult leader, Charles Dederich, the founder of Synanon, which began as a tough-love drug-treatment program and became—in Pawel's gentle locution—"an alternative lifestyle community." Chavez visited Dederich's compound in the Sierras (where women routinely had their heads shaved as a sign of obedience) and was impressed. Pawel writes:

Chavez envied Synanon's efficient operation. The cars all ran, the campus was immaculate, the organization never struggled for money.

He was also taken with a Synanon practice called "The Game," in which people were put in the center of a small arena and accused of disloyalty and incompetence while a crowd watched their humiliation. Chavez brought the Game back to La Paz and began to use it on his followers, among them some of the UFW's most dedicated volunteers. In a vast purge, he exiled or fired many of them, leaving wounds that remain tender to this day. He began to hold the actual farmworkers in contempt: "Every time we look at them," he said during a tape-recorded meeting at La Paz, "they want more money. Like pigs, you know. Here we're slaving, and we're starving and the goddamn workers don't give a shit about anything."

Chavez seemed to have gone around the bend. He decided to start a new religious order. He flew to Manila during martial law in 1977 and was officially hosted by Ferdinand Marcos, whose regime he praised, to the horror and loud indignation of human-rights advocates around the world.

By the time of Chavez's death, the powerful tide of union contracts for California farmworkers, which the grape strike had seemed to augur, had slowed to the merest trickle. As a young man, Chavez had set out to secure decent wages and working conditions for California's migrant workers; anyone taking a car trip through the "Salad Bowl of the World" can see that for the most part, these workers have neither.

For decades, Chavez has been almost an abstraction, a collection of gestures and images (the halting speech, the plaid shirt, the eagerness to perform penance for the smallest transgressions) suggesting more an icon than a human being. Here in California, Chavez has reached civic sainthood. Indeed, you can trace a good many of the giants among the state's shifting pantheon by looking at the history of one of my former elementary schools. When Berkeley became the first city in the United States to integrate its school system without a court order, my white friends and I were bused to an institution in the heart of the black ghetto called Columbus School. In the fullness of time, its name was changed to Rosa Parks School; the irony of busing white kids to a school named for Rosa Parks never seemed fully unintentional to me. Now this school has a strong YouTube presence for the videos of its Cesar Chavez Day play, an annual event in which bilingual first-graders dressed as Mexican farmworkers carry *Sí, Se Puede* signs and sing "*De Colores.*" The implication is that just as Columbus and Parks made their mark on America, so did Chavez make his lasting mark on California.

In fact, no one could be more irrelevant to the California of today, and particularly to its poor, Hispanic immigrant population, than Chavez. He linked improvement of workers' lives to a limitation on the bottomless labor pool, but today, low-wage, marginalized, and exploited workers from Mexico and Central America number not in the tens of thousands, as in the '60s, but in the millions. Globalization is the epitome of capitalism, and nowhere is it more alive than in California. When I was a child in the '60s, professional-class families did not have a variety of Hispanic workers—maids, nannies, gardeners—toiling in and around their households. Most faculty wives in Berkeley had a once-a-week "cleaning lady," but those women were blacks, not Latinas. A few of the posher families had gardeners, but those men were Japanese, and they were employed for their expertise in cultivating California plants, not for their willingness to "mow, blow, and go."

Growing up here when I did meant believing your state was the most blessed place in the world. We were certain—both those who lived in the Republican, Beach Boys paradises of Southern California and those who lived in the liberal enclaves of Berkeley and Santa Monica—that our state would always be able to take care of its citizens. The working class would be transformed (by dint of the aerospace industry and the sunny climate) into the most comfortable middle class in the world, with backyard swimming pools and self-starting barbecue grills for everyone. The poor would be taken care of, too, whether that meant boycotting grapes, or opening libraries until every rough neighborhood had books (and Reading Lady volunteers) for everyone.

But all of that is gone now.

The state is broken, bankrupt, mean. The schools are a misery, and the once-famous parks are so crowded on weekends that you might as well not go, unless you arrive at first light to stake your claim. The vision of civic improvement has given way to self-service and consumer indulgence. Where the mighty Berkeley Co-op once stood on Shattuck and Cedar—where I once rattled the can for Chavez, as shoppers (each one a part owner) went in to buy no-frills, honestly purveyed, and often unappealing food—is now a specialty market of the Whole Foods variety, with an endless olive bar and a hundred cheeses.

When I took my boy up the state to visit Cesar's old haunts, we drove into the Tehachapi Mountains to see the compound at La Paz, now home to the controversial National Farm Workers Service Center, which sits on a war chest of millions of dollars. The place was largely deserted and very spooky. In Delano, the famous Forty Acres, site of the cooperative gas station and of Chavez's twenty-five-day fast, was bleak and unvisited. We found a crust of old snow on Chavez's grave in Keene, and a cold wind in Delano. We spent the night in Fresno, and my hopes even for the Blossom Trail were low. But we followed the 99 down to Fowler, tacked east toward Sanger, and then, without warning, there we were.

"Stop the car," Conor said, and although I am usually loath to walk a farmer's land without permission, we had to step out into that cloud of pale color. We found ourselves in an Arthur Rackham illustration: the boughs bending over our heads were heavy with white blossoms, the ground was covered in moss that was in places deep green and in others brown, like worn velvet. I kept turning back to make sure the car was still in sight, but then I gave up my last hesitation and we pushed deeper and deeper into the orchard, until all we could see were the trees. At 65 degrees, the air felt chilly enough for a couple of Californians to keep their sweaters on. In harvest season, the temperature will climb to over 100 degrees many days, and the rubbed velvet of the spring will have given way to a choking dust. Almost none of the workers breathing it will have a union contract, few will be here legally, and the deals they strike with growers will hinge on only one factor: how many other desperate people need work. California agriculture has always had a dark side. But—whether you're eating a ripe piece of fruit in your kitchen or standing in a fairy-tale field of blossoms on a cool spring morning—forgetting about all of that is so blessedly easy. Chavez shunned nothing more fervently than the easy way; and nothing makes me feel further away from the passions and certainty of my youth than my eagerness, now, to take it.

THE 36-HOUR DINNER PARTY

Michael Pollan

HERE'S THE CONCEIT: Build a single wood fire and, over the course of thirty-plus hours, use it to roast, braise, bake, simmer and grill as many different dishes as possible—for lunch, dinner, breakfast and lunch again. The main ingredients: one whole goat from the McCormack Ranch in Rio Vista, Calif.; several crates of seasonal produce (and a case of olive oil) from Hudson Ranch in Napa; a basket of morels and porcini gathered near Mount Shasta; an assortment of spices from Boulettes Larder in San Francisco; and a couple of cases of wine from Kermit Lynch in Berkeley. The setting: a shady backyard in Napa (but picture suburban subdivision, not vineyard estate), where a big country table stretches out beneath the canopy of a mulberry tree. The cast: three accomplished Bay Area chefs (Mike and Jenny Emanuel—whose kitchen and backyard we've commandeered for the weekend—and Melissa Fernandez), one gifted baker (Chad Robertson), one jack of all culinary trades (Anthony Tassinello) and two amateurs (me and my seventeen-year-old son, Isaac). The guests: all of the above, plus a rotating crew of spouses, children, friends and neighbors. The fire: almond, oak and mulberry logs burning in a cob oven that Mike Emanuel built with the help of some friends in 2006. A cob, or earth, oven is a primitive, domed cooking device that can be made from layers of mud, clay, straw, stucco, even manure; the earthy mixture, the cob, can endure much higher heat, and hold it much longer, than an indoor oven can. Emanuel's incarnation, which he built "to bring together family and friends for extended feasts," stands five feet tall with a thirty-inch hearth and looks like a cartoon character: a visitor from a planet of chubby, eyeless, big-mouthed monsters.

The inspiration for this pyro-gastronomical experiment was the communal ovens still found burning in some towns around the Mediterranean, centers of social gravity where, each morning, people bring their proofed, or risen, loaves to be baked. (Each loaf bears a signature slash so you can be sure the one you get back is your own.) But after the bread is out of the oven, people show up with a variety of other dishes to wring every last B.T.U. from the day's fire: pizzas while the oven is still blazing and then, as the day goes on, gentle braises or even pots of yogurt to capture the last heat and flavors of the dying embers.

The idea is to make the most efficient use of precious firewood and to keep the heat (and the danger) of the cook fire some distance from everybody's homes. But what appeals to me about the tradition is how the communal oven also becomes a focus for social life ("focus" is Latin for "hearth"), a place to gather and gossip and escape the solitude of cooking at home. Shared meals have always been about community, about what happens among family and friends—even enemies—when they gather around a table to eat; but once upon a time, before every family had its own kitchen in which Mom labored more or less alone, cooking was itself a social activity, one that fostered community and conversation around the chopping board or cook fire long before the meal was served.

Our own backyard experiment with a communal oven, which unfolded last June over the first weekend of summer, was in spirit obviously more playful than practical. But when Mike offered to organize and host what amounted to a thirty-six-hour dinner party, I was immediately intrigued: could an around-the-clock cook fire still exert the same social force? I barely knew most of the people with whom I'd be spending the weekend, and I wondered how well two days of working side by side and eating at the same table would wear on everyone. I also wondered about the food—whether four meals teased from a single fire, three of them from one goat, would get a little monotonous. But then, my previous experience of cooking with fire was pretty much limited to grilling slabs of meat on a Weber. I had no idea just how many different things one fire could do.

SATURDAY

9:22 A.M. Mike has laid the fire in the mouth of the oven: a tidy pyramid of crumpled newspaper, kindling and split logs. He waited for Isaac and me to show up before lighting it. Isaac lets Mike's twelve-year-old son, Will, do the honors. The oven's draft must be good, because the fire leaps to life almost instantly. The shape of the oven and the size of its single opening are designed to draw in air along the floor, then conduct it around the curving back and roof of the dome before exhausting it at the top of the opening. Within minutes, fat tongues of flame are licking at the top of its mouth, reaching out. This fire will burn straight through the weekend, though not always in this oven: to bake bread, we'll need to remove the burning logs and embers to a fire pit nearby—a concrete ring of partly buried sewer pipe—and then transfer them back. The most important cooking implement of the weekend will turn out to be a shovel.

10 A.M. While we wait for the oven to become hot enough to fire pizzas, Mike and Melissa break down the goat on the table outside. The rest of us mostly watch, lending a steadying hand from time to time. Ten days ago, Mike and I drove to the ranch to choose our animal and watch an itinerant butcher slaughter and dress it; Mike says the experience made him want to honor our goat by wasting as little of it as possible. Melissa is small but strong and has a sure hand with the hacksaw and the butcher knife; within twenty minutes the goat is transformed into considerably more appetizing cuts of meat: the baron, or hindquarters, and the saddle (both to be roasted for tonight's dinner); two racks of ribs (for tomorrow's lunch); the shoulders (destined for an overnight braise); and the scraps, which Anthony collects to make a sugo—a slow-cooked Italian meat sauce—for tonight's first course and to make sausage for the pizzas. Mike cuts a few slivers from the loin and passes them around; a ceremonial tasting of the uncooked animal is, he explains, "a butcher's privilege." The raw meat is surprisingly sweet and tender. It's so good, in fact, that we decide to make some crudo, or goat tartare, for an appetizer.

11 A.M. We break into small groups to prep for lunch, some of us working inside in the kitchen, others outside at the big table. Everybody is chopping and chatting—those of us who know one another, catching up; those of us who don't, getting acquainted. My lunchtime job is to assemble, with Isaac's help, a shaved vegetable salad—a julienne of everything that the farmer at Hudson Ranch, Scott Boggs, picked for us: fennel, carrots, radishes, cabbage, summer squash and green beans, all tossed with lemon juice, olive oil, pounded garlic, fresh herbs and salt. Over the top, I shave a few papery slices of fresh porcini and Parmesan. In the kitchen, Melissa is simmering a stock made from the goat's head, organs and bones while Anthony is grinding meat for sausage, sprinkling it with fennel pollen. Out by the fire, Chad, the baker, is starting to stretch his pizza dough, which he mixed last night.

1 P.M. Using a thermometer gun, which measures the temperature wherever you aim its infrared beam, Chad has determined that the floor of the oven is between 700 and 900 degrees, hot enough to cook a pizza in four or five minutes. He invites people over to make their pizzas from a variety of toppings that Melissa, Anthony and Mike prepared: sautéed squid, several kinds of cheese, goat sausage, morels, porcini, chopped herbs and green and yellow coins of summer squash. Chad shows us how to stretch a ball of dough over our fists and rotate it until it is paper thin. After we decorate our pies, Melissa, who ran the pizza oven at Chez Panisse for six years, shows us how to use the long-handled paddle to quarter-turn the pie in the oven as soon as the section of crust nearest the burning logs begins to balloon and blister. I think of professional chefs as control freaks, but Melissa and Chad are happy to let go and let everyone try their hand. So what if some of the pizzas aren't perfect circles? Isaac makes a goat-sausage-and-mushroom pizza that he declares the best he's ever tasted. I have to agree: Chad's crust is crisp but with a chewy interior, and all the toppings are nicely inflected by wood smoke.

3 P.M. After a leisurely lunch well oiled by a few bottles of rosé, everyone is ready for a snooze, but Mike reminds us that there's dinner to prep and bread to bake and a fire that needs our attention. Chad has proofed several loaves of his big country bread. (This may be the most coveted loaf in the Bay Area, selling out every evening at Tartine, his bakery in the Mission.) Mike helps him shovel all the burning logs and embers out of the oven and into the fire pit to even out the heat in the oven and eliminate the smoke. Even without a fire in it, the oven holds heat remarkably well: the gun clocks the back of the oven at 550 degrees, perfect for bread. But the floor must be hotter, because the bottom of the first loaf blackens before it has fully risen and crusted. Chad slides in a "sacrificial loaf"—one he bakes solely to cool the oven floor. By the time he slides in the next one, conditions are good though still not ideal. Chad says the dome of the oven is too high to give the tops of the loaves the hard, dark crust he's aiming for. Everyone else thinks the bread came out wonderfully moist and chewy, but Chad is not thrilled, and his relationship with the oven will remain testy all weekend.

6 P.M. Once all the loaves are out, we shovel the fire back into the oven and add logs to build up heat for the roast. I hold back some of the burning embers in the fire pit, where I plan to roast the root vegetables in a bed of ashes. Called rescoldo, this is a method described by the Argentine chef Francis Mallmann in his book *Seven Fires*: bury whole beets, turnips, carrots and any other root vegetables in the ashes of a dying fire; dig them out a couple of hours later, dust off the ashes (or peel the vegetables, if you don't like eating a little ash) and serve. Immediately I face my first fire-management challenge: the dying fire is a little too dead, so I have to add kindling and resuscitate it by blowing through a four-foot-long steel straw that Mike has for just this purpose. Soon, however, the fire is blazing and threatens to burn my vegetables beyond a crisp, so I now have to stifle it by shoveling in more ash. My first lesson about cooking with live fire: at any given moment, there is either too much of it or not quite enough; the sweet spot is hard to find and fleeting.

6:50 P.M. While I was worrying my fire and root vegetables, Mike and Melissa, who have emerged as something of a leadership team, were prepping the roasts, giving the baron and the saddle a deep-tissue massage with a mixture of pounded herbs and garlic and then wrapping them in a beautiful white lace of caul fat, the sort of item professional chefs just seem to have around. I'm beginning to appreciate Mike's genius for what chefs call the mise en place: making certain everything we could possibly need is at hand; never once have we had to run out to the store for a missing ingredient. Another lesson. I'm also impressed by the ease with which these cooks collaborate, how they can go back and forth from taking the lead on a dish to playing sous chef. These meals are a group endeavor, and everyone seems happy to share authorship. Except, that is, for the two bakers—Anthony and Chad—who occupy their own private bubbles of activity. Not sure why, but perhaps because baking demands more precision and therefore tighter control.

The oven is hovering between 450 and 500 degrees when Mike slides in the roasting pan. In the kitchen, meanwhile, Melissa is stirring a big pot of extremely slow-cooked polenta and tending to the goat sugo, while Anthony is whipping eggs for his dessert. He's assembling individual pots with slabs of spongecake soaked in sparkling wine and topped by wedges of fresh apricots and a sabayon: an airy custard of whipped eggs and cream tinted with saffron threads. The dessert needs to be ready to go into the oven when the roast comes out; oven traffic is building.

7:30 P.M. While we wait for the roasts to finish, Anthony brings out a platter of one of the few dishes untouched by our fire, his crudo: a rough dice of raw goat tenderloin with lemon juice, olive oil and a drizzle of raw egg yolk, served on a bed of rocket (aka arugula) and shaved raw porcini. Federal food-safety authorities would not approve of Anthony's dish, but spooned onto toasts made over the fire pit, the crudo is luscious: lemony, silky and cool.

7:45 P.M. The captivating scents emanating from the oven are drawing people outside and into its orbit. A few neighbors magically appear through an opening in the back fence, wondering what's cooking.

Unidentified children and puppies are suddenly underfoot. The gravitational field of the cook fire seems to have enlarged our little community, so Jenny sets a few more places at the big table.

8 P.M. When Mike and Melissa pull the roasts from the oven, putting them on the lip to rest, I set about retrieving the fire-roasted root vegetables, which requires a treasure hunt. The beets and turnips I can find, excavating among the ashes with a long pair of tongs, but the carrots have vaporized: the fire seems to have eaten them. I dust off as much ash as possible and put the vegetables, which are nicely charred and smell fantastic, on a platter. Isaac voices skepticism.

8:30 P.M. We sit down to dinner at last, starting with Melissa's sugo over polenta. The dish is unbelievably rich, owing no doubt to the goat-head stock, the organ meats in the sugo and the long, slow cooking of the polenta. (Melissa also soaked it overnight, "blooming" and slightly fermenting the corn meal.) Mike carves the roasts; the meat, which is mild and sweet, has a perfect ratio of deeply browned, smoky crust to pink interior. To accompany it, Anthony has chopped a salsa verde, made extra-astringent by the addition of fresh grape leaves. Opinion is divided on my roasted root vegetables, with Isaac firmly in the rejectionist camp. The beets and turnips are nicely caramelized and aromatic, but the ash coating takes some mental adjustment that not everyone can manage.

It is a long, loquacious and delicious dinner, made more special by the fact that virtually everyone at the table had a hand in preparing it. I feel as if I've already learned a lot cooking with this crew, especially about working together and trading ideas. Each dish might have a lead cook, but other cooks will contribute a technique or flavoring—dozens of tasting spoons have been passed around—so that the final product becomes something more or less new, even to its author. Already I'm better acquainted with everyone in the easy way that seems to happen when people work together, especially at tasks, like kitchen prep, that leave plenty of mental space for talking. The flow of conversation has been desultory, drifting from summer plans to the World Cup (playing earlier in the living room), kids, other meals, the work at hand. But it is the working together at less-than-all-consuming tasks that seems to be forging our motley crew (far flung in age and background) into something that feels like a community. Sometimes getting to know people is easier done side by side than it is face to face.

9:45 P.M. Anthony has left us to tend to his apricots, which emerge from the oven fragrant and caramelized with perfect black tips. Their sabayon blanket is blazingly bright yellow-orange from the saffron—apricot on apricot—and the flavor is as intensely layered as the color: honeyed ripe fruit, sweet spices, wine and wood smoke.

10:30 P.M. Mike, easily the most compulsive and conscientious member of our group, pops up from the table to go to work on the braise for tomorrow's lunch, something no one else is quite ready to confront. But the fire, fading now, is just right: 400 degrees and subsiding slowly. For tomorrow's meals, the culinary inspiration has shifted from Italy to other shores of the Mediterranean: Morocco and the Middle East. The goat shoulder has been marinating all day in harissa. In a big, old crock, Mike and Melissa bed down the shoulder on a mirepoix and add a couple of cinnamon sticks, slices of preserved lemon and handfuls of Persian mint and fresh green coriander seeds. Over that, they pour what's left of the goat stock and some white wine. To seal the crock as tightly as possible, I retrieve some of Chad's surplus dough from the compost, roll it into a thick rope and use it to caulk the top of the pot before Mike slides it into the oven and closes the door.

11 P.M. Indefatigable Mike has yet one more dish he wants to tease from our fire, using its fading heat to ferment some goat's-milk yogurt. He inoculates a crock of milk with a spoonful of yogurt and then sets it in a water bath on top of the oven to gently heat overnight. Now we're done for the day. Everyone except Anthony is too tired to take up Mike on his offer to watch *The Baker's Wife*, the Pagnol film, projected on the back wall of his house. The rest of us head off to bed.

SUNDAY

6 A.M. [This entry is based on reports; I'm still asleep.] Mike jumps out of bed in his underwear to check on the braise. The fire is all but completely out, but the braise is done and looks perfect, the top of the shoulder crusted in deep brown bark and the liquid thickened to a rich paste. The goat's milk, however, has curdled: too much heat. Undeterred, Mike adds a pinch of salt to the curds and puts them in a cheesecloth to drain, hoping to salvage a farmer's cheese for our breakfast.

8:30 A.M. The core group reassembles in the backyard for breakfast. Mike has coaxed the fire in the oven back to life. I'm starting to think of the fire as a creature with its own moods and appetites; now it needs to be fed. Chad has kindled a second fire in the pit and is toasting slices of yesterday's bread. Melissa, meanwhile, has prepped an unexpectedly intricate yet goat-free breakfast: in individual clay pots, she arranged sautéed porcini on a bed of blanched amaranth greens picked from Mike's garden. Over that, she cracked an egg and drizzled some cream. The pots go into the oven for several minutes, and when they come out she gives each a dollop of green-tomato chutney and dusts them with dukkah, an Egyptian spice-and-nut blend. All I can say about dukkah is that it does extraordinary things to an egg, as does wreathing cream briefly in wood smoke. But breakfast cannot be entirely goat-free: Mike's accidental farmer's cheese turned out to be delicate and sweet. One of the best bites of the weekend, if not of all time, is of a slice of Chad's toast spread with Mike's cheese and Jenny's apricot jam and then liberally sprinkled with dukkah. It takes a village to make some toast, apparently, but this is one sublime piece of toast.

9:38 A.M. We're still at the breakfast table when Mike starts pouring glasses of Vouvray to mark the twenty-four hours that have passed since we lighted the fire. By now, having shared so much eating and drinking and cooking, everyone feels comfortable enough not to have to talk; we've all entered the same psychological space. Even so, the Vouvray strikes me as ill advised, because we still have one more big meal to prep, this one for the largest group yet—the twenty-five or so friends, spouses, neighbors and local farmers expected for lunch. But no one else seems concerned; the mood is mellow in the extreme.

10:30 A.M. The pace starts to pick up. Melissa goes to work on the braise, removing the bones and skimming the fat. I take charge of the goat kabobs. Working with meat that Mike has ground with Moroccan spices, I form it around skewers like naked sausages: kefta, they're called. Chad is off by himself by the oven rolling dough for some flatbread pitas; bakers are solitaries, I decide. Prematurely, perhaps, because at the big table Isaac is helping Anthony pit Bing cherries and, using an old-timey wooden ice cream maker, hand-cranking frozen goat's-milk yogurt for dessert. (Mike finally nailed the yogurt, but on a hot plate inside.) The cranking is arduous, so Anthony recruits everyone, guests included, to take a turn as the price of dessert. The pitted cherries, with the addition of cinnamon, orange zest and eau de vie, go into a crock that will go into the fire to roast briefly.

11:30 A.M. Mike and I have rigged a pseudo-tandoori oven for the kabobs: a big clay garden pot half filled with hot coals stolen from the oven and topped with the pot's saucer. But it works only so-so: to fit under the lid, the skewers need to be planted in the hot coals at a fairly steep angle, and even after I improvise a tinfoil cap for each of them, sort of like the hand guard on a sword, the meat still wants to slide down into the ashes. So I move the skewers onto the grill over the fire pit, sharing space with Melissa, who is grilling the goat racks, obsessively turning them this way and that over the open fire.

12:30 P.M. Fire traffic is building again: Chad needs to get into the oven to bake his flatbreads (on a very hot fire), Melissa needs to reheat the braise, Anthony wants to roast his cherries at a lower temp and Mike's got a rice pilaf he needs to crisp. They work it out: build a big fire to bake the flatbreads and then bring down the heat by shoveling the burning logs into the fire pit.

1:30 P.M. Lunch turns out to be a sprawling, semi-spontaneous party. Word (and aroma) of our doings has gotten around, and a few more neighbors show up. It's a good thing, too, because we have a ton of food—all of today's creations plus a considerable amount of distinguished leftovers. Mike has also invited several of the folks who produced the ingredients we've been cooking. A dozen beautiful platters of food crowd the big table, the handiwork of so many gifted hands working together. I count at least seven dishes made from that one goat and this thirty-hour-old fire, so many complex variations on such a simple theme.

Lunchtime spreads out liquidly over the rest of the day, the adults lingering at the table, Isaac and Will strumming their guitars, the little kids playing with the dogs. The food is delicious, the chops perfectly grilled, the pitas soft and puffy and perfect for stuffing with meat and Mike's goat's-milk yogurt sauce—and the now-obligatory dukkah. But by now the food feels almost beside the point. I realize I've gotten at least as much pleasure from working together to create these meals as I have from eating them. Sometimes producing things is more gratifying—and more conducive to building community—than consuming them, I decide. Our guests seem merry and convivial, but there's something special about the camaraderie of the kitchen crew.

After Anthony pulls his crock of roasted cherries from the oven, we let the fire die, just short of thirty-six hours after lighting it. This fire has been protean, and the big-mouthed oven, which by now seems more like a character in our drama than a prop, has been prodigious in its output. I raise a glass to offer a toast, first to our hosts, then, of course, to the goat and lastly to all the cooks at the table. It seems to me that one of the many, many things our fire produced is a sense of community, as cook fires have probably always done, but especially among those of us who worked to bring all this food to the table. So I add to my toast an impromptu announcement, unauthorized but, I'm hoping, true: that Mike and Jenny have graciously agreed to host the second annual live-fire weekend next summer, thereby turning our improbable experiment into a tradition.

from *THE COOKBOOK COLLECTOR*

Allegra Goodman

SHE WAS LATE to work. Half an hour late, forty-five minutes late. George sat at his desk at Yorick's and called Jess's home number, but no one answered. He began to call the Tree House and then hung up.

His old black telephone sat silent on his desk. The boxes he had stacked near European History remained unpacked. She'd quit. That was the most likely scenario. She had decided to leave but hadn't bothered to give notice. That was usually the way with students. She had run off with her boyfriend, an amphibious creature George had met just once in passing at the Farmers' Market, where Jess hailed George from a booth selling root vegetables.

"I want you to meet someone!" she called out in her friendly way. Then she drew Leon from the shadows, as one might draw a dark slug off a lettuce leaf. The boyfriend was a tall Russian, or Armenian perhaps, with slippery black hair and olive skin, and eyes of an unusually pale, druggy shade of blue. The better to see you with, my dear, thought George. "This is Leon," Jess said.

"Hey," said Leon as George extended his hand.

"This is my boss, George," Jess told Leon.

Leon sized up George. "You're the bookseller."

"I am."

"Good for you," said Leon as though George were a child or a student or a dog performing some stupid trick. "What's selling these days?"

George frowned. "Nothing you'd like."

How quickly Jess had traded slacker Noah for sinister Leon. She was now over an hour late, later than she had ever been. Maybe she had not run off with Leon. Maybe she was dead.

He walked to the shop window, which Jess had set up with a display for Shakespeare's birthday. Used paperbacks of the Histories and Comedies framed a leather-bound Complete Works, and a *Tales from Shakespeare* in two volumes, very fine condition, with illustrations by Arthur Rackham. She had opened one volume to display a color plate of barefoot Miranda dancing with fairies on her father's island, but George had vetoed that idea, closing the book to save its spine and protect its colors from the sun.

No one outside even stopped to look. The fine fall weather kept people out of dark little bookstores. He told himself this, although on rainy winter days, he tended toward the other opinion, concluding that few would venture out to browse when they could stay home and order books online or reread books they already possessed. Vanity, vanity. Instantly accessible, infinitely searchable, the Internet precluded physical transactions, so that there was little point to keeping a bookshop, even in Berkeley. Moments of discovery in the store were sweet but all too rare: the reunion of a customer with the long-sought *Zen and the Art of Motorcycle Maintenance*, the discovery of Linus Pauling's copy of *On the Origin of Species*. Why live for such occasions? He only felt lonelier afterward.

He pushed away those melancholy thoughts and looked ahead to dinner. He had invited Nick, and his friend Raj as well. He had his own dissolute companions—or by the end of the night he'd make them so. There would be no wives or girlfriends, only good food and drink, George's favorite kind of evening. Why, then, was Jess late today? She was holding him up. He had planned to leave early so that he could pick up dessert (he didn't bake) and begin cooking.

The bell rang, and as the shop door opened, George backed away from the window lest he seem anxious. Surprised, he recognized the woman who walked in: not Jess, but Sandra.

"Welcome," he said, noting her cloth bag. She had come just twice over the past nine months, and each time she had brought an ordinary book. A first-edition *Fannie Farmer,* and an old *Mastering the Art of French Cooking*. He had offered only ten dollars for the last, and she had left Yorick's in a huff. Then he concluded that, when it came to her uncle's estate, Sandra had already sold him the crown jewels, such as they were. "Another cookbook for me?"

"No." She pushed her long hair back over her shoulders, a gesture surprisingly young for a woman so gray.

"May I help you find something?"

"No." She stood quite still before him. "What I would like," she said, and she spoke with precision, "is to take you to the house."

"To your house!"

"My uncle's house," she amended. "The house he left me. I'm interested in an appraisal."

Why now? he thought. And why him? Did she want a second opinion? Or was he the first? Just how desperate was she?

"Some of the books are valuable."

Let me be the judge of that, he thought.

"Some are unique."

"How many are there?"

"Currently," she said, "eight hundred and seventy-three."

The number startled him, because it was bigger than he expected, and more exact.

"Sorting out that many will take time."

"That's just it; time is of the essence," she told him. "Would it be possible for you to come this afternoon?"

With some humor, he considered his empty store. "Sure."

"I'll show you."

"I'd have to lock up," he said. Jess should have been there to cover for him.

He stuck a Post-it on the glass shop door. "Back in an hour."

Then he dashed off instructions for Jess, who had a key. He took his fountain pen and covered a note card quickly with his small tight cursive:

> J.—I assume you're writing a new theory of moral sentiments or testifying against Pacific Lumber. In either case, the books have not been shelved. Take care of that and break down the boxes!—G.

They took George's car, because Sandra didn't drive, and they drove through Elmwood with its beetle-browed old bungalows. Towering hedges of eugenia nearly obscured Sandra's home from Russell Street. Her uncle must have bought the place for about a dollar, thought George, as he picked his way through a jungle of ornamental plum, live oak, and Australian tea trees, trailing their branches luxuriantly. There were figs and lemons, roses and giant rhododendrons, all overrun with thorny blackberry canes.

"Watch out for the cat," Sandra told George as he followed her up peeling steps to the front porch.

She gestured for George to step in close behind her as she unlocked the door. Like a furry missile, the black-and-gray cat launched himself, trying to escape outdoors. George blocked him with his legs. Sandra scooped him up in her arms. "Down, Geoffrey," she ordered, as if chastising a dog, and she dumped the animal onto a couch draped in dark green slipcovers. Geoffrey jumped onto the back of this well-protected piece of furniture and glared at her with furrowed brow and narrowed eyes.

The living room was stuffed with armchairs, end tables and bookcases, stacks of magazines and yellowed newspapers. Empty antique birdcages filled the front bay window. Abandoned pagodas. Flanking the dining table, open cabinets displayed bowls and goblets of dusty ruby-colored cut glass. A phalanx of botanical engravings adorned the walls. No bright tulips or orchids here. The engravings were all pale green and gray, portraying and anatomizing moss and lichens. Odd choices, George thought. Geoffrey purred, and instinctively, as he leaned over the green couch for a closer look, George touched the cat's soft fur.

"He bites," said Sandra.

Too late. George gasped as the cat nipped his finger.

"I warned you." Sandra's voice rose.

The wound looked like two pinpricks, the puncture marks of a tiny vampire.

"I told you. I said watch out for the cat. He's a very..."

She disappeared into the next room, and George followed her into a kitchen that smelled of bananas and wheat germ and rotting plums.

The paint on the cabinets was chipped, the countertops stacked with dishes and small New Age appliances: rice cooker, yogurt maker, fruit dehydrator. Little cacti lined the windowsills. Prickly cacti, hairy cacti; spiky, round, bulbous, hostile little plants of every kind.

"He was my uncle's cat," Sandra explained. "He was abused when he was younger. My uncle found him and took him in, and then when my uncle passed..."

Ignoring this sob story, George marched to the sink.

"He felt abandoned," Sandra said.

George turned on the tap and a cloud of fruit flies rose from the drain. Disgusted, he held his finger under the running water.

"Let me get you some iodine," said Sandra. "Let me..." Her voice trailed off again. "You do still want to see the books?"

"That's what I'm here for."

She had turned her back to open the kitchen cabinets. For a moment he thought she was searching for the iodine, and then he saw them. Leather-bound, cloth-bound, quartos and folios, books of every size. The cabinets were stacked with books. Not a dish or cup in sight. Only books. Sandra bent and opened the lower cabinets. Not a single pot or pan. Just books. She stood on a chair to reach the cabinet above the refrigerator. Books there as well.

George stepped away from the sink without noticing that he had left the water running. Injury forgotten, he gazed in awe. He leaned against the counter and stared at bindings of hooped leather, red morocco, black and gold. Sandra opened a drawer, and there lay *Le Livre de Cuisine*. She opened the drawer below and he took out *The Accomplisht Cook: or, The Art and Mystery of Cookery.* He opened the book at random: *Section XIII: The First Section for dressing of fish, Shewing divers ways, and the most excellent, for dressing Carps, either Boiled, Stewed, Broiled, Roasted, or Baked, &c.* He had never tried to roast a carp. *Take a live carp, draw and wash it, and take away the gall, and milt, or spawn; then make a pudding with some grated manchet, some almond-paste, cream, currans, grated nutmeg, raw yolks of eggs, sugar, caraway-seed candied, or any peel, some lemon* *and salt, then make a stiff pudding and...*The cook in him wanted to read on, but the collector was distracted by the array in cabinets beneath, above, below.

Where should he begin? How could he approach, let alone assess a trove like this? Books like these would take a specialist, a Lowenstein or Wheaton. The sheer numbers were overwhelming. The antiquity. And the strangeness of it all, the perversity of substituting cookbooks for utensils, domestic treatises for pots and pans, words for cups, recipes for spoons and spatulas and cutlery. Still cradling *The Accomplisht Cook,* George tried to comprehend the open cabinets and drawers before him. He did not make a sound until Sandra opened the oven. Then a cry escaped. Books piled even here, arrayed in boxes on cookie sheets! The collector had converted oven racks to stacks.

"Where did he find these?" George murmured to Sandra.

She shook her head. "After the War," she said, "when he was young. But he kept them in boxes until he retired, and then slowly he unpacked them, and shelved them here. He didn't cook."

George knelt before the open oven. He slid the top rack out partway and took a flat box in his two hands, keeping it level, as one might support a cake. "Oh, my God," he murmured. Inside the box lay *La Cuisine Classique,* volume two, bound in worn red morocco.

He opened the book, and scraps of paper fluttered to the floor.

"What's this?"

The book was stuffed with folded notebook paper, even index cards, the precious volume interleaved with notes. George looked up at Sandra in alarm. "These aren't acid-free. You see this?" He held up a note card covered with black writing. "The acid in this card will eat your book alive. This has to go."

Notes and even newspaper clippings. The nineteenth-century volume was stuffed with what looked like shopping lists and pages torn from address books, thin typing paper brittle with age. Black ink leached onto the title page.

"You don't keep folios like this," he told Sandra. "Not in ovens! Look at this." The collector's block printing stained recipes for aspic, and smudged an engraved illustration of eight desserts, including *pralinées aux fruit* and *abricots à la Portugaise.* What had the man been thinking? Notes in permanent black ink pressed between these pages? He pulled out a folded article from *The New York Times.* An obituary for Samuel Chamberlain.

"He asked me to keep everything," Sandra said.

George wasn't listening. "Do you see this? A paper clip!" The silver wire clipped several scraps of paper to a recipe for *petites meringues à l'ananas.* George pulled it off, and showed Sandra the rusty impression left behind. "This is criminal."

The paper clip upset him most of all. And there were others. A rare cookbook with lavish illustrations required lavish care. What George saw here were pages stained and crimped. "Have you opened these?" George demanded.

She shook her head.

"Have you seen their condition?"

"I try not to...I don't want to crack the bindings," she said.

He did not believe her. Who could resist cracking books like these? He wanted to open them right now, one after another on the kitchen table. He wanted to shuck these books like oysters in their shells.

"He asked me to keep the collection together," she said.

George caressed a quarto bound in brown leather, hooped at the spine, secured with a gold clasp curiously wrought with scalloped, spiraling designs, engraved initials *CWM,* and the date 1735. Inside the book a title page printed in prickly gothic letters: *Das Brandenburgiche Koch-Buch.* Oh, glorious. The frontispiece depicted men and maidservants dressing fowl, and roasting meat over a roaring fire. Through a stone archway the lady of the house watched over all, raising her right index finger to instruct the staff. She held a great key in her other hand. The key to the house? To the spices? To cookery itself? In a reverie, George turned the page—and discovered folded typing paper.

He exploded. "You cannot stuff a book like this. Do you understand?"

"These are my uncle's notes."

"He was not a scholar," George said, for he could not imagine a scholar imposing his notes on books like these.

"Yes, he was. He was a lichenologist." She watched as George unfolded the brittle piece of typing paper. "He was very well known—in his field," she added anxiously. "His name was Tom McClintock. He held the Bancroft Chair in..."

But George was lost in the thicket of McClintock's words—poetry cross-referenced with recipes: *I prithee, let me bring thee where crabs grow (iii crabbes and oysters) / And I with my long nails will dig thee pignuts, / Show thee a jay's nest and instruct thee how / To snare the nimble marmoset; / I'll bring thee to clustering filberts (xiii iellyes, puddings, other made-Dishes)...*

"He taught at Cal for almost forty years," Sandra said.

George had found another paper, covered with hand-printed lines—part love poem, part recipe, part threat:...*snare you, dress you, cut you with the bone still in. Mince you small with suit and marrow, take sweet Creame, yolkes of Eggs, a few Razins of the Sun*...An ink drawing illustrated these lines. A nude woman lying on a tablecloth. She lay on her side, all line and tapered leg, head resting on her hand. The drawing was expressive, despite its small scale. The subtlest marks indicated the arch of her foot, her brow, her full breasts.

"What have we here?" George asked, even as Sandra snatched the paper from his hands and folded it again.

"My uncle was a very scholarly, modest...," Sandra began.

"And what was he doing with these books?"

"I don't know," she whispered in reply.

And George wanted the collection then. He wanted it, notes and all, to read and puzzle over. He wanted days and weeks with these rare books and their strange apparatus, the notes and drawings of their collector. He would satisfy his curiosity. But first, "I'll need to bring in an antiquarian. I have a friend—"

The front door rattled and Sandra jumped, hand on her heart.

"What was that?"

"Only the mailman," she said. "He frightened me."

George looked warily at her. She was far too nervous, far too gray—ashen-faced, really—wide-eyed, shaken.

"I'm afraid," Sandra said.

Oh, God, thought George, but he asked, "What are you afraid of?"

She mulled the question. "I'm afraid in general."

"Afraid of selling?"

"I need to sell, but I'm afraid of him."

"Your uncle's gone," George reminded her.

"Yes, I know," said Sandra, but her voice trembled. "He's dead, and I'm going to betray him."

from ***ENTANGLED***

Don Asher and Lois Goodwill

CONTRASTS

FROM THE START, I could have sworn the ex-priest was gay.

I thought things were going more or less swimmingly, twenty-two uninterrupted years of late-life, youth-tinged romance: sharing the same bed, hers—we maintained separate homes a few blocks apart—nightly dinners when I didn't have a piano-playing gig, weekly movies, an occasional play or concert, ardent periodic lovemaking (blessed Viagra), our days our own and valued as such. We never considered setting up housekeeping; for one thing, my daily practicing or less formal screwing around (her term for improvisations) on my battered Kranich & Bach baby grand would unhinge her. Though she had grown up (in Montreal) during the big band era, swing/jazz—my passion and, along with a handful of published books and magazine pieces, my bread and butter—left her untouched, a mild fancy for Sinatra CDs aside. It was a mutually comfortable arrangement. Marriage was not an option; inclination and inertia aside, her divorce settlement would levy a hefty financial penalty if she were to remarry.

There were minor notes of discord over the years (which she attributed to "domestication"), occasional dark clouds shadowing the horizon, but nothing that couldn't be ignored, deflected, or weathered. We're different breeds. I'm reserved (I believe and have been told), unexcitable in the normal course of events, unadventurous outside my music and writing—which may have to do with age—mild-mannered, sentimental. Sarah has attitude, is strong, resolute (flirting with stubborn), unfailingly honest, unforgiving when crossed, a won't-suffer-fools-gladly kind of lady—traits she carries easily, that from my vantage are commendable, and that I sometimes regard with a stir of envy. A mutual friend once confided to me, "It's very hard to win an argument with Sarah," which I've found to be invariably true.

Travel has long been a sticking point between us. Over the years I've become a confirmed non-traveler, a hater of long car trips, of airplanes, terminals, and hotels, packing and unpacking. Happily tethered to writing desk and piano bench, my two contained, city-anchored vocations, I relish the even tempo, the unchanging pattern of my days.

My older brother, Herbie, a wealthy retired businessman, raised a red flag early on. He calls from Fort Lauderdale a couple of times a month. "How's it going?" he asks. "You need any money? Looks like your Giants are going in the tank again...And how's the little lady?"

"Fine. As always she sends her best."

"She still taking trips without you?"

"She is."

"Alone?"

"With a group, usually, or a friend."

"You oughta change your M.O. Take one trip with her, you might enjoy it."

"I went to Sedona with her three years ago for a week. It's a desert area, the annual rainfall is fairly low. Though it was November she insisted I pack my bathing trunks and tennis racket. It rained for five straight days. The temperature never cleared fifty-eight. It was like summer in San Francisco but with steady rain instead of fog. After two days all the tourists but us had fled the area."

"Where the hell is Sedona?"

"Arizona."

"Ari-*zona*? That's a hop and a skip. All I'm telling you, kid, is be careful. Make some concessions, or one of these days you're gonna get whacked. She's gallivanting around Europe, Asia, wherever, meeting people, living it up, and you're sitting on your ass in Frisco like a frog on a log."

I'm not sure just how or when the wanderlust of my early years vanished, but it seems irretrievable. At thirty-two, restless, stifling in a smokestack town, I pulled up my New England stakes for good. I abandoned Worcester ("Worn hunched Worcester, dingy queen dowager of southern New England redbrick towns," I wrote, overwrote, in my journal) and a tenured teaching position in the Massachusetts school system for the mecca of San Francisco, lured by tales of the Barbary Coast and the Beats, of a high-up alabaster city where sables mingled with sandals and a Mediterranean light prevailed. Brother Herbie, on a stolid conservative track in those days, tried to dissuade me. "What are you going to do in California you can't do here—mingle with the fruits and nuts? Experience an earthquake firsthand? Don't be a schmuck. Get married, raise a family, move up in the school system. On weekends you can tinkle your piano, write your little stories. Your roots are here. You'll end up an itinerant, a bum like Uncle Phil's brother." The advice splashed over me and rolled off. With my worldly savings of just under two thousand dollars, with no West Coast contacts or extra-state teaching credential and no prospects beyond the publication of a couple of undistinguished short stories and an ability to render competently on piano a repertoire of Tin Pan Alley favorites, I beat my way across the summer heartland in a rattletrap Ford Falcon, peeling off the highway onto back roads, exploring riverbanks and whistle stops, thrilling to each new vista—Nat King Cole's "Route 66," my own national anthem, bouncing from the car speaker.

In Frisco (I'd soon learn of a deep native aversion to that raffish diminutive) the two grand kept me afloat while I hustled piano-playing gigs, wrote of California things—bridges and surfing and flower children, cool jazz and the flowering of rock—and used the freewheeling rollercoaster city as a base for further excursions.

Some fifteen years after I had left dear dead Worcester (*Wŏŏs-tuh*, I instructed West Coasters) in the dust, the upbeat song of the road inexplicably began winding down like a 78 on an old stand-up Victrola. It happened gradually, measure by measure, as does the aging process itself, nature gently affording us time to accommodate. Something alien had infiltrated my bloodstream, leaving an insidious languor. It was as if the tempo of a tune, briskly set, had begun to drag—the pianist's hands tiring, the drummer's foot turned leaden—and with the diminishing beat, melodic and harmonic invention wilted. Year by year, beat by beat (nature making its accommodation), vistas narrowed, enterprise flagged, comfort overcame daring. The bridges, indispensable arteries jutting from the shining city's heart, now bristled with imagined menace: monster traffic jams, unavoidable collisions, earthquakes. Once again I had become insular. The anthem's lyrics underwent a major transition:

You'll see your castle in Spain
Through your windowpane
Back in your own backyard

Sarah is a vagabond, a road freak; her blood is laced with broken highway stripes and jet fuel. France, Spain, North Africa, Italy, China—all in the past couple of years—with friends who, like her, always seem keen to lift off, or go on university-sponsored group excursions, or an occasional solo venture. Early in our relationship, before she became fully aware of my self-imposed restraints, she proposed a three-week trip to rural Japan. Three weeks in *rural* Japan: it sounded like the booby prize in a competition where you came in dead last. I thought about this daunting prospect for half a minute and graciously declined, as I would future overseas proposals. She became gradually inured to my obstinacy, resigned to what seemed at the time a nonthreatening clash of preferences.

If jazz is the heart-song that drives my life, it is *fado*, the Portuguese chanteys celebrating the longing for distant shores, that circulate in Sarah's veins. She is both amused and exasperated by my stubbornness and chides me at every opportunity. If a piano gig requires that I cross the Bay Bridge to—land ho!—Oakland, and the money is too good to turn down, she'll ask if my passport is in order and if I've had the proper inoculations. It is a testament to the strength of our other ties that at the time the ex-priest came along we were still together.

THE UBIQUITOUS PRIEST

Sarah is closing in on seventy; I'm ten years her senior. Why should anything change at this stage of our lives? Except neither of us is acting our age. Her morning regimen of vigorous seven-to-eight-mile walk/runs (undeterred by rain, obliterating fog, precipitous hills) is followed by office appointments with clients—she has a small practice in clinical psychology, established after returning to school in her early fifties for a doctorate (let's hear it for Dr. Sarah Brown)—volunteer work for nonprofit agencies, board meetings, women's club activities, faxes, emails. (I use pencil and a lined yellow pad for my writing—the tactile guiding and shaping indispensable to me are akin, I imagine, to the guitarist's choice to pluck with fingertips rather than pick. I do not envy her computer literacy.)

Getting dressed, preparing to leave her place around 8:30 a.m., from the second-story bedroom window I watch her stride off into brimming sunlight/swirling fog/spitting rain. I marvel at the vivacity of her gait, brisk, sure-footed, arms cockily swinging, short silvery hair bobbing metronomically, a delicious sway to the fetching hips and behind—the pace and carriage of a woman half her age. I'm not a walker. My exercise—and lifelong outdoor passion—is singles tennis. "We don't do many daytime things together. You could teach me," she once suggested with a seductive smile.

"It's a bit late for you to pick up the game," I answered gingerly, in case she was serious.

"Relax, stop gulping your drink. I was teasing. Total absence of skills aside, it's not my shtick, as you showbiz people say."

Now, would you think an ex-Jesuit priest—a rangy seventy-year-old Irishman with a cropped white beard, an unspecific gay air about him—could wreak havoc on a pair of nonpracticing Jews in the October/November of their lives? He had officiated at the nondenominational wedding of Sarah's youngest son to a sweet French girl ten months earlier, and he and Sarah had become friendly. She had never before met him; he'd been recommended for the job by a member of Sarah's club. At the reception following the ceremony, both held at a Marin County yacht club, he asked her to dance. An energetic, moderately skilled jitterbugger, he had the bridegroom's mother happily flushing from exertion. (I'm a non-dancer; I suspect most musicians are. When our junior and senior proms came along, we were usually on the bandstand, not prancing out front.) It turned out he rented an apartment in our neighborhood. Learning of Sarah's daily walking regimen, he proposed joining her one morning. She accepted: someone to share the long invigorating miles with. Now I'd watch her from the window as she set out to occasionally meet him halfway between residences. If I inquired, she was always forthcoming. ("Vernon's joining me this morning.") No need not to be. As I've said, I figured the big amiable guy was gay.

I began to spot his name more and more often in her agenda book, which usually lay open to the current week on her small kitchen corner table. I'd sometimes glance at it in passing, to refresh my memory of her announced plans on nights I was working. Usually she filled me in on her evening plans, but my attention span for nonessential info is short, and the details wouldn't always stick. I'm not a peeper; my purpose was to inform myself so I could casually ask how the lecture was, the dance performance, the touted new restaurant; how are Harriet, Michelle, Judie? Sarah is a precision planner, and I'm sure she appreciated this attention to detail. Good: always alert where you're concerned, babe, no proceedings too trivial.

*Aurora Theatre 8 pm. Vernon has tickets...SF Ballet Opera House 8. V picks me up...Lunch with V 12:30 his place. His friend Jim, also ex-priest, may join us...*One weekend noon she and V came to Moose's, the parkside North Beach restaurant where I regularly play for Sunday brunch. Not unusual: she occasionally brought one or more of her woman friends or colleagues to hear me. On my first break I joined them for coffee. Vernon hadn't much to say. He smiled steadily, if weakly, but seemed withdrawn, reticent; it was the first time I'd spent more than a few minutes in his company, and he struck me as fairly insipid. He wore pressed jeans and a horizontally striped short-sleeve jersey; his white bristly beard made me think of sandpaper, and his blue eyes almost twinkled. I don't know why I was feeling twinges of uneasiness at this point—maybe because Sarah, carrying the brunt of the conversation, seemed so *at ease* with him. I was as sure as I could be the sucker took a left turn. I mean, he had that aura about him that you come to sense after living for a time in San Francisco. There was the way he carried himself, for instance (I know I'm reaching here), not *mincing* exactly, but...measured. And wasn't his voice a touch feathery for such a big man?

Some five months after her son's wedding I came home from a gig close to midnight and found Sarah still dressed, reclining on the sofa, an open *New Yorker* facedown on her stomach. Even if she had gone out for the night, she was invariably in bed this late, reading or sleeping.

"How was the evening?" she asked.

"Crowded and noisy, resulting in minuscule tips."

"You've remarked on that before. People can't distinguish the songs you're playing..."

"That's my theory. How was your walk with the Jesus guy this morning? Did you sing in the rain?"

"I wish you wouldn't use that expression. We did not sing. We marched fearlessly. It was cold, it was wet. But forget the walk." She smiled slyly up at me. "Guess who I found out today isn't gay?"

I can rarely feel the pulse beating in my neck without laying a finger there. Right then I felt it. "The ubiquitous priest," I said.

Her eyes got larger, the smile deepened. "You came up with that awfully quick."

"Who else? Aren't we talking about him? And I can't think of another mutual acquaintance about whom you'd pose that question."

"My, we're precise and formal. But then you're a writer as well as a piano player."

"How, exactly, did you find out?" The words emerged spaced, weighted; my mouth had gone bone-dry.

"A revelation. I have my sources."

"So, has he hit on you?"

"Not yet." The smile—part foxy, part pleased—never left her face.

"And what would be your response if he did?"

"That that part of my life is with you."

The pulse in my neck slowed. I pulled off my tie. "I had multiple requests tonight for the abominable score from *Phantom*."

"And you dutifully complied."

"It's my M.O.—if I know it I'll play it. Babe, I'm beat. You coming to bed?"

"Soon." But the smile lingered in the crook of her mouth, almost a baiting look. A tiny curl of jealousy fluttered in my chest like a trapped moth. As well as I think I know Sarah, it isn't always easy to tell where she's coming from. She can blow both sweet and tart.

SARAH'S JOURNAL

May 19, 2006

Walk with V this morning—his idea. Weather predicted foul. Offered him an out, a rain check. Nonsense, he said, whatever comes I'm up for it. Good for him. Rather than pick me up here I suggested we meet halfway, at the Park Hill corner. Needlessly cautious as I'd told D we might be walking together. Still, he's been acting a tad edgy about the connection.

Five-plus miles of chilling cold, periodic cloudbursts. Hardly felt it, impervious, conversation easy—fluid! Drew him out about his growing up, the decision to join the Jesuits, his life since leaving the order (twenty years ago). Pace brisk, my two steps to his one, soaked stalwart warriors braving the elements. The man is funny, observant, charming—all in an understated sort of way. Halfway through the wet slog he slowed the pace and dropped the bombshell, asked how I saw our relationship. "Friendship, of course," I said. "I want to be candid," he said. "I had hoped for more than friendship"—which momentarily knocked me off my stride. The hunky ex-priest is straight! Gathered myself, told him I'm flattered but it's not possible, that part of my life is with Don. He pressed, said it was time again for a woman in his life. Intrigued, I asked about the "again"—his history with women—feeling a bit like my clinician self, wanting to understand him better. He recounted two significant but short-lived romances, both now well behind him: a woman who turned out to have an alcohol problem that became increasingly apparent as they traveled Europe, the other with magical mystical beliefs that he thought implied psychosis—flaws rendering each lady unsuitable. Told him I'd think through my list of friends but am really not too eager to find him someone—let him do his own finding, especially since I find him so dangerously attractive.

On the way back conversation moved to a more neutral ground: our shared professions, our newness with each other and an undeniable chemistry spawned on the dance floor at Chris and Nicole's wedding and last week's club dinner dance. (D had a gig, yet might have offered to hire a sub and gone grudgingly with me, and I'd've had to drag him onto the floor.) The man is really a stellar dancer, nimble and adroit, especially on fast tempos—showing moves I doubt he learned in the seminary! Explained that one of the first things he'd done after leaving the order was sign up for Afro-Cuban dance lessons. Fascinating he'd so artfully prepare himself for the socializing you'd assume is lacking in the Jesuit life. Something he said that night at the club stays with me: "I'm not above showing off the old razzle-dazzle"—while deftly spinning me around, the soul of patience between tunes as I caught my breath. Now, as we approached his place, thoroughly drenched, he suggested I come in for coffee and dry off. We were three blocks from my house. Tempted, I gave him my most winning smile, said, "But then I'd get wet all over again, wouldn't I?"

Restless tonight. Read for hours waiting up for D. Dropped the sex-switch bombshell on him but little else about the walk. He looked stunned, apprehensive, asked if V had made a move on me, wanted reassurance the friendship remained platonic.

I gave him that.

May 27

Why am I so lured by this man? I am captivated for sure, almost as if I were back in junior high. I would choose a route home from school, usually past the football field, that might allow me a glimpse of a boy I fancied. In those days I probably would have been shy and blushing had I actually encountered the object of my affections. But some fifty-five years later I am quite elated if I run into my new friend out front loading stuff into his car or returning from his gym down the hill from our shared street. I happily stop and chat with him when we meet "though not really by chance."

He notices my activewear, commenting on the blue nylon jacket and icy blue Polarfleece vest that protect me from whatever weather San Francisco will spring on me over the two hours of my solo walk. "Did you have your colors done?" he asks. "Everything complements you!" I do choose my wardrobe, even my running clothes, with care. I take pleasure in color, especially blue, and here is this man who pays attention and acknowledges his awareness of how I look. D is decidedly disinterested in matters of style and color; I remember having to explain to him exactly what microfiber and Polarfleece are. And I am quite sure that the color of whatever I may be wearing is well below the threshold of his awareness. Still, not good enough reason to be so excited by the new man, nor to think of abandoning a relationship of many years.

Is it just because Vernon is a new man? And I am new to him. Does that give our random meetings a charge? Could be...certainly it is exciting to be noticed, if only for the becoming colors of my outfits. Or is that all V is responding to? I think not—his face brightens, as must mine, when we encounter each other on the rim of the park or in his driveway. Does he too long for someone to share his thoughts and pleasures or concerns?

On the cusp of seventy, facing life as a senior—wait a minute, you're already there!—with its accompanying sadness and yearning, am I seeking one last chance to relive my youth, try to satisfy my yearning? It could be all that and more...

With the deepening of the friendship, I find myself increasingly intrigued. He dresses well. I appreciate that; the former husband was in men's wear and I've always liked to see people dressed with style. Dear D must be prodded and coaxed to wear a decent pair of shoes. "These are perfectly good old tennis shoes, serviceable and comfortable," he insisted. Took me years to get him to buy a pair of casual sturdy walking shoes, and on too many movie dates he "forgot" to wear the Rockports, showing up in his beloved worn-out tennies. Again not sufficient reason to leave him, but...

V likes to garden. D's scant interest in plants/ flowers precludes any sharing in that direction. I take enormous pleasure in my small garden and the plants I rotate on the deck. My orchid collection is a focus of my living room. V is taken with the grouping, even offers advice on their care. Does D even know the dozen or so specimens in the room? He might dutifully pause to admire a display I point out in a store or restaurant. He did once bring me a bouquet—left over from some private party gig.

V's funny flirty emails are charming. Odd to think of electronics as sexy, especially for those of us who grew into adulthood without computers and cell phones. He uses his cell to call me if he is away from home. D has no computer, no cell phone, and has had a problem realizing that he must hit END when he calls and leaves a message on my machine from anyplace where they provide a cordless phone for him to call from. I have returned home more than once to twenty minutes of background noise recorded on my machine from some café where he has a gig and hasn't ended his call after leaving a message. Sweet that he calls—but oh the fun of email and silly forwards from the Internet and discussions of the ethics of doing psychotherapy electronically.

And then too, the newness and the promise, the hope of more. Enough to beguile this old lady!

GOODBYE MY FANCY

D. A. Powell

FOR YEARS NOW, we've been crisscrossing
    this same largesse of valley.
It has provided for us, plenty. You've been
    my homoerotic sidekick, Bryan.
Excuse me. Ryan. There. You see?
I am promiscuous with even my own wit.
    & I can never keep you straight.

All the boys of recent memory
    have been like this: *accomplice,*
        adjutant, aide-de-camp.
I should just toss you my thesaurus.
    There are words for the kind
        of love we have,
though none of them quite suffice.
    Well. Why be verbose?
This is—to put it quite demotic—
        how we roll.

Whether stopping off in Stanislaus
    so I could nibble me some ribs,
or taking the back road up to Dixon
    for your taste of hot tamale,
we've served each other well.
        Oh, we're a fine pair.
We also know exactly what to order.

Eventually, they kick us out
    at the Silver Dollar Saloon.
Buck up, my little buckaroo.
    Every Western ends this way:
        Sunset. Chaps.
The valley's just like San Francisco,
    but without so many kissers.

    The warbler has two notes
that he prefers from all his repertoire.
    But there are others he reserves
        for loftier joys, profound sadness,
as well as his most savage flights of fancy.

These he also reserves for you.

HOW TO DATE A FLYING MEXICAN

Daniel Olivas

RULE 1: DON'T TELL ANYONE ABOUT THE FLYING PART

AFTER THE SECOND night Conchita witnessed Moisés flying in his backyard under the moonlight, and after the first night they shared her bed (which happened to be the second night she witnessed him flying in his backyard under the moonlight), she realized that no one, not even her sister Julieta, could learn of her new novio's extraordinary talent. What would people think? Certainly gossip would spread throughout the neighborhood, eventually migrating south out of Los Angeles and down below the border to Conchita's hometown of Ocotlán via whispered phone calls, wisecracking e-mails, and even terse though revealing postcards. Yes, the chisme would most certainly creep out of the city limits, inexorably spreading like a noxious fog, finally reaching all of her friends and family, who would shake their collective head about poor Conchita Lozano de la Peña finally going loca. And, of course they would proclaim, such madness involved lust. See what happens when you don't settle down like all good Catholic Mexican women and marry a man who can give you children and something to look forward to in old age! No God-fearing woman should enter her sixth decade of life—as Conchita had two years earlier—without having walked down the aisle to accept the sacrament of marriage. And it makes no matter that Conchita certainly doesn't look her age with skin as smooth as Indian pottery combined with a voluptuous figure that would knock the false teeth out of any mature (and eligible) man. But that's the problem, you see. Too much fun, not enough pain. And now Conchita thinks she has fallen in love with a Mexican who can fly. ¡Ay Chihuahua!

So, you see, no one can find out about her novio's penchant for flying. Period. Conchita's good fortune cannot be tarnished by this slightly odd behavior. While keeping this secret, she will proudly introduce him to her comadres at tardeadas, quinceañeras, and funerals even if they already recognized Moisés Rojo as Conchita's recently widowed but still vigorous next-door neighbor. And people will, indeed, nod with approval because this woman (¡finalmente!) has found a solid, handsome, and age-appropriate gentleman who maybe—just maybe—will ask her to marry him. And perhaps—they will say—Conchita will come to her senses after all these years of "dating" charming but useless men and allow the Holy Catholic and Apostolic Church to bless their union in a proper Mexican wedding. Because in God's eyes, it is never too late for sinners as long as they are still living and breathing and taking up space on this miraculous place we call Earth.

When Conchita finally broached the subject with Moisés—about his flying, not marriage—he held up his right hand, palm out to his new love, and corrected her: "I do not fly, mi amor," he said softly. "I levitate."

"And what exactly is the difference?" she asked.

"Planes fly," he explained. "Birds and mosquitoes and kites fly. People levitate."

"Oh," said Conchita. "That's clear. But what should I tell people?"

Moisés only shrugged. A few minutes later, when Conchita attempted to return to the topic, Moisés grabbed her shoulders and kissed her full on the mouth. Conchita surrendered to his taste, smell, and touch as if this were their first kiss. Moisés pulled back and looked into his novia's eyes.

"Tell people whatever you wish," he said. "To me, it makes no difference."

And so it was: Conchita decided never to share her secret with anyone.

RULE 2: DON'T TRY TO UNDERSTAND HOW HE DOES IT

Other than the flying part, Conchita found Moisés to be quite normal. He ate, slept, read the paper, and loved her as any ordinary man would. When Conchita asked him one day why she couldn't fly unless she held his hand (in which case she would rise effortlessly from the earth as if she were filled with helium), Moisés, of course, corrected her terminology ("I levitate, I don't fly") and then explained that after his wife died, he had fallen out of balance. So he took up yoga and transcendental meditation.

"How did you learn of these things?" asked Conchita.

"I went online to Ask.com and typed in: OUT OF BALANCE," he said. "I found many excellent Web sites and articles."

"And?" Conchita pressed.

"And after much study, I became a disciple."

"A disciple of what?"

"Of balance, mi amor," Moisés answered. "Balance."

"And if I studied yoga and transcendental meditation," ventured Conchita, "I, too, could learn to fly?"

"Of course not," he said. "I read nothing of levitation. It just happened one night as I sat in the lotus position while chanting my mantra."

Conchita skipped asking what a mantra was but nonetheless continued her cross-examination on the crucial issue at hand: "Must you have moonlight to fly?"

"No, no," said Moisés, betraying a bit of impatience. "This is not magic. It is pure physics."

"I knew it!" exclaimed Conchita. "No magic, just magnetic fields, right?"

At this, Moisés simply sniffed and reached for his cup of coffee. Conchita stood at her kitchen sink waiting for an answer to her question.

"You make the richest coffee I've ever tasted," Moisés finally offered. "What do you do to make it so delicious?"

"It's my mother's little secret," she said, pleased by the compliment but annoyed at the evasion.

Sensing Conchita's conflicting emotions, Moisés said: "Magnetic fields could certainly be at work."

To this, Conchita smiled and refilled her lover's cup with fresh coffee.

RULE 3: DON'T LIE ABOUT IT TO YOUR DEAD MOTHER

On the third night they shared her bed, Conchita's late mother, Belén, appeared to her daughter. Moisés snored softly, curled up like a milk-drowsed baby, while Conchita sat by his side, propped up on two pillows, surveying her new and quite delightful situation. And then, in a blink, there stood Belén at the foot of her bed dressed in the pretty floral print she'd been buried in, holding a cup of coffee and puffing on a fat, hand-rolled cigarette.

"Ay, mija," said Belén after she exhaled a large billow of white smoke. "Another man?"

"Mamá," whispered Conchita. "How long have you been watching?"

"Oh, mija, I saw the whole thing."

"¡Ay Dios mío!" exclaimed Conchita through tight lips. "This is so embarrassing!"

"Don't worry, mija," said Belén. "I'm dead. Nothing embarrasses me. You ought to see what your sisters do."

Conchita was partially placated by this thought but she wondered if, in fact, her younger sisters really enjoyed themselves with their men and whether they were having more fun than she. But her mother interrupted such musings.

"So, mija, your new man flies, eh?"

"I don't know what you mean, Mamá," said Conchita as she crossed her arms and turned to gaze upon a slumbering Moisés.

"Don't lie to your mother," said Belén. "The Fourth Commandment forbids it, as it is numbered by the Roman Catholic Church."

Silence.

"It is useless anyway," reasoned Belén. "I know all. Mothers always do."

Conchita knew that her mother spoke the truth.

"So, otra vez, mija, I ask you: Does your new man fly?"

"If mothers know all," said Conchita with a sly smile, "why do you ask?"

"Because mothers want their children to admit things," she scolded. "Does your novio fly?"

"No, Mamá, he levitates," said Conchita as she turned to face her mother. "Planes fly. And so do mosquitoes and birds and other things. But people levitate."

"Ni modo," said Belén with a wave of her cigarette. "It's all the same. He's up in the air like a plane or a bird or a mosquito or whatever." With that, Belén sipped her coffee and let out a little burp.

"But his special talent doesn't make him a bad person, Mamá," said Conchita, feeling a bit defensive.

"You're right," said Belén. "Sabes qué, mija, before I met your papá, I dated a man who could do things with his mouth that were simply miraculous."

"No, Mamá, I don't need to hear this."

"Oh, mija, that man," continued Belén, "that man could make *me* fly!"

Belén let out a little laugh as her mind wandered to ancient memories.

And Conchita let out a sigh.

"His name was Francisco," said Belén after a few moments.

Conchita blinked. "You mean the butcher?"

Belén nodded, took another sip of coffee, and then puffed heartily on her fat cigarette. At that moment, Moisés woke with a start.

"Did you say something?" he asked without opening his eyes.

Belén blew a kiss to her daughter and disappeared.

"No, mi cielo," said Conchita. "Back to sleep, it was nothing."

"Have you been smoking?" asked Moisés as he sniffed the air.

"No, mi cielo, no," said Conchita as she pushed down her pillows and snuggled near her man. "You know I don't smoke."

Moisés closed his eyes and started to snore softly.

RULE 4: DON'T GROW WEAK IN YOUR RESOLVE TO KEEP THE SECRET

Each morning before 7:30 a.m. except on Sundays, Conchita asks Moisés to go back home. It's not because she doesn't appreciate the intimacy that only long, lazy hours in bed can bring. No. It's because her sister Julieta drops by each morning at 7:30 a.m. sharp, Monday through Saturday, to end her power walk and have a little chat with her hermana. After sharing a little family time, Julieta walks home, showers, and meets her husband at their camera shop for another full day of keeping their fussy customers happy. Having Moisés leave before Julieta arrives is not for Julieta's benefit. Not at all. Julieta knows that, throughout the years, her older sister has enjoyed almost countless men. And being sisters, they have shared many naughty stories, though most of them came from Conchita, not Julieta. In reality, Conchita wanted to spare Moisés the embarrassment of having to socialize with Julieta after spending the night in Conchita's warm, entertaining bed. He was a sensitive man who read books, enjoyed art, and, most important, was still healing from his wife's death though he tried mightily to hide his grief from Conchita.

So, Conchita would wake to her buzzing alarm clock at 6:00 a.m., slide herself on top of Moisés for a delicious bit of lovemaking, serve a wonderful breakfast of tamales de puerco and hot coffee along with the newspaper, and then direct her man out the front door. Moisés obliged without argument, subdued by love, food, and the morning news. He'd walk next door to his home, shower, and then meditate in his living room while Conchita and Julieta visited with each other.

During the first two weeks Conchita had enjoyed her new relationship, Julieta used her morning visits to pepper her older sister with questions. Julieta's preliminary queries were somewhat benign and quite general, such as: "Does he snore?" And: "What's his favorite food?" But then after a couple of days, Julieta dug deep with: "How often do you make love?" And: "How big a wedding do you want?" Such questions didn't bother Conchita. Indeed, she'd be insulted if Julieta failed to probe into her love life. But one morning, she surprised Conchita with a particularly insightful query.

"What makes Moisés different from all the other men you've been with?" she asked as Conchita served coffee.

This was precisely the kind of question that Conchita had feared. She'd always shared with Julieta the deepest, most personal elements of her dating life even though Julieta, after drinking up every delicious detail, would eventually scold her older sister for not settling down. Would it hurt if Conchita revealed this little secret to her best audience? What's the worst that could happen? Julieta would think she's crazy? No big deal. But perhaps Conchita shouldn't move too fast on this. Maybe she could drop little crumbs of information to see how Julieta reacts.

"He's very spiritual," answered Conchita, relying on every ounce of self-control that she could muster.

Julieta perked up. "Spiritual?" she asked. "You mean he prays to todos los santos and goes to Mass a lot?"

"Not quite," answered Conchita, looking over to the kitchen window.

"Well, what do you mean, hermana?"

Conchita turned back to her sister, brought the coffee cup to her lips, and said: "He meditates."

"Meditates?"

Conchita drank and then slowly lowered her cup until it met the wooden tabletop with a muffled *clink*. She nodded and waited.

"Meditates?" Julieta spat out again. "What is he, some kind of... of...of...agnostic?"

"Well, I wouldn't say that."

"But, meditation?" continued Julieta. "What kind of man meditates? What's wrong with saying a rosary? That works for me. It works for all good Catholics, right? A good rosary and I'm ready for bed and a good night's sleep."

At that moment, Conchita realized that it would be a mistake to tell her sister that in addition to meditation, Moisés also levitated. So much for sharing.

RULE 5: DON'T GOOGLE THE WORD "LEVITATION"

The same morning Conchita decided, once and for all, that it would be best not to share with Julieta her little secret, she decided to do some research on her novio's special talent. She typed in "levitation" on Google and got over two million hits. Too many to go through. How could she limit her search? Ah! One of the books Moisés loved to read was entitled *The Gateway to Eastern Mysticism*. Conchita added the words "eastern mysticism" to "levitation" and got 5,263 hits. Much more manageable. After going through several web sites, she found one that seemed promising. The first paragraph explained this phenomenon:

> The reported instances of levitations have been observed in connection with hauntings, shamanistic trances, mystical rapture, mediumship, magic, bewitchments, and (of course) possessions of various types (e.g., satanic or demonic). Based on documented events, many if not most levitations last a short time, perhaps only a few seconds or minutes. In the field of parapsychology, levitation is considered by many as a phenomenon of telekinesis, also known as "mind over matter."

The first part sent an electrical current of panic through Conchita's entire body. Hauntings? Satanic possessions? ¡Dios mío! What did she get herself into? She pushed on:

> Not a small number of saints and mystics reportedly levitated as proof of God's great power over the incarnate form, in holy rapture, or because of their saintly nature. Reputable reports documented the abilities of the seventeenth-century saint Joseph of Cupertino, who could levitate. Indeed, the reports indicated that he could fly in the air for longer periods of time than ever documented with other similar instances of levitation. Conversely, in Eastern mysticism, levitation is an act made possible by mastering concentration as well as breathing techniques that are at the core of the universal life energy.

Ah! Saints! Perhaps Moisés was a modern santo! Conchita wiped her upper lip with the back of her hand and began to calm down. Maybe levitation wasn't so odd after all. She went to Wikipedia, typed in "St. Joseph of Cupertino," and read:

> Saint Joseph of Cupertino (Italian: San Giuseppe da Copertino) (June 17, 1603–September 18, 1663) was an Italian saint. He was said to have been remarkably unclever, but prone to miraculous levitation and intense ecstatic visions that left him gaping. In turn, he is recognized as the patron saint of air travelers, aviators, astronauts, people with a mental handicap, test takers, and weak students. He was canonized in the year 1767.

Conchita read about Joseph's father, who was a carpenter and a charitable man. But he died before poor Joseph was even born, leaving his wife, Francesca Panara, "destitute and pregnant with the future saint." Conchita eventually came to this:

> As a child, Joseph was remarkably slow witted. He loved God a lot and built an altar. This was where he prayed the rosary. He suffered from painful ulcers during his childhood. After a hermit applied oil from the lamp burning before a picture of Our Lady of Grace, Joseph was completely cured from his painful ulcers. He was given the pejorative nickname "the Gaper," due to his habit of staring blankly into space. He was also said to have had a violent temper.

Such miserable lives these saints lived, thought Conchita. Clearly, that's why they became santos. ¿No? But what of levitation? Conchita wanted to know the details. She scanned the article further, her heart beating fast. This Joseph of Cupertino was a real misfit who had been teased endlessly by his classmates when he had holy visions at the age of eight. Eight! So young to be seeing things. Because of his bad temper and limited education, he had been turned away, at the age of seventeen, by the Friars Minor Conventuals. Eventually, Joseph was admitted as a Capuchin, but was soon removed when his constant fits of ecstasy proved him unsuitable. In his early twenties, he was admitted into a Franciscan friary near Cupertino. The article continued:

> On October 4, 1630, the town of Cupertino held a procession on the feast day of Saint Francis of Assisi. Joseph was assisting in the procession when he suddenly soared into the sky, where he remained hovering over the crowd. When he descended and realized what had happened, he became so embarrassed that he fled to his mother's house and hid. This was the first of many flights, which soon earned him the nickname "The Flying Saint."

And finally, she read that when this saint heard the names of Jesus or Mary, the singing of hymns during the feast of St. Francis, or while praying at Mass, he would go into a trance and soar into the air, "remaining there until a superior commanded him under obedience to revive." His superiors eventually hid him away because his levitations caused great public disturbances. But he also gave off a sweet smell because he was pure. Poor St. Joseph of Cupertino! A prisoner of his own holiness. And would that be her new man's fate if anyone discovered his secret? Would the government or even the Catholic Church want to hide Moisés away so as not to cause public disturbances? No, it was clear to Conchita. Moisés must keep his levitation a secret from all. Period. End of story.

RULE 6: DON'T FORGET TO BREATHE

Conchita and Moisés made a compact. If she taught him the secret of her delicious coffee, he'd teach her how to meditate. Moisés quickly mastered Conchita's brewing techniques. However, introducing Conchita to the art of meditation was an entirely different affair. Oh, she easily became skilled at sitting in the lotus position due in large part to her great flexibility, which also made her a delight in bed. But Conchita wrestled mightily with the meditation part of it.

"I'm distracted," she complained as she sat on his living room carpet. "I can't keep my mind from bouncing from thing to thing."

Moisés counseled her: "Mi amor, the most important moment in meditation is when you realize that you are, in fact, distracted."

"¡No es cierto!"

"Yes, it is true," he cooed. "Say to yourself: I am now distracted."

"But I can't empty my mind," she protested.

Moisés said, "Meditation is *not* the absence of thought."

Conchita opened her eyes and turned to her man, who kneeled next to her.

"What the hell is it, then?" she asked.

Moisés gently turned Conchita's head, closed her eyes with his fingertips, and pressed his right palm onto her lower back, his left onto her abdomen.

"Don't forget to breathe," he said.

Conchita obeyed her teacher and inhaled deeply.

"Now exhale," he instructed. "Let your thoughts come and go without clinging to them so that you can focus on the meditation."

Conchita inhaled deeply again. And after a few moments, she exhaled with a soft *woosh*.

This is really stupid, she thought. I'm such a pendeja.

"Tomorrow," said Moisés, "we'll discover your mantra."

"Perfecto," said Conchita. "Perfecto."

"Do you mean it?"

"Yes," said Conchita. "I've always wondered what kind of mantra I would have when I grew old and senile."

SUMMING UP: LET US REVIEW

First, never, under any circumstances, let anyone know that your new lover can fly. This will cause great consternation with your family and friends and might lead to the government or Catholic Church locking him up to prevent public disturbances.

Second, don't lie to your dead mother about it. She is dead, after all, so she won't be disturbed by the news. Besides, nothing escapes her so you might as well fess up. The Fourth Commandment (as it is numbered by the Roman Catholic Church) is, indeed, the most important one of all. At least for dead mothers, that is.

Third, do not conduct Internet research on your lover's levitation skills. What you find will only cause great agitation and make you perspire profusely. Sometimes controlled ignorance is the only way to get through life.

Fourth, enjoy your flying Mexican. Life is short and we all need to take delight where we can find it. A corollary to this is that you should learn to accept your lover's special talents even if they're annoying.

And finally, we hope that you remember the most important lesson of all: Do not forget to breathe.

EARTHQUAKE

Rob Roberge

IT MAKES THE COWS, especially the blind one, crazy as all hell and it screws with the bank machines. You're at a bar in Arcata and the A's are playing the Giants on TV and the quake hits three hundred miles south. You see it, but you don't feel it. It fucks with Ricky Henderson a whole lot more than you. When you get home, drunk, you find out about the cows.

They're running all around the yard, smashing into the sides of the house and the dead 1974 Forest Green LTD that sits next to your Subaru in the gravel driveway. You are from the East. From a city. You didn't know cows could run. You never dreamed they could be frightening.

You made a mistake moving here—the earthquake has nothing to do with this, you were long gone before this hit—and you're moving the day after tomorrow.

You live at the dead end of a dirt road in McKinleyville, California. 1963 B Avenue and you find it strange that the house sits in a town named after one assassinated president, and your address is the year of another's.

You live with Buzzard Wendell. You placed an ad and he answered it.

Buzzard Wendell, in his mid-forties, is wanted by the federal government, the California Parks Authority, the Audubon societies of three states, and both the local and the national Friends of Animals.

He fought in Viet Nam for three tours and lost his right leg, just below the knee joint—a career Marine who, after a series of nervous breakdowns, became an errand boy for Mrs. Kissinger before quitting the corps in the early '80s and starting his second career, which was hurting and killing animals protected by the US Government's Endangered Species Act.

Buzzard Wendell has a praying mantis earring, dipped in shellac for preservation. He has a Florida black panther tail on his Harley. A necklace made from the teeth of Oregon sea lions. His gear bag is an armadillo shell. His boots are alligator.

He comes to the house in oil-stained Levi's, a slight limp caused by his prosthetic, a "Loud Pipes Saves Lives" t-shirt, and a nine millimeter tucked into his wide brown belt at the small of his back.

Buzzard Wendell is a walking junkyard of death and he takes the room next to yours in the house.

You get home and you're pinned in your car. You open the door a couple of times, but a cow slams into your door and you stay inside. The back window of the LTD is smashed in. You think you might die. Killed by cows.

Buzzard drops all five of them—you didn't know there were five, until they're dead and still and the cold air steams around their wounds, there was no way they seemed so few in number, you would have guessed ten at least—and the world goes quiet.

"Thanks," you say to Buzzard as you head into the house. You are still drunk and this is the strangest night you've had in a while.

He shrugs. "They were suffering," he says.

The next day, you go down to the bank to get the rest of your money. You never close an account. This is what you do—you take money out down to the last twenty and leave the rest. You keep moving—you'll have money all over the country. The machines don't work. The earthquake knocked all the bank machines down. Your money is tied up in natural disasters and technology.

You move, eventually, back East. People ask you about earthquakes.

"They fuck with cows and they screw up bank machines," you tell them.

"Really?" they say. "Bank machines?"

PARANORMAL ACTIVITY

Stef Willen

WHEN THE Trinity River Lumber Mill burned down I had reached a new summit in my romantic life. The view was painfully obvious: My attraction to older, unavailable women was not a good strategy. Crushing on women with crow's feet who walk away from me shortly after I engage them in conversation and being smitten by ladies who show signs of graying and of being in a committed relationship was leaving me lonely. I plunged a flag into my newly crested epiphany: Life is short. Go after what you want, stop staring at it and wishing it would talk to you. Go! Go! Go!

But the only place I went was Weaverville, California, home of Trinity River Lumber Mill. Husked in flannel, capped with a hard hat, I sat with similarly clad millwrights who helped me sort bushings into A, B, and Q hubs. I didn't learn to overcome my fears and walk up to available women in bars, slosh some bourbon on them and say "Nice pants." I learned to tell the difference between 120, 140, and 78 chain and that Nipples look nothing like nipples.

When I heard that the fire was estimated to cause over ten million dollars worth of damage, I booked a room at a local B&B for the entire month. The bonhomie was a nice counterpart to spending my days untangling every last coupler, every last anything that looked like something, from a Mobius strip of electrical wiring and pulley chain. I could lounge in the parlor on a Victorian medallion-back sofa and flop my hand into one of several nearby bowls of bon bons, pop two into my mouth at once. Things were fine—boringly fine—until Nicole, the owner of the inn, softly rapped her knuckles on the entryway and informed me that I was sharing the sofa with a ghost, and that's why the cat had been acting so strange.

"Do you see it?" I asked.

"No, I can't see them," she said looking all around the room. "But Bob does. He told me this morning that our place has ghosts. Then he pointed in here and said she was on the couch with you."

She?

That's when Bob, her boyfriend, slunk in, wearing some kind of duster. Bob was cute in an Alan Jackson sort of way, and I wanted to like him. But he lacked boundaries. Every evening he'd sit across from me in the parlor and watch me type. I'd hear him uncross and re-cross his legs. If I glanced up, he'd start talking about the rodeo, and *gawl*, how he missed ridin' bulls. When Bob was ignored for long stretches of time, he'd make a noisy ordeal out of leaving but not without stopping in front of me and pulling out his last card—even if it was "Did you know I have a special power?" Yesterday, I learned that Bob's special power was guessing the gender of unborn things (his cousin, his nephew, Nicole's baby colt). Now, where I saw empty chairs and throw pillows, he claimed to see the souls of people who were not of this world.

Bob explained that there were three other ghosts that hung out in the parlor, a young couple and an older fellow named James who once threw a pen at him. He said the girl, She, was a middle-aged woman, probably from the 1800s. Then he added that she liked to watch me work. I tried to shoot Bob a look that said *Bullshit. It's you who likes to watch me work*, but he told me to come see Princess.

Princess is Bob's orange cat, and it was true, she was acting strange. She hadn't joined me in the parlor like usual for the past few mornings, and now she was wedged between an Apple computer monitor and the kitchen wall.

I don't believe in ghosts. I chalk sightings of them up to gas leaks, tricks of light, the electromagnetic field, or a dire need for attention. I was once hired to inventory the famous haunted Mt. Lassen Hotel after it caught fire, and I became a temporary hero for being the only person who would go into "the murder room," and record what had been left untouched since a man was brutally stabbed 40 times two decades ago. I was supposed to have felt a cold draft, sensed someone watching me, heard something go bang, gotten pushed. Of course, the scariest thing that happened was that I forgot to turn my Dictaphone on and had to start over after fifteen minutes of talking to myself.

But, when I looked at Princess and saw her hair bristling as her dilated pupils slowly tracked the movements of something behind us, I got scared. Bob may be full of shit, but Princess was the only living thing in the house that didn't need to see something that wasn't there to make life more interesting—and the cat *was* seeing something.

For nearly five minutes, the three of us huddled around that cat. I hadn't told Nicole anything personal, and I would never tell Bob anything personal. Yet, somehow, right then, they could not misunderstand me, or me them. Like an earthquake brings you close to strangers, the "ghost" in the parlor made my world fall down around me a little, just enough to make me feel like hugging them. Nicole's long silvery hair was pulled over her left breast and some of Bob's salt and peppered chest hair poked out where he'd buttoned his flannel; he was older than I thought. It was the sweetest thing about him. I almost touched them both. Then, Nicole said, "Well, I've got to go to Costco."

They asked if I was okay alone because Bob had to go mend a fence. I said sure and something about not really believing in ghosts anyway. But I was beginning to think I was not okay alone; that despite my many smug pronouncements, I'd never been okay alone—that life was one long trick of deceiving yourself, figuring yourself out, then deceiving yourself better. On that note, I summoned the courage to go to the parlor and stare at the couch.

I tried to look through it, like the couch was one of those 3D stereogram images and some transparent middle-aged woman giving me a lustful look would flow forth from the cushion pattern. Nothing manifested, but across the room, Nicole's dried grass and flower bunch moved ever so slightly. The baseboard heater? A ghost from the 1800s who liked me? I had an incredible urge to go gussy up.

In the shower I became slightly afraid of the other three disembodied souls. Who had this James guy been? Maybe the kind of guy who always wished he could slip through walls to see naked girls showering. Perhaps the young married couple spiced up their afterlife by writing things on steamed-up mirrors, like "We're here" or "Boo-yah!" I had locked the door, which was kind of quaint. But, it made me feel safer, able to really do a good job washing my hair and then blow-drying it with a big round brush so it had volume and curl. I put my makeup on slow and careful so I looked like I wasn't wearing any. Except for lipstick. I put that on red. Then I walked down the stairs feeling sexy, and decided the woman waiting for me in the parlor looked just like Catherine Keener. An ectoplasmic Catherine Keener in some kind of 19th century dress.

The parlor was still empty, but entering it felt thick and warm and scary like walking into a blind date. I sat myself down on the middle of the rug so as not to be too forward and accidentally sit on her. I could feel the air in the room moving around, even through the hairs on my bare arms. I was aware of everything. I grabbed a book off the coffee table called *Fifty Places to Fly Fish Before You Die* and pretended to read.

About two minutes had passed when something gently covered my hand. It felt like a warm electric blanket if you could feel the electric part. I had been leaning most of my weight on that hand, which could explain the weird sensation, but maybe this is my problem—I never let anyone close, I always explain them away. So, I raised an eyebrow and looked over my shoulder. I saw my hand on an oriental rug. As I stared at it, the florid patterns seem to rise up and float in the air. This could be my astigmatism, or it could be my chance to believe a ghost had taken my hand, a ghost who looked like Catherine Keener.

I leaned into her a little, and She didn't do anything haunting like make me feel alone after I already believed in her, and I didn't do anything heartbreaking like act like she didn't exist when we were in the same room. I closed my eyes and felt myself fall further into a warmth, and it was exactly like falling into the dress of a beautiful woman, all the way to the buttons. The warmth was real. It was maybe really happening; her arms wrapping around my waist, her breasts against my back, her face nuzzling into my neck so our cheeks were about to graze, her thick splendid dark hair about to slide over my shoulder.

Then there was a hollow knock. I opened my eyes and She was gone, but on the porch there was a soul still trapped inside a body and it was carrying some sort of jug.

"Pear wine?" Bob asked as I let him in. I told him no, and then no again when he winked and asked if anyone had bothered me while he was gone. It was just too humbling to maybe have something in common with Bob. Or to be trying to. But, I tried again that night. It was my last chance as Nicole was closing the inn for a month, and I had to book a room at the Motel 8 where there would be no creaks, no framed black and white photos of grainy faces long departed. I would probably just come back from the mill, toss my dirty clothes in a corner, order a small pizza and sit on the bed winking at girls on match.com. Then those girls would write some unforgivable thing back like, "What up gurl?" or "LOL!" Or, maybe they'd just write back too soon, and it'd be over for me. I deserved someone who wasn't so easy, someone who took her sweet time revealing herself to me.

I opened my bedroom door a crack, changed into sexy underwear, put on tinted lip balm, and got into bed and waited. Maybe I'd fall asleep and slowly awaken to her weight on the mattress and then her weight rolling on top of me, cloaking me in a careful and sweet way. I would be scared, but I would not be afraid of intimacy and ask, "Who are you and what do you want with me?" I would say nothing and just lie there unable to move.

In the morning, I awoke with no sign my life had changed. If I wanted to, I could argue that I didn't remember putting the pillow exactly where it was, but that wasn't nearly as exciting as what Bob had discovered. As I stood in the kitchen, waiting for Nicole to get my bill, he pointed to the laundry room door and told me all about the squeak he heard at 5 a.m., how the doorknob slowly turned and an old, old woman carrying a laundry basket came out, didn't acknowledge him, and vanished into the dining room.

I stared at the brass doorknob and thought about the tedious mountain of metal I had to inventory at the mill. Part of me was jealous of Bob. I wished that I could hear a squeak and believe humans can transcend their earthly existence. But I could feel that I was going back to being myself: someone who doesn't believe in making bigger mysteries to solve smaller ones. I knew that at some point, perhaps under the popcorn ceiling of that night's Motel 8, I would have to admit that the simplest explanation for my brief, unrequited romance wasn't that She exists, and I had fallen into her arms, but that I had found yet another way to start falling for someone who wasn't really there. I mean, who is more unavailable than a ghost from the last century who you only sort of convinced yourself you felt and don't really believe in? No one. Not even Catherine Keener.

I resolved to call the US Geological survey when I got home to see if there was any seismic activity in the area that only cats can feel. I would research whether it's possible some mechanical unit produces a sound that wigs out felines but is inaudible to humans. I would consider the possibility of finding older, available women attractive.

I hugged Nicole goodbye and gave Bob a couple quick pats on the shoulder. Then I put on lipstick and took the long way to my car, past the parlor, so I could imagine, just once more, that someone who wasn't a possibility might rise up from the couch, think I'm beautiful, then float away from me.

FOUR GAMES PLAYED WHILE RIDING THE BUS

Alexandra Teague

I.

THE COUPLE ACROSS the aisle is playing Rock, Paper, Scissors.
Over and over their hands touch. Under and over,
and Rock is always beaten by Paper's soft drapery,
though Rock's crushing of Scissors has more military
pomp, while Scissors are always a cut above Paper.
The elegance of childhood rules defining nature.
Amazing, I think, not that adults would play,
but that the game has brought into the rush-hour fray
this tacit silence: each one deciding only as they move
the shapes their own fists guard. With each smooth
sleight of hand, they're turning *It's better like this;*
it's not. Let's don't. Let's do. My love, I know your tricks;
You never will...into swift One, Two, Three.
Each turn risking strength exposed as vulnerability.

II.

Maybe Alzheimer's is angelic possession,
the mind's repetitive wings beating sense
for all it's worth. *God-damn talking bus.*
God-damn talking bus, says the old man
at each announcement. And doesn't everyone
agree really, though our askance glances impress
that calls for silence ought to come in silence?

Please vacate front seats for seniors—God-damn
talking bus—*and the disabled.* Each sing-song
echo more mechanical, we raise embarrassed
newspapers or drink from empty coffee cups.
But after he climbs off and the voice goes on,
No eating or drinking on Muni, someone says
below their breath, *Oh, won't you just shut up?*

III.

The French-Algerian self-proclaimed genius painter
in a scarf and burgundy fedora on the hottest October
evening this San Francisco reasons, *But I'm not wearing
any socks or underwear,* and he shows us by baring
his ankles, adding, *six pieces, counting my shoes.*
After the quiet minute in which we each, impromptu,
tally, one friend says *seven,* another *five,* and I, blushing,
four, and just like that—fully dressed—lose. The evening
is down to hairpins of light outside the bus windows,
the plastic seats smooth as skin, and in the seconds that follow
this shared revelation, we ride silently toward the dark
as though we have found a new, more serious art:
not to paint the town, but to watch it, hour by hour, strip,
each loss wagered on this companionship.

IV.

Near the back of the bus, a man sits down and deals
three cards into his lap. One, the king, is marked.
He says, *These two lose, the king card wins. These
two lose, the king card wins. Not these; the red card.
If you got money and you got heart, you can win
yourself some money now.* With shuffling sleight
of hand, he turns them up, but no one will play him.
The king is bent. *These two lose, the king card's high.*

If you got twenty, and you got heart. Will no one play
because the game is rigged to favor us, because we
pity him his fumbling fast hands as they lay
the bent card down, or do we fear the con that surely
waits? No matter the cards, we know these blues:
if you got money and you got heart, you can always lose.

OFF-LIMITS
(IN WHICH THE BITCHY VIRGIN NO ONE CAN GET WITH VISITS A GAY BAR)

Briandaniel Oglesby

TOO YOUNG TO enter The Hole legally, and not pretty enough to flirt their way past the bouncer, the sparkly uglies smoke outside the fenced patio, flicking ashes into the gutter and butts into the street. They swallow pills like breath mints. These lost boys are waiting for some drunken oldster to stumble from the throbbing gay bar, someone they can charm into buying them a forty, who'll take them to the moon with a flare of crystal meth, who'll make them feel young, which they are, and beautiful, which they are not. They are children of the night, and the oldsters are the only ones who can afford them. Saliva will be exchanged, semen swallowed, someone robbed, someone infected, someone hurt. The sparkly uglies glower at me as I flit by them, my ID already out, and I smile back.

I'm here to make someone fall in love with me, and I will smile again and again.

I hear, "Cholo" muttered under a breath, and then someone corrects, "More like chol*a*."

The bouncer is bald and bulging, a barbed wire tattoo climbing his arm like a varicose vein, encircling a cartoonish grinning penis on his shoulder. He's a bear. Not my type. He glances at my ID, I'm twenty-five, and he smashes a stamp onto my hand. I flash him a smile, thank him, call him "Honey," and leave him to watch the sparkly uglies alone.

The patio fence is high for privacy, necessary for a place like The Hole in a city like Sacramento, and the patio is roofed so that even on rainy nights the smokers can suck their cigarettes dry. Only a handful of smokers are outside now. Two lesbian heavies press against each other, almost ready to kiss, but not quite, still in that stage where they're erasing everyone around them.

I pass yellowing infecteds, disease in their dark eyes, their skin leather, and they watch me as they light cigarettes from Bics, pretending to be sensuous, seductive, and clean. I avoid their looks because I don't want them to cat-call me. Infecteds are the dalits, a caste off limits.

The music is painfully loud inside The Hole, thumping like a drag queen's heartbeat. It smells of plasticide bodyspray, sweat, and cigarette smoke. The lights are low to hide the ugly of the uglies, and walls shimmer because they are covered in red, sagging velvet. Framed black-and-white photographs dimple the billowing velvet. Some are of old-time movie stars, Cary Grant, Humphrey Bogart, Lauren Bacall. Some are of naked male bodies, muscular, with a dark tassel of pubic hair ornamenting semi-erect members. Some are of topless women leaning against tile walls and curtains, looking like pinups cut from World War II *Playboys*. They are all white. The glass is thick over these pictures of perfect bodies; they cannot be touched.

Levi the bartender hisses colorful well drinks and amber Budweisers into pint glasses from the hoses at the bar. I'm not even at the bar and he's already poured my Diet Coke, virgin. I offer a dollar bill because I know he'll wave it away, and he waves it away. He adds four maraschino cherries.

The music quiets, someone announces the drag show in a few minutes.

"You sure I can't drop in something harder, Raul?" Levi asks.

"Levi, my love, a Diet Coke a day keeps the plastic surgeon away," I say. "Liquor makes thicker." I bite a cherry and slide into a barstool.

"How the hell am I going to get you drunk and take advantage of you?"

He wants to fuck me. He's older than I am by a good decade, missing a tooth, and tonight he's already a little drunk or high. It won't happen and we both know it.

"Not tonight," I tell him, and blow him a kiss, which we both know serves as the only payment I can afford. The music picks up, so we don't have to talk.

Someone brushes past me and I tense.

The oldsters across the bar eye me. No one has a job these days except old fucks like them, because of old fucks like them. I hate the oldsters instantly; they stole all the money.

The Hole will get more crowded soon, populated by the desperate, the depressed, who'll burn what little money they have at The Hole because they need to drink and don't want to drink alone. They'll first buy Budweiser because it's cheap, and then rum or tequila or something mixed with vodka because it works better as the night wears on.

But now the bar's population is sparse, so the oldsters eye me. They are sipping cosmopolitans and martinis, which they will also buy for whatever young thing they fancy. They are hunting in a pack, these wealthy middle-aged queens. They can afford to be direct.

"Want to be my Latin lover?" one oldster shouts over the thumping Lady Gaga.

"Not tonight," I shout back. I laugh and wink. Maybe when I'm older, but by then I'll be with someone who is not you.

"Aw. C'mon. Levi, get my Latin lover some tequila, and make it Patrón, not the cheap Cuervo crap."

"Leave him alone, you old fucks," snaps Levi, who can say such things to them because they also want to fuck him.

I am the Bitchy Virgin No One Can Get With. Not Levi, not the aging queens, no one.

I guard my drink as if the oldsters have it in them to slip me Rohypnol, stir, chew another cherry. Levi is complaining about his love life, his back to me. He downs the shot of Patrón the oldster buys for him instead of me. I slip a cherry stem into my mouth, tongue it into a knot.

"Oye Levi!" I wave.

Levi pivots, the gap from his missing tooth flashing. "You want another round?" Levi asks, reaching for my half-empty glass.

As he refills it, I stick my tongue out and show him the knotted stem. I show it only to him, but the oldsters can see it, too.

He shakes his head. "You are a tease," he says. He leaves the pint of Diet Coke on the counter. "Next time, it will be full calorie."

"You love me for being a bitch, mi amor," I say.

I leave the knotted stem on the counter.

The bar is filling because the drag show is going to start soon. Levi is occupied filling plastic cups with Budweiser. I push off from the counter and head toward the writhing dance floor. I don't join, just watch. A group of lesbians I've talked with on previous nights invite me to join, and I shake my still half-full drink and mouth, "Later." They are having such fun.

The pretty white bois don't make eye contact with me. Their eyes dart away. A quick glance is all you need. Are you worth it? The pretty white bois throb in the music, wrap themselves around each other. No. I'm not worth it.

A dried ugly introduces himself to me. He smells of Axe. There's a flake of dandruff on his eyebrow; I watch it so he thinks I'm making eye contact. I forget his name as he says it. He's not my type, but bless him for trying, and I do bless him, I grin, smile, and laugh, because I know he's joking about something, and I don't care what. I reward his valiant attempts with something he can pretend is flirtation. I clutch my stomach as I laugh. He's going to fall in love with me.

I'll shake him off when I'm ready and he'll feel awful for a few minutes, but then he'll realize that he tried, he tried!, and that's what matters, right? He was brave, he took a risk, that's what matters, he'll think to himself, now proud. Tonight, when he touches himself, he'll think of me.

He's almost falling in love with me and his hand grazes mine and I pull away.

"Want to dance?" he asks.

I can see how he'll look when he gets old. His teeth will only get yellower. His thinning hair will continue to vanish until there's more scalp than hair. His body will wilt. He's finished.

"Want to dance?" he asks again. He wants to kiss me. I'm beautiful to him.

"Later, dear," I lie. I rattle the ice left in my glass. "I'm enjoying the drag show," I lie. A drag king is onstage trying to boss her way through something Jimmy Hendrix. The king is pathetic, as too many kings are, struggling to appear masculine, with spirit-gummed facial hair, flannel and jeans, a backwards baseball cap. Her feminine face and thick chest betray her. She's trying so hard, but it's a costume. Sad.

I push away, disappear, hope the dried ugly finds someone else, someone not me. Never me.

Piss puddles the bathroom floor. A clot of what I hope is chewing tobacco rings the toilet and the door to the stall is gone, probably a good thing, and I'm standing at the urinal. Men are relieving themselves one after another in the stall next to me. I'm waiting. Nothing happens. I can't squeeze anything from my bladder. I smell piss and Band-Aids. I'm out in the open. I'm afraid someone will grab me. My bladder is full, but nothing comes. I'm frozen. I want everyone to leave. I want to scream, "No! I just have a shy bladder! I'm not waiting for a blow job, you perverts! I'm not!" in case any of the men who enter and exit the stall next to me, one after the other, think otherwise.

I'm home behind a door with a thousand locks. No one can see me.

A trickle. Enough. Finally.

The beast makes too much noise. He wheezes when he talks and he talks too much. His round face bobs on his round body. He's wearing makeup and Abercrombie. He looks like a nesting doll. Open him up and inside of him are more round Abercrombie beasts.

I do not discourage him.

"Are you a top or bottom?" the beast finally asks. "Don't tell me you're versa. I hate them bitches. All fucking queer studied and shit. Like I care if I'm buying into a hetero-normalicity, or whatever. Bitch, I don't care. Make up your mind."

I savor this. "Virgin," I say with a shrug. The beast's eyes bug.

"Liar," says the beast. "I don't believe you. I DON'T believe you. How old are you?"

"Twenty-five." I've had this conversation a thousand times. I enjoy it. His shock is flattering. It means I'm beautiful.

"That's gotta be some sort of record. Bitch, you've never sucked—"

"I told you I'm a virgin." I sound annoyed at the beast.

"Sucking is *not* sex."

How a beast like him can find sex astounds me.

"Why?" he asks.

My standards are higher than yours, so I'm the Bitchy Virgin No One Can Get With. I'm pristine. I have no diseases yellowing my skin or boiling pustules on my genitals. I take no medications to keep me breathing like the septic dalits. There is no poison inside me at all. "Because," I offer.

"You've kissed a guy, right?"

I nod.

"You waiting for the one true love?"

No. A better offer.

The beast finds a reason to leave. I'm the Bitchy Virgin No One Can Get With, and he sure as hell isn't changing that. Not tonight.

I watch as the beautiful boy whispers to a girl. She is the hag to his fag, but she is thin and pretty. He's white, blond, blue-eyed, and American Pie. I want to swoop by him, say, "Let's dance," and grab his hand like a five-year-old and take him onto the dance floor. Even better: I want him to see me and see that I cannot approach him. He'll like the shy ones and so he'll come to me. He'll take me by the hand onto the dance floor. He'll have a thing for brown boys. We'll dance, close enough that the oldsters will tremble in envy like they have Parkinson's, and an optimistic ugly will sidle up to us, grind against us, and we'll shake the ugly off with a glare. The beautiful boy will whisper, "Let's go outside," and we'll pick up our drinks from his skinny hag. Outside he'll light a cigarette and I will take a drag from it even though I've never smoked. He'll offer me a sip of his beer and I will sip it even though I don't drink. This alcohol mixed with his saliva will give me courage; I'll laugh, take the cigarette from his mouth, swallow another puff. "I've never done this before," I'll say. And he'll fall in love with me. "I'll teach you," he'll say, and he'll lower the cigarette and he'll lean in, and I'll lean in too, and we'll lean together until we're breathing each other's air and you could pass one piece of paper between us, but not two.

I wish I could taste him.

He kisses the girl.

He's a breeder, I realize, he's trawling for the pretty hags, the girls made randy by watching boys dry hump on the dance floor. An opportunist. The worst form of ally. He's hoping that dumb faggy fucks like me grab his ass and flirt just enough so he can feel attractive. I hate him.

I am also relieved. I never approach, never make a move. I'm the Bitchy Virgin No One Can Get With. I'm untouchable. It's safer.

An oldster is talking to me now, outside, on the patio. He brought me outside because it was too loud inside and he wanted to talk. I've forgotten his name already. His face is too clean, poisoned with Botox. It looks airbrushed. Like a lawn saturated with weed and pest killer, nothing lives in that face. His eyebrows look painted, his hair sculpted, his teeth bleached, but his body sags. He's the type that comes every night to drink. He comes in here looking for love, for sex, for *something*, getting fat on liqueurs and bar food. He is doughy. I've forgotten his name, so I call him Doughboy.

Doughboy is telling me about the cities he's visited and I'm pretending that I'm interested in Paris, London, Rio. I'm laughing, smiling, showing my teeth, making this old Doughboy want me so bad he aches. Lean in. Don't touch. No touching. Show him the teeth. Don't touch me. Doughboy puts his hand on my side, and I back away, spin, and laugh.

He's pretending to be young. He's lying, and I hate him for lying, for being fat and old and ugly and fake, for poisoning his face, for having a job and money when no one else has either, for being alone at his age. For liking me. For making me reject him because he likes me.

He asks for my phone number.

"Sorry," I say. "I only date men my age." Doughboy turns red, his dead, Botoxed forehead almost wrinkling. I want to ask him, Why are you single? I want to ask him, Why haven't you found someone your own age? Why the fuck are you chasing guys like me? What the hell is wrong with you, old fuck?

I sip my Diet Coke, my third. He thinks I'm interested in his stories of Rio and Paris, in conversation. He's confused. The Hole is not a place where conversation is the agenda. The Hole is a place where conversation is a tactic used to pursue another agenda, an agenda of the body, not the mind, of salt, sex, liquid, and flesh. But here I am, a saint, the sweet Virgin Maria, interested in what the Doughboy has to say, but not in the Doughboy.

"Hey," he says, loud. "I asked you for your number. You dicking me around?"

He's supposed to wander away, embarrassed for chatting up the twenty-five-year-old. He's supposed to stumble into someone his own age.

"What do you mean?" I play innocent.

"I asked for your phone number. We've been talking for like fifteen minutes." Ten actually. "I'm not *imagining* the chemistry. I'm not crazy."

I shake my head, you poor fucking old sap. "I'm sorry. Those are my rules."

Doughboy wants to spit on me. Were it not for the Botox, his face would be contorting like a baby's. "We've been talking for like half an hour and *all* I asked was for your phone number."

I've forgotten his name. "Sir, if you're looking for a date, you should pick up someone closer to your own age," you old fuck whose name I've forgotten. "I'm here to *meet* people."

He kicks a chair, which clatters to the concrete, and now everyone is looking. We're entertainment.

"Why are you *fucking* with me?"

"Sir, I'm not, sir."

"Why? You a breeder, spic?"

"I can see why you're still single."

"BITCH!" His hands are doughy, soft, and it hurts less than I expected when he hits me, but it does hurt. I'm tossed back, the lights spinning, and a glass shatters, and I'm on the glass, I'm on the ground, looking up at feet, at shoes, at knees, where everyone looks the same. The thick, tattooed arms of the bouncer are on Doughboy, dragging him away, and he's shouting at me, something like "Bitchbitchbitch!" and I'm wet, covered in my drink and his, glass under me, sharp but not cutting, and the floor is sticky and they're all watching me, my body splayed out on the gummy sewer of alcohol, of ash and butts, of vomit, of sweat and blood and semen, of disease, and it's all sticking to my arms, my back, my neck, my hair, and everyone is looking at me like I've done something wrong, like I'm some drunk, and that's when they bend down, the angels, and I'm lifted, rescued, by the beautiful breeder boy and the drag king dressed like Jimmy Hendrix, who suddenly, up close, looks masculine, and they pick me up, and they ask if I'm okay, and I'm not. "He's drunk," I say, "I told him no, I didn't do anything." I hurt in a thousand places and I want to cry.

I hear Levi's voice through the music and rabble, I hear his voice, "Banned! Banned for life!" I hear his voice. "Tell Raul it's okay, bitch is BANNED!"

I'm a thousand years old, my face tingles, and I let them hold my weight. Someone hands the beautiful breeder boy a new drink for me, Diet Coke and cherries from Levi, another gift from my Levi. I feel them brushing off the glass and cigarette butts and I don't want them to stop. I want to curl up with them, become theirs, only theirs, before I'm just another one of the uglies, the oldsters, desperate and broken, before it's too late.

WIND GIRL

Francesca Lia Block

Santa anas like the hot breath of my angry sexy city
heartlessly tossed orchids over
into plates of jasmine rice

inside the chocolate fountains swirled
and i blew through
in hot pink satin shoes

a goblin found me later barefoot and lost outside
dancing in the heated breeze
showering him with petals
he asked me to dinner and the wedding band
glinted harshly on his hand
oh no i said and danced
away

a troll found me
he fed me lotus root and soba with green tea
touched my face so tenderly
i gave him my dream
where he said to me
put on your beaded dress
and come to vienna
but his father had just died and he
was angry at the world
he told me that there was nothing
after death

when i tried to say my father was a horse
for those moments in the field
oh no he said
oh no i said and danced
away

i called the elf
i went out with this man i said
because you told me not to wait
but i missed you

i don't love you he said
and it's not fair to you or your sweet kids

i realized i had helped him over me
that night in the hotel
like the other elf who came into my bed
days after his mother's death

i don't love you said the elf again
oh no i said and danced
away

i called the bear
he was listening to desert bands
he knew there was something after death
his father had been a red tail hawk
i told him we should never fuck
maybe we'd stay friends forever
maybe if i never tried to save him
or be saved
i would never lose him
like the rest

i met a banshee at the café
we drank green tea rice milk bobas

which is why i'm still awake
and writing these disjointed words
she said *you are doing them*
a public service girl
but what of you?
i love you like the air i said
i love you like my moon
and i am yours
and i will never dance
away

IN THE THIRD KIND OF FOG

Jon Carroll

THE FIRST TIME I saw Limantour Beach was in 1975, about two days after we'd moved into a little time-share cabin on Silverhills Road outside Point Reyes Station. Tracy—the woman who would become my wife—and I did not know each other very well; the cabin had been a matter of opportunity and impulse. We knew little about the Point Reyes National Seashore either; that first week we took roads mostly at random, knowing that we would eventually fetch up at someplace beautiful.

On Point Reyes, all roads are the right road.

We discovered that there are at least three types of fog at Point Reyes. One is the thick blowy kind, almost the density of whipped cream, that turns everything into a mystery story, one perhaps titled "Where's That Landmark?" The second kind is a low dense overcast, the meteorological equivalent of a bout of black depression. The third kind hangs low and still over the landscape, drippy and calm and, if you're dressed for it, infinitely romantic.

As you might have guessed, we encountered Limantour in the third kind of fog. There was hardly anyone on the broad beach because of the gloomy weather; even the gulls were muted. Each end of the sand disappeared into mist; the beach was so featureless we had no idea which direction we were walking. It was very much like our state of mind at the time; very misty and very unsure where we were going. We walked for a long time without reaching anything in particular; then we walked back.

As we were walking back to the parking lot, I saw what at first I thought was a mirage—an all-white deer in the low coastal scrub perhaps 100 feet from where I was standing. It disappeared almost immediately, and I thought perhaps I had conflated the animal out of sundry bushes and trees. At best, I decided, I had seen a brown deer turned white in the fog.

Then I saw it again, more clearly. It was a white deer, as real as the ground under my feet and as metaphorical as a Yeats poem. They're European deer, brought to parts of this country—Texas and Georgia mostly—as game animals. Their population at Point Reyes grew rapidly, and the park has made numerous and controversial attempts to keep the deer in check through trapping, relocation, contraception, and shooting. But all this was in the future, and I was in a haze of awe. These white deer mostly live in the wilder southern end of the peninsula; I was lucky to see them at Limantour and even luckier to see them my first time there.

White deer on a foggy day on a quiet beach with my new sweetie—it forever linked Limantour and romance in my mind.

Limantour is a spit of land created by longshore drift currents. At the northeast end of the spit is a channel into Drakes Estero, a spectacular spread of water and land, and the more modest Estero de Limantour.

Harbor seals swim just outside the line of breakers on Limantour Beach, and pelicans skim over the water, occasionally taking a headfirst plunge to snare some unwary fish. Sandpipers skitter along the hard sand near the waterline. On the inland side of the spit is a wetlands, popular with egrets, mallards, and (in the winter) wigeon and elegant canvasback ducks. The occasional great blue heron pays a visit. And, need one add, gulls gulls gulls.

One of the unexpected joys of Limantour is that far tip of the spit, where harbor seals bask and cuddle on the sand islands just offshore in the channel. I have watched them for hours; they are occasionally clownish and always magnificent. It has occurred to me occasionally that the seals consider Limantour a prime people-viewing area.

I am not alone in my affection for Limantour; thousands of people make the pilgrimage every year. And yet the beach is so large, and the sand dunes so accommodating to privacy, that you can always feel alone there even on the nicest weekend days. In the winter when the wind is blowing a stiff thirty miles an hour off the point, you can actually *be* alone, and that ain't bad either.

Some years ago now Tracy and I lived in Inverness, a tiny town on the Point Reyes Peninsula. It was a golden time filled with good cheer and good company. One of our visitors was Jacques d'Amboise, just retired from his job as a principal dancer with the New York City Ballet. He was looking around for something to do, and we were trying to decide whether I would be a good ghost writer for him.

My two daughters were utterly entranced by Jacques. He was something of a force of nature, a man of great energy and good humor. He was up before we were, preparing breakfast and entertaining the girls.

In the afternoon, we would take a walk somewhere on the point, out to the lighthouse or down by Drakes Estero or, in this case, over the hill to Limantour. It was one of those crystal Bay Area winter days. The Farallones were visible on the horizon; Chimney Rock out by the point seemed as close as my hand. It was toward sunset, and the broad beach was still well populated by strollers and kite fliers.

Jacques suddenly had an idea; he often suddenly had ideas. He wanted to teach our daughters, then seven and eleven, the *Wizard of Oz* dance. You know the one: Dorothy and the Scarecrow and the Tin Man and the Lion are "off to see the Wizard, the wonderful Wizard of Oz," and they are dancing down the yellow brick road all happy. (This is before the flying monkeys, but you knew that.)

So he stood between my daughters, took their hands, said "This dance is so easy"—dances were always easy when he did them—and off they went down the sands of Limantour, into the setting sun, skipping and singing and disappearing into the dusk. I just stood and stared. It was a magic moment of unalloyed joy. Eventually I saw them come back the other way, all smiles, still dancing, as the waves kissed their feet and pelicans flew by.

And it all happened at Limantour. It could have happened somewhere else, but it didn't.

The last time I saw Limantour was two weeks ago. I'm a bit older now, and my enthusiasm for walking up sand dunes has decreased somewhat. I was with my granddaughter, who is now nine. This was the second time she'd been to Limantour, and she enjoyed playing tag with the waves as much as my children had.

Seaweed had washed up on the beach that day, and I found a particularly splendid example, a twelve-foot-long whiplike brown clammy rope of bull kelp, with a giant bulb at one end. I began twirling it around, first at knee level and then higher and higher until, with some effort, I had it going over my head. I had to turn my whole body to keep it going, and I got dizzy pretty quickly.

I sat down on the sand to regain my balance. But Tracy had a great idea, and spun the seaweed like a gargantuan jump rope, so our granddaughter could jump over it. Almost immediately, I took the other end, and we created a giant ungainly jump rope. Tracy, seeking firmer footing, went down to the water's edge, thus leading the squealing grandchild into the shallow water. She jumped and jumped; Tracy and I turned and turned. While one part of me was hefting the giant seaweed, another part was standing at a distance, watching the whole thing, delighted to be part of the experience; happy to be alive, happy to be home, happy to enjoy yet another day at my favorite beach.

And it all happened at Limantour. It could have happened somewhere else, but it didn't.

FELLOW CONSERVATIVES

Jonathan Rowe

OUT HERE ON the edge of the continent, where the force fields of respectability and convention run thin, we like to think of ourselves as progressive, in an undogmatic way. But really we are conservative, when you get down to it. We are alert constantly to the capacity for evil in human nature, especially in the form of greed, and greed's designs upon the land. We are skeptical of the version of progress that the corporate market pushes at us. We embrace the wisdom of the past, especially as embodied in the natives of this place.

Russell Kirk, the intellectual progenitor of modern conservative thought, marked these as central tendencies of what he called the "conservative mind." (Kirk would not be pleased by what claims that banner today, but that's another matter.) We revere the land and take a dim view of change, and if those are not conservative inclinations, then nothing is.

Unlike the conservatism that prevails in Washington, ours is not pliant to moneyed interest or calculated for political advantage. It represents the strange fate that befalls the progressive in a commercial culture that turns everything into a commodity for gain. Yet this does not exempt us from the karmic conundrums that attend efforts to resist change or turn back the clock. Nor does it make us immune to the blind spots that can occur when a sense of virtue is wrapped up too tightly in the preservation of a status quo, even an ecological one.

Create a national park, restore a wetland, and people want to drive out here to partake of them. Start to create a local food economy, and more people come who are less interested in the landscape than in the food. The town fills with cars. Parking becomes a problem. A place in which ecology is practically a religion becomes, on summer weekends, a hot spot on air pollution maps.

We locals become a little cranky and walk around with a debate inside our heads. We like our neighbors who have started the ventures that help attract these crowds. We want them to succeed. We support local economy, organic food, all of it. Yet each success takes us a little further from what we thought we wanted to be—or at least from what this place used to be. It also drives up real estate prices, so that people who made the community what it is can no longer afford to be part of it.

It is not a new dilemma—the failure of success. But it has a particular and ironic twist in a place where people thought they were going to be different. It eats at us, the way our certitudes keep colliding; and this is what makes local points of contention—a footbridge over a creek, or an oyster farm on Tomales Bay—so symbolically hyper-charged, almost like conflicts in the Middle East. The disagreements are over competing versions of good and therefore become projection screens for the tensions that beset us not just from the outside, but from inside as well.

Walking—good. Sustainable aquaculture—good. Local food economy—good. How do such goods become bads? It is hard enough to battle developers. Now the fight is over objects of our own desire too. We feel a need to draw a line. But where, and how—especially when we are part of what we have to draw the line against?

We build our homes at the edge of this stunning landscape—well, let's call the spade here, in this stunning landscape. Then we get our backs up at those who would intrude upon it with their footsteps, or a sustainable livelihood, or a second unit that enables the owner to afford the first. We create our own understated and ecologically responsible versions of better homes and gardens, and then wonder why the town cannot remain forever the rough-edged remnant of the Old West it still is in our minds.

As somebody once put it, the one who builds the house is the developer; the one who lives in it is the environmentalist. Yet we are not unself-conscious people. The paradoxes—I put this gently—of our oppositions rest uneasily in us, along with the awareness that we are a privileged group to begin with—we who oppose privilege on principle—just for being here. We find ourselves a little like those people who, in middle age, begin to suspect that they have become the parent they rebelled against, and that their rebellion somehow binds them to that parent all the more.

This quandary is not new to me. From the time I first came to West Marin fifteen years ago, I have felt that I had walked back into a drama I've been through before. I spent my teen years at the tip of Cape Cod, which is as far east as Point Reyes Station is west. My mother's husband was an artist-craftsman who owned a shop—and later apartments—in Provincetown, where the land ends, and from which the next stop is England. The Pilgrims landed there before they went on to Plymouth.

P'town, as it is called, is a compact little village along a narrow strip between the bay and the dunes. Physically and geographically, it is very different from West Marin. The Cape at that point is less than two miles wide; the open spaces are out to sea. History overhangs the place in the form of a tower that commemorates the Pilgrim landing.

And yet P'town in those days was similar too. The traditional economy was based on food. Where we have cows, P'town had fish. More precisely, it had a fishing fleet that worked the bay and the Georges Banks beyond. The old-timers were Portuguese fishermen, tough, swarthy guys who went out for a week or more and who still walked barefoot down Commercial Street in winter. As out here, there were decaying remnants of a railroad. It had once carried the fish to Boston, which is one hundred twenty miles by land, though only about fifty by sea.

What P'town shared most with West Marin was a sense of being beyond the pull of social constraint. It was a separate world; you could go for years without a coat and tie. Artists and writers were drawn to the rustic authenticity where they were close enough to Boston and New York for a quick visit to a publisher or gallery. Eugene O'Neill started the Provincetown Playhouse. Norman Mailer, Stanley Kunitz, and a host of others followed.

What drew them drew another group as well—-gays, who came in summer droves and let it all hang out in ways they couldn't even in New York back then. The result was a mélange like no place else. There was traditional P'town, embodied in the fishing fleet and Portuguese Bakery, with its flipper bread and tangy soup. And then there was Mr. Kenneth with his hat shop; the female impersonator lounge singer at the Crown and Anchor Inn; the lesbian bar called the Ace of Spades, which jutted out into the bay and from the deck of which throaty laughter could be heard late into the night; and the Atlantic House down the alley where the homoerotica in the men's room could make even a gay sailor blush. A town council dominated by people with names like Santos and Cabral looked upon it all with a Mediterranean shrug. (The business brought to their bars and restaurants didn't hurt.)

It was a rich mix, and a fragile one. As with so many places, P'town was done in by what made it so attractive; its uniqueness turned on itself. The tourist shops metastasized. Fudge became more prevalent than fish. The gay self-presentation became more circus-y and contrived. Wooden cottages were spiffed up. Rough turned into quaint; the nooks and crannies of affordability disappeared. The year-round population diminished; merchants had fewer customers in the winter months. Meanwhile, artists without trust funds could no longer pay the rents—nor could very many others.

If the shoe doesn't fit enough already, there's more. Outside of town, a new national park—the Cape Cod National Seashore—made the lower Cape (the end furthest out, though also the furthest north) all the more attractive, and the existing real estate all the more valuable. The park saved a precious landscape—within its boundaries. Outside them, development came like mange. The marsh across the road from the Goose Hummock outdoor shop in Orleans, which I passed on my way to school each day, is now the Cranberry Cove Plaza. You could be anywhere. Much of the Cape is that way now. It pains me to go back.

In the parts that aren't spoiled, moreover, an Aunt Sally landscape has replaced the Huck Finn version—preserved, but with a precious quality, and woe to him or her who tracks dirt across the rug. Deer hunting season used to be a little like a Jewish holiday in New York, with empty desks at Nauset High School. Now the woods are houses. The guys go to New Hampshire to hunt. There was a dune colony just outside of P'town, near Pilgrim Lake, where adventuresome souls lived off the grid in summer in driftwood shacks. The Park Service took it down.

The dune colony was a little like the summer encampment at White House Pool, halfway between Point Reyes and Inverness, where young people in the 1960s took refuge when they had to relinquish their winter rentals to the owners. The informal campsite couldn't happen now; and what is relief to some is a sense of loss to others, leaving us with a nagging question as to whether there might have been another way—one that maintained our rougher edges and the social dimension of our landscape.

That Cape experience helped to shape my conservative side, in the Kirkean sense. Washington conservatives see evil mainly in government and in a teeming penumbra of Communists, gays, Muslims, and liberals that never give them rest. I see evil more in money—not money itself but the love of it, the cupidity, which threatens always to ruin that which is precious and beyond price.

That weighs on me when I see development creeping out from Petaluma, Fairfax, and Novato, and the story poles that go up periodically around town, and when I think about the potential ripples from an upgraded Grandi Building in Point Reyes Station. When I watch the parade on Western Weekend, I flash back to the P'town equivalent, the annual Blessing of the Fleet. It is still a celebration, if anything louder and more garish than before. But there is no more fleet, just a sad assemblage of rusting hulks at the town pier. The fish market there once did a brisk business. Town kids dived for coins nearby. Now they are gone; and it is hard not to wonder whether our ranches will go the same way and the pick-ups in town become mainly exurban accoutrements for the hauling of landscaping equipment and organic garden supplies.

Edmund Burke, that proto-conservative, worried about the unique local cultures that the Jacobins of the French Revolution would destroy with their rationalistic planning. The real estate market is a Jacobin by other means. Yes, the bulwarks here are stronger than they were on the Cape. We have county planning and the Coastal Commission, where the Cape back then had neither. Still, money doesn't sleep, and plenty of damage can be done within the existing "envelope," as the planners call it.

But then I remember the kid—myself—whose family lived on tourists, as did most of the people I knew. My mother and her husband were at the shop until 9:00 or 10:00 every night. I worked on a golf course and in a grocery store where the customers were tourists too. "The season," as we called it, ran from Memorial Day to Labor Day—three months in which to make the nut for the year. There was gloom at the dinner table on rainy weekends, and even more when the bad weather stretched on for days.

That memory tempers my annoyance now at the traffic. Cars mean customers, and something besides spaghetti on the dinner table. I find myself asking merchants in town how the season's going. I hope they don't think I'm nosey; part of me thinks I'm still one of them. There is grumbling in town about the tourists. We grumbled too—about the ones who pawed the merchandise, and let their kids run wild, and never bought anything. My mother's husband had a thing about the tourists from Canada, of all places, and the women who should have left the Bermuda shorts at home.

But I cannot get too down on tourists. I've been tempted, as when a contentious fellow shouted curses at me and my young son when we didn't vacate a parking space as he expected. Still, our merchants need the business if there is to be a local economy and a Main Street with shops and life. Those lines of upscale motorcycle fantasists on Sundays help keep the Bovine Bakery open for the rest of us. And for all the traffic, it is a kind that is dependent upon the landscape and thus provides an economic base for it.

Do we really expect taxpayers to pay for a park and then let it become a private viewscape for those fortunate enough to be situated nearby? No matter what we do or don't do, there is a price. Even if we try to build a wall around West Marin, our community still will change because of who gets to live within the wall and who doesn't. From a strictly ecological standpoint that might not seem so bad to some. The Rockefeller estate in Westchester County, north of Manhattan, has preserved almost 3,500 acres of mainly woodland. You look at the surrounding sprawl and feel grateful for the enclave, much of which is open to the public.

But most of us humans cannot live on ecology alone. There is a social ecology here as well as a natural one; inhabitants as well as habitat. Our town is symbiotic with ranchers, ranch-hands, tradesmen, along with the artists and musicians, who together comprise a human web within the natural one to make the place unique. Yet for all the effort to preserve the landscape out here, not much has been devoted to the integrity of the town itself and the social ecology it embodies. This is a great opportunity. Our biggest contribution to the larger ecological cause could be in finding new ways for the social and the natural to co-exist.

Sustainability without settlement is a non sequitur, and one to which Western environmental movements are prone. I sometimes sense in the complaints about tourists—and in the opposition to such things as an oyster farm—an indifference to livelihood generally and to the practicalities of daily life. This is the classic astigmatism of the conservative gentry; and it is no less myopic because it is connected now to ecology and landscape.

Not long ago I too might have shared it. Then I married a woman from the Philippines and began to visit her family on their rice farm there. It is a rural landscape in a way that ours no longer is. The roads are dirt. There is no plumbing. Chickens and goats run about in the yard. When it is time to prepare dinner, my wife's mother goes out back with a knife.

Yet for all this it is a domesticated landscape. Practically every inch is accounted for, and must be in a land that is so populous and poor. There are efforts in that country to restore clearcut mountainsides and protect remaining forests. But the concept of "wilderness" in the American sense does not exist. My wife had never encountered it until she moved here. For most of the world wilderness is a luxury for those whose income and sustenance comes from someplace else.

Untouched places are important, where they actually exist. But for most of humanity the challenge is to live on and with the land in a way that doesn't ruin it; to embrace that challenge in West Marin might help us unravel the conundrum of change. Main Street and landscape are connected. If we want a town that is not just a quaint tourist destination, then we had better support the ranches and dairy farms—and perhaps even an oyster farm—that sustain the agrarian version. No ranches, no feed barn.

A range of housing is important too, to prevent the town from becoming too upscale and precious. Socially and environmentally, it is hardly ideal that so many of our service workers must drive in from Rohnert Park and Santa Rosa each day. This means, among other things, encouraging second units, especially close in. It means filling in the town so we can leave the landscape alone.

Organizations such as the Community Land Trust Association of West Marin (CLAM) and the Marin Agricultural Land Trust (MALT) have been doing yeoman work along these lines. Why not extend the techniques by which MALT has helped preserve the landscape to the town itself? If we can buy development rights to ranchland, for example, why not to town land?

Why not establish a town trust and buy key parcels ourselves? It could help keep out invasive uses, and the rents on existing or created housing or shops could provide a funding base for local purposes.

Such a trust might also purchase parcels in town to create common places where the social ecology can flourish. One of the constants in Provincetown through the years has been the benches outside the town hall on Commercial Street. No matter how expensive and tacky the place becomes—and it is both—the benches do not discriminate. Anyone can sit there to take in the passing scene.

This is social open space. Stinson Beach has a town green. Every town should, especially ones that want to maintain a noncommercial dimension and continuity with the past, as we conservatives want to do.

I know a person who bemoans change in town and the visitors who flock here. This person's house wasn't even built when another friend up the road first moved in. There are old-timers who were here before both of them; from their standpoint, the first to move in was a hippie, the other gentry, and both took some getting used to. I have seen pictures from the early 1900s of locomotives coming down the middle of Main Street and the entire northeast side devoted to a railroad yard. That's not a past that anyone I know wants to go back to.

There is a geology of memory out here, an accretion of reference points for the better yesterday. We tend to think the story starts when we enter; yet our own entrance might have been someone else's jarring change. The point is not that one house justifies another ad infinitum until the landscape is full. It is that we need to approach the question with humility and an awareness that the process that enabled us to be here is going to continue in some form.

We need to leave some play in the line and some room for humans in the ecological scheme. Nature as a concept would not exist without us. The one thing we can say for certain is that the town will be different in thirty years, just as it is different now than thirty years ago. Once upon a time, the Dance Palace was in the Cabaline. Point Reyes Books was a natural food store. Building Supply was in the Grandi Building, and there was a dance studio above it.

That process will continue, and this is not necessarily to be regretted. If the change is indigenous and inventive—as it can be—we could look at the results and think, "Hmmm, not so bad." A generation ago, a burst of local energy gave rise to the Dance Palace, the Point Reyes Clinic, and other civic institutions that are warp and woof of the community today. That change is our normal. If we can bequeath a new normal such as that, then we conservatives will be able to rest in peace.

THE BLUE

Camille T. Dungy

ONE WILL LIVE to see the Caterpillar rut everything
they walk on—seacliff buckwheat cleared, relentless
ice plant to replace it, the wild fields bisected
by the scenic highway, canyons covered with cul-de-sacs,
gas stations, comfortable homes, the whole habitat
along this coastal stretch endangered, everything,
everyone, everywhere in it in danger as well—
but now they're logging the one stilling hawk
Smith sights, the conspiring grasses' shh shhhh ssh,
the coreopsis Mattoni's boot barely spares,
and, netted, a solitary blue butterfly. Smith
ahead of him chasing the stream, Mattoni wonders
if he plans to swim again. Just like that
the spell breaks. It's years later, Mattoni lecturing
on his struggling butterfly. How fragile.

If his daughter spooled out the fabric
she's chosen for her wedding gown,
raw taffeta, burled, a bright-hued tan,
perhaps Mattoni would remember
how those dunes looked from a distance,
the fabric, balanced between her arms,
making valleys in the valley, the fan
above her mimicking the breeze.
He and his friend loved everything
softly undulating under the coyest wind,

and the rough truth as they walked
through the land's scratch and scrabble
and no one was there, then, besides Mattoni
and his friend, walking along Dolan's Creek,
in that part of California they hated
to share. The ocean a mile or so off
anything but passive so that even there,
in the canyon, they sometimes heard it smack
and pull well-braced rocks. The breeze,
basic: salty, bitter, sour, sweet. Smith trying
to identify the scent, tearing leaves
of manzanita, yelling, "This is it. Here! This is it!"
his hand to his nose, his eyes, having finally seen
the source of his pleasure, alive.

In the lab, after the accident, he remembered it,
the butterfly. How good a swimmer Smith had been,
how rough the currents there at Half Moon Bay, his friend
alone with reel and rod—Mattoni back at school
early that year, his summer finished too soon—
then all of them together in the sneaker wave,
and before that the ridge, congregations of pinking
blossoms, and one of them bowing, scaring up the living,
the frail and flighty beast too beautiful
to never be pinned, those nights Mattoni worked
without his friend, he remembered too.
He called the butterfly Smith's Blue.

SILVER GIRL

Angie Chau

ON THE FOURTH of July we glide through the winding roads of Mt. Tam with the top down. Tree tops sway and leaves shimmer like tinsel when the moon hits just right. Over the railing the Pacific Coast is as placid as a lake tonight. Amphi's dad takes the curves hard and fast. He pumps even harder when Aretha Franklin goes off on her scat. Her lungs are like the gale winds of the Bay. But still Larry puts the music loud. He's a jazz musician. He plays trumpet. He's deaf in one ear from his years next to a speaker.

Amphi and I are squeezed together in the front bucket seat. We're bundled up in matching sweaters and blue jeans and scream with the turns of our stomachs. We're hunched over with the heat high. Our noses nestled against the vents, cheeks touching. We like the hot-cold look of reddened cheeks, chapped lips, the wind through our hair. We like how it feels even better. Amphi's dad says we're complicated women. Already we groove on contradiction. I like being called a woman. My father would call us kids.

My father would say, roll up the windows and turn the heat off. He would say, either-or, why both? My father's at home tonight. He's bathing in the blue light of his sitcoms. His bared feet are crossed at the ankles, propped up on the coffee table. He's rubbing them together when he says, "Sure you don't want to stay home with us? Mom's making *pho* and we can watch the fireworks on TV." His two big toes are bruised from cheap shoes, steep hills, the weight of the mail on his back.

At the top of the mountain Larry parks on a dirt shoulder. Amphi and I run to the cliff's edge. She screams, "Last one to the wall!" I'm sprinting fast, lungs full, out of breath. Beyond us, the city lights beckon. The sprawling hills stretch until they roll underwater. I imagine swimming in a sea of silver stars.

Amphi is ahead of me spinning and pirouetting, jumping so high she defies gravity. My best friend looks like those princesses they draw in children's fairy tales. She has sweet clear eyes and Botticelli lips and a blaze of auburn hair always in perfect disarray from riding in her dad's convertible. The top of her head skims the tip of a maple leaf and for a fleeting moment she is crowned. I watch afraid if I blink she might disappear forever.

Last month, on the last day of junior high, we pricked our fingers and swore we'd remain Bo Diddley and Wonder Woman, soul sisters forever. Come September she'll be starting high school at the Arts Academy. For now we pretend that the summer will be endless, that the fall will never arrive.

When I told my parents I wanted to go to the Arts Academy, too, they said we couldn't afford it.

I said, "I could apply for a scholarship."

My father said, "That's not a guarantee."

I said, "What happens if I get in?" My father changed the channel. The remote is wrapped in plastic. It is like everything in our house.

Amphi and I lean on the wall. The moss is cool. It tickles our elbows. We can see the entire peninsula, all five bridges. We call out their names: the Golden Gate and the Bay Bridge, the Richmond and the San Mateo. Our words bounce back in the wind. Way out in the distance we can see the Dumbarton too. That's how clear it is tonight. It's so far away it looks like a stray piece of string.

From the car, Aretha is belting out a gospel. She sounds like a velvet storm you could drown in. Amphi calls to Larry but his head is buried in the trunk. She rolls her eyes and says, "At least your dad isn't always in his own world."

I remember the first time I spent the night at their house. Larry came home and started playing the piano at one in the morning. He sounded like Chet Baker singing "Smoke Gets in Your Eyes," with a voice so timid it trembled. He was tapping his foot and because the piano bench had a wobbly leg it added an extra beat against the hardwood floors. He nodded at us and then at the wide open windows and the moonlight. His tweed bowler hat tipped over his brow. Amphi screamed, "Come on Dad! Don't you know the time?" A breeze swept through and flapped the calendar pages on the wall. Larry grinned and played on. I couldn't help it, I grinned too.

My father doesn't like sleepovers. He says no proper girl would ever spend the night away, or even want to for that matter. As punishment, he sits me down with a date book. "High school's next year and every minute counts." Six to seven—swim practice. Seven to eight—breakfast with flashcards. After school, violin lessons from four to five. Five to six—French tutor. Six to seven—dinner. Seven to nine—homework. Nine to ten—relax. "You're scheduling in a relax hour?"

"When else would you do it?" he asks. He picks up the remote. *Three's Company* is on tonight. It's his favorite show. He laughs along with the laugh track. Larry calls it a laugh trap.

Larry slams the trunk and its tinny echo slices through the warmth of the night. When he approaches I can still hear the music play. It's muffled but I can tell it's Aretha singing, "Bridge Over Troubled Water."

Larry catches my eye and says, "Hey silver girl."

Amphi says, "If she's silver girl, who am I?"

He says, "You're gold."

My father once told me about the ancient Kingdom of Angkor Wat. How the royal family sprinkled gold dust on themselves. How they were seen by their public only one night of the year, on the eve of the harvest moon. Their naked bodies glowed beneath firelight and when the embers died, they vanished. The villagers thought they were gods. I wondered what it was like for them the rest of the year.

Amphi glances at the paper bag cradled in Larry's arm and asks, "What took so long?" He hops up and sits on top of the wall. We copy him and climb on too, me on one side, Amphi on the other. Our legs hang over the ledge. I know my father wouldn't approve. He says teasing death is only fun when you don't know what it smells like.

The tree tops below our feet look like baby broccoli heads. I ask, "Did you pack sandwiches in there?" We haven't had dinner yet.

Larry sets his brown bag down. He says, "I'm not hungry. But we can get food on the way back." He flicks his cigarette butt. When I kick it the red ashes spray.

He says, "What d'ya know, those are practically fluorescent in the moonlight."

Amphi says, "Her dad polishes her sneakers. And guess who did her hair?"

I say, "It's just because I can't reach the back by myself."

Amphi says, "Dad, you've never helped me curl my hair."

"You've never asked."

"No," she says, "it's because when Kristen was around I wasn't allowed more than fifteen minutes in the bathroom."

The first night Larry met Amphi's soon-to-be step mom, he came home craving his deceased mother's *puttanesca*. It didn't matter that it was around midnight and he had to wake us up. I chopped tomatoes. Amphi diced onions. And while Larry minced the anchovy fillets this was the story he told.

He'd been in Sausalito at his regular Saturday night gig at a place everyone called the No Name because it literally had no name. "There's no sign, just a door," he said. You push through a heavy wooden block and then you're in an open air bar like an old-fashioned Spanish courtyard. "I've never really dug blondes before," he said, "but..." But maybe it was how the bar had white Christmas lights hanging from the trees and she looked like a little angel with her platinum hair framing her face in wisps. Or maybe it was how she drank Shirley Temples one after another. Or how even from the stage he could see that she was shivering. He said to me, "She's practically your size."

During the break he grabbed his jacket and offered it to her. Up close she had the saddest eyes he'd ever seen. They were "bewitching." He said her name, "Kristen," and then repeated it again in a reverent whisper. I promised on the spot that one day a man would say my name with that much awe. "That one's gonna break my heart," he said, "but I don't care."

We played Sinatra records and rolled up the rug and Amphi and I took turns letting Larry spin us on the hardwood floors and out to the porch and then down to the front lawn where the dew was sticky between my toes. In the lilac hours of daylight, the sheets pulled up to my chin, I dreamt about the shimmy and women who looked like angels, and the promise of flight.

Tonight Larry denies Kristen's spell. He's pretending things didn't change when she came around. "That's hogwash," he says, "Baloney!"

I'm so hungry I can hear my stomach growl. At my house my parents shove food down your throat the second you walk through the door. If you don't eat anything, they'll put a papaya in your backpack or give you some persimmons to take home to your parents.

At Amphi's house we eat at odd hours and drink coffee. We sit in the shadows of the living room where it's dark and musty and smells like old wood and roasted coffee and we listen to Larry's jazz albums. He makes coffee drinks from his fancy Italian espresso machine while we write down "the vibe" we get from the song. "How's the piano talking to the sax? What are the sounds saying to you?" Larry encourages us to express ourselves.

My father doesn't like that I'm always staying the night away. "Is there something wrong with our home?" He tells me that in Vietnam, the word "sleepover" doesn't exist.

I say words like "privacy" and "passion" aren't in the Vietnamese language either. "Does that mean they don't exist?"

"You're getting mouthy," he says. "See what the sleepovers are doing to your attitude?" I like that "mouthy" is used the same way in English and in Vietnamese. Finding these connections helps me feel better.

I've started writing. Mostly it's nonsense. I use the things littered on Amphi's living room floor as paper. I write on grocery bags and pizza boxes, candy wrappers and cigarette packs. I make lists. Stone, beat, dark.

The only present Larry ever gave me was a journal. It had a thick red cover with thick crisp paper inside. "Copy this down for me will ya?" He gave me a pizza box I'd written a poem on. He said he might make it into a song.

I came home and asked my parents, "Why don't we talk more?"

My father said, "We talk plenty." He switched back to the TV.

One day I said, "We watch too much TV."

My father said, "But we watch TV to improve our English. You said you wanted us to talk more."

My parents understand practical functional English. They have learned the English of ESL, the language of getting from A to B, questions, commands, directions, a job in a new country. They speak in the language of survival. We are boat people, refugees. Sometimes when we talk it's as if we're drifting apart at sea.

My father's diplomas are water stained. They're yellowing and hanging on the wall above the TV. He says you can choose to be a doctor. They help others and are respected in society. He says you can choose to be an engineer. Decent paycheck and math comes easy to you. He says be a professor, excellent benefits and the students will keep you young.

Amphi's dad says, "Follow your passion."

Out toward the East, Larry points to the hydraulic boatlifts and says, "George Lucas was sitting right here looking out at 'em when he got the idea for the AT-ATs in *The Empire Strikes Back*." The boatlifts look mystical and foreboding, rising out from the sea like post-industrial dragons. Although I've heard some people call them dinosaurs and others call them Dobermans, I know them as guardians. They stand at attention on the edge of the coast. They're perched and ready, here to protect the inhabitants of the Bay. If my parents knew this maybe they wouldn't stay tucked inside their box all the time, hidden behind two deadbolts and a squeaky screen door.

Larry once played a gig at the Lucas Ranch estates. He was instructed to wear a tux and bring a blindfold. Kristen didn't like the idea of him going alone. She said that if Larry loved her he would sneak her in.

She could pretend to be a backup dancer. "It could be my big break," she said. When Larry said it was out of his hands, Kristen said, "Everything slips through your hands." She squeezed hers into tight fists. The biceps she'd gained from teaching her Taut-N-Tone class bulged.

Later that night, Amphi overheard Kristen saying she was too young to have given up her acting career for him and for a daughter who wasn't even hers. That's when Amphi told me about the survey. They did a survey where they asked a bunch of people, if you were on a sinking ship and you could only save either your spouse or your child, who would you pick? Ninety percent of the women chose the kid and ninety percent of the men chose the wife.

Amphi asked me, "Who would your father choose?"

Larry balances on one arm, lifts his hips off the wall, and fumbles for his back pocket. Amphi says, "Careful, you're scaring me." He pulls out a corkscrew and uncorks the bottle from his bag.

The day before Kristen left, we had a big barbeque in their back yard with his sponsor and her sponsor and all of their other AA friends to celebrate Larry's two-year chip. We grilled fish and shrimp, tofu and tempeh burgers. Amphi and I volunteered to circulate with the trays of sushi. The coolers were all iced up brimming with Calistogas and Martinelli's, sodas and juices. Larry and Kristen seemed happy, arms around each other, all kisses and affection. (I'd never seen my parents hug). But the very next day, Kristen's leotards and leg warmers and her rainbow array of high top sneakers were all packed into her duffel bags and gone. Since then Larry's been drinking again. He's barely picked up his trumpet. He doesn't even finish his scales before going off for yet another drive.

Amphi and Larry are talking about the *Star Wars* movies and she asks, "Dad, do you think I'm pretty enough to be an actress?"

He says, "You'd rule the world hon, if you didn't let your own fears get in the way."

Amphi is looking into the night sky, dreaming stars and smiling. She says, "I wonder when the fireworks will start." They're huddled together and she puts her head on his shoulder. It is silent all around except for the chirring of crickets. It sounds like escaping in the middle of the night. It is the sound of hope and fear stuffed so deep it coos.

My father says, "Your mother and I risked our lives to come here. I know you'll make us proud. I know you'll care for us when we're old." He massages his feet. He soaks them in a big pot of warm water and sits back on the couch. Often he'll ask me, "How did I get reincarnated from a man to a mule all in a lifetime? Why go on at all?"

I didn't say anything, but it made me think about the year I wrote him a poem for Father's Day. I wanted him to know how much he meant to me. When he thanked me he said, "Work on your handwriting, poor penmanship gives off a poor impression." I'd written it in pencil, erased often, couldn't make it perfect enough. In the end, I'd given him an embarrassment of fingerprints and sweeping graphite smudges.

A warm wind passes and we sigh. We can see out past the Marin Headlands and then the very faint beam from the lighthouse on Angel Island. Right beside the old Russian forts is the island prison of Alcatraz. Beyond it is San Quentin and Larry just stares. He takes small sips and closes his eyes after each one.

He swigs from his bottle and sets it down with a chink. I watch his Adam's apple bobbing up and down, up and down, two gulps total. He wipes his mouth with the back of his hand then taps my knee. "Hold this will ya?" Larry hunches over and springs to his feet like a cat. He's squatting with his hands on the ledge and butt in the air.

Amphi says, "Stop, you're not funny."

He says, "Relax, hon." With a great push of the forearms, Larry pops to his feet and stands upright. His arms point straight out like airplane wings. Amphi screams when he wobbles cliff side. With one foot in front of the other, he walks the length of the wall like a tightrope walker.

Amphi says, "If you love me, you'll cut it out."

Larry says, "Love's not like that, hon. Remember, everyone's gotta live their own life."

"But doesn't loving someone mean protecting them and keeping them from making mistakes?" Her voice is getting higher.

Larry says, "But everyone's gotta find their own way."

"Right," I say, "Isn't love about freedom? Loving someone unconditionally? Loving them despite their mistakes?"

Amphi says, "You two are nuts! Finding your own way? And freedom?" Her voice is insistent now, sharp. I look over but Amphi won't look at us. Her shoulders are slumped and she keeps her eyes straight ahead looking out at the prison and city lights.

She says, "I don't feel good Dad. Can we go home?"

"The fireworks will start up soon," he says.

"Please."

"What's wrong?" he asks.

"I have a headache."

"I'd hate to go when we just got here," he says.

She says, "If Kristen weren't feeling good we would have been in that car yesterday."

And instantly, Larry jumps down. He holds her chin in his hand and says, "Come on, don't do that. You're my number one lady. You know I love you." They walk off arm in arm to go look for aspirin. I can't think of the last time my father and I even touched.

Larry's wine bottle is wedged between my thighs. When I lift it, it's heavier than I'd imagined. I put the spout to my nose. It smells bad. The first sip warms my throat. The taste is unclear. First it's sour, and then it's bitter, then it has a little sweet aftertaste. I try again and I take a bigger drink this time. It's easier when you just gulp it. It makes my head hot. It makes my skull soften, my neck looser. I drink more.

In front of me, the view is both so grand and so small all at once. Sometimes I think it's the smallness that scares me. That I will suffocate beneath the plastic. But then the bigness scares me too. Look at all those stars and seas, the lights that go on endlessly, red and white ribbons of traffic speeding by, everyone going somewhere and wanting something. Even the Dobermans look mean.

The scholarship deadline is three days away. Beneath my bed, I have my manila envelope stuffed with my poems, transcripts, letters of recommendation, a self-addressed stamped envelope. I'm just waiting on Larry now. He's been saying that he's almost done with the song. He says, "With poet-songwriter on your application, you're a shoe-in."

I kick my heels against the wall and watch the sediment as it crumbles. When I lean forward the rush of it is freeing. I hang off the edge, facedown. I want to see how far I can go before I feel like falling. I sip more wine. It's delicious. I smile back at the night seduced by those winking lights.

I think I see a deer running, a pair of wet shining eyes behind a bush. I lean farther out. The wine falls from my lap. The bottle clinks against rocks as it rolls down the mountain.

Back at the car Amphi is sitting on the rear bumper with her arms folded to her chest. She's tapping her foot furiously and looking away from Larry. He's in the driver's seat. His head is on the steering wheel. His hand is in a fist on the dash. I see him turning the key but the car won't start.

Amphi says, "The battery's dead. Dad shouldn't have left the music on."

"Does your dad have jumpers?"

Larry screams, "Damn-it."

Amphi says, "What do you think?"

"I guess they wouldn't have helped even if he did though right?" We're up on the peak of Mt. Tamalpais and Larry took side streets and illegal fire trails and nobody is around at all. The entire predicament makes me bust up. I can't stop laughing. I can barely stand it. I'm rolling on the pavement.

Larry stands over me. "If your parents knew, kiddo," he says and shakes his head. But then he turns his attention to the car. "Let's try and jump start it." Larry says that he'll push, Amphi'll drive, and I'm in the passenger seat. The idea is that at the first turn off, Amphi will pull in. Larry's going to walk down the hill and meet us there.

She's behind the wheel and freaking out.

"I'll do it," I say, "I want to drive!"

They say, "Yeah right!"

Larry says, "Now, when I say so, let go of the clutch. That's all you've gotta do." He's out of breath as he pushes the car along.

"I don't know," she says. "I just don't know."

Larry insists she'll be fine. He says, "I have all my faith in you, honey."

The engine fires up and we cheer. The wheels skirt the edge of the road. We scream at the top of our lungs. We're careening down the hill and then the fireworks start. Beautiful blossoms burst everywhere. We are up so high we see five shows: the one in Mill Valley and Richmond, Oakland and San Francisco, San Rafael too. There are pinwheels and starbursts and sparklers and rockets. Everything is in flight. Umbrellas of red and purple rain down blues and greens. I put my face to the sky. The heavens are near and the world lies before us, that's what Larry always says. It is warm. It smells like a bakery. The fireworks look like cupcake sprinkles and my mouth is open wide.

CLUB ICARUS

Matt W. Miller

WE'RE NO MORE than a few silver
seconds in the air when that winged
and cocky boy gets sucked
into a turbine sparking off a fire
that rips the starboard wing
away from the fuselage, shucking
passengers out and raining
us over northern California, dozens
of us dropping towards the bay
and you can imagine the screams,
I'm sure, the prayers cast up
then down the twirling sky,
and yet here's my daughter
laughing the whole way
down, her yellow hair whipping
around her first teeth smile,
as she titters at the tilted
wonder of what was happening,
rolling airborne over and over,
as we all drop like sacks of wet
clay and for a second I want to snag
her, to show her how frightened
she should be, so I can hug
her safe one last time, but the way
she looks laughing I just can't

and so as the brick of the bay
comes up to kiss my back I watch
my little girl giggling, grinning
floppy-cheeked into the wind
and then, damn, if I don't see, right
before the world splits my sides,
wings all her own butterfly
from her back and lift her
laughing back into the blue.

from ***THE GREAT NIGHT***

Chris Adrian

IT TOOK THEM both a long time to understand that the boy was sick, though she would point out that she was the first to notice he was unhappy, and had sought to remedy his discontent with sweeter treats and more delightful distractions. She thought it was evidence that she loved him more, how she noticed first that something was wrong, and she said as much to her husband, when they were still trying to outdo each other in love for the child, before he became sick enough to demonstrate to them that they both loved him equally and immeasurably.

Neither of them had any experience with illness. They had each taken many mortal lovers but had cast them off before they could become old or infirm, and all their previous changelings had stayed healthy until they were returned to the mortal world. "There was no way you could have known," said Dr. Blork, the junior partner in the two-person team that oversaw the boy's care, on their very first visit with him. "Every parent feels they ought to have caught it earlier, but really it's the same for everyone, and you couldn't have done any better than you did. In fact, you did great. You did perfect." He was trying to make them feel better, to assuage a perceived guilt, but at that point neither Titania nor her husband really knew what guilt was, not ever having felt it in all their long days.

They were in the hospital, not far from the park on the hill under which they made their home, in the middle of the night—early for them, since they slept all day under the hill and had taught the boy to do the same—but the doctors, Beadle and Blork, were obviously fatigued. The four of them were sitting at a table in a small windowless conference room, the doctors on one side, the parents on the other. The boy was back in his room, drugged with morphine, sleeping peacefully for the first time in days. The doctors were explaining things, earnestly and patiently, but Titania was having trouble following along and found herself distracted by the notion that she should be delighted by the newness of this experience, for she and her husband had always been seekers after novelty, and yet already she did not like this at all.

"A boy should not be sick," she said suddenly to Dr. Blork, cutting him off as he was beginning to describe some of the side effects of the treatment they were proposing. "A boy should play...that is his *whole* purpose."

"It's hard to see him like this," Dr. Blork said, after a glance at his superior, "and I'm so sorry that your beautiful boy is so sick. It's going to be a long haul, and he may be sicker before he's better, but we'll get him through it." He started talking again about specifics, the drugs they would use—the names seemed rather demonic to her—and the timing of the treatments, which parts could be done at home and which parts must be done in the hospital. This was suddenly very boring. She waved her hand at them, a gesture practiced over centuries, and even though there was no magic in it, Blork was instantly silent.

"You will do your mortal thing," she said sadly. "I know all I need to know."

"Pardon me?" said Dr. Blork.

"Leukemia!" said Oberon, breaking the silence he'd kept all through the meeting. "Leukemia!" he said again, and it sounded as if he were somehow trying out the idea behind the word. He was smiling and crying into his beautiful beard. "Can you cure it?"

"Yes!" said Dr. Blork. But Dr. Beadle said, "Maybe."

She could not remember the quarrel that brought her the boy. A real or perceived dalliance or slight, a transgression on her part or her husband's—who knew? They had been quarreling for as long as they had been in love. She forgot the quarrels as soon as they were resolved, except for a vague sense, when they fought about something, that they had fought about it before. But the gifts her husband brought her to reconcile—even when she was at fault—she never forgot. The boy was one of those gifts, brought home to the hill, stolen from its crib in the dark of morning and presented to her by dawn. "That is not sufficient to your crime against me," she remembered saying, and remembered as well that she barely paid the child any mind during her restless sleep, except to push it away from her when it rolled too close. Oberon had rubbed poppies on its eyes to quiet its crying, so it was still sleeping soundly when she woke. For a while she lay on her back, watching the stars come out on the ceiling of her grotto, listening to the little snores. Oberon was snoring more magnificently. She turned on her side to better look at the child, and noticed for the first time how comely it was, how round and smooth were its face and shoulders and belly, how soft-appearing and lustrous was its hair. It made a troubled face as it slept. She put her hand out to touch the child, very lightly. Right away it sighed and lost the troubled look, but then it gave a little moan. She draped her hand over its shoulder, and when it did not quiet she rolled it closer to her. It stopped moaning only when she held it in her arms, and put her nose in its hair, and breathed in its scent—poppies and milk and warm earth. Oberon had woken and was looking at her and smiling, propped on one elbow with a hand against his ear, the other lost under the sheets, but she could hear him scratching himself. "Do you like it?" he asked.

"I am indifferent to it," she said, holding the boy closer, and squeezing him, and putting her face in his neck.

"This place is so ugly," Titania said. "Can anything be done about that?" She was talking to the oncology social worker, one of a stream of visiting strangers who came to the room, a woman who had described herself as a person to whom one might address problems or questions that no one else could solve or answer. Nonmedical things, she had said. You know—everything else!

"But you've made the room just lovely," the woman said. Her name was Alice or Alexandra or Antonia. Titania had a hard time keeping track of all the mortal names, except for Beadle and Blork, but those were distinctive and actually rather faerie-like. Alice gestured expansively around the room and smiled, not seeing what was actually there. She saw paper stars hanging from the ceiling, and cards and posters on the wall, and a homey bedspread upon the mattress, but faeries had come to carpet the room with grass, to pave the walls with stone and set them with jewels, and blow a cover of clouds to hide the horrible suspended ceiling. And the bedspread was no ordinary blanket but the boy's own dear Beastie, a flat headless creature of soft fur that loved him like a dog and tried to follow him out of the room whenever they took him away for some new test or procedure.

"I don't mean the room," Titania said, "I mean everything else. This whole place. And the people, of course...Where did you find them? Look at you, for instance. Are you deliberately homely? And that Dr. Blork—hideous! He is beyond help, but you...I could do you up."

Alice cocked her head. She did not hear exactly what Titania was saying. Everything was filtered through the same disguising glamour that hid the light in Titania's face, that gave her splendid gown the appearance of a track suit, that made the boy appear clothed when they brought him in, when in fact he had been naked. The same spell made it appear that he had a name, though his parents had only ever called him Boy, never having learned his mortal name, because he was the only boy under the hill. The same spell sustained the impression that Titania worked as a hairdresser and that Oberon owned an organic orchard and that their names were Trudy and Bob.

"You need to take care of yourself," Alice said, thinking Titania was complaining about feeling ugly. "It might feel a little selfish, but you can't take care of him if you can't take care of yourself. Did you know we have a manicurist who comes every Wednesday?"

"You are so sweet," Titania said, "even if you are homely. Did you ever wish you had the eyes of a cat?"

"A hat? You can buy one downstairs. For when his hair falls out, you mean. That's weeks away, you know. But the baseball caps are awfully cute. But listen, not everybody wants to talk about this at first, and not everybody has to. I'm getting ahead of myself...of ourselves."

"Or would you rather be a cat entirely? Yes, I think that would make you lovely." Titania raised her hands and closed her eyes, seeking for words sufficient to the spell she had in mind. They came to her in an image, words printed on a little girl's purse she had glimpsed in the waiting room outside the surgical suites downstairs. She started to speak them—*Hello, Kitty!*—but Oberon walked in before she had the first syllable out.

"What are you doing to the nurse?" he asked her.

"She's the social worker. And we were only talking." Alice's head was turned to the side and she was staring at Titania with a mixture of curiosity and devotion. The glamour had slipped as Titania was about to strike, and the woman had seen her true face. "Her name is Alice."

"Stop playing," Oberon said. "He's almost finished. Don't you want to be there when he wakes?" The boy was downstairs getting things done to him; a needle in his hip to take the marrow from his bones and another in his neck to give him an IV that would last through the weeks and months of the treatment.

"I'll just stay here and wait," she said, sitting on the bed and idly petting the Beastie when it sidled up to her.

"He'll be looking for you," Oberon said.

"You'll be there."

"He'll ask for you."

"Tell him I'm waiting here with his Beastie." She lifted it into her lap, as if to show him the truth of what she was saying but also to demonstrate that she was settling in. Alice, still standing between them, was looking back and forth, catching glimpses of their majesty, as their mounting anger caused them to let it slip, and getting drunker on them.

"Did I give you your meal tickets yet?" Alice asked them. "The cafeteria is really not so bad, for what it is."

"You'd rather laze about than comfort him. Do you love him at all?"

"More than you do, and more than you'll ever understand. You like to see him undone and ailing, but I can't bear to look at him like that." She had drugged the child herself many times, when he was younger, but now she could not stand to see him in the vulnerable, unnatural sleep the anesthesia brought.

"Those are very normal feelings," said Alice. "I validate those feelings. Haven't I been saying how hard it is to see him like this?" She turned to Oberon. "Haven't I?"

"Heartless and cowardly," Oberon said. "A most unattractive combination."

"That's normal too," Alice said. "The anger. But don't you know it's not her that you're angry at?"

"You stupid sour cock," said Titania, and then they just called each other names, back and forth, getting angrier and angrier at each other while Alice turned back and forth so swiftly it seemed she was spinning.

"How can I make you understand how totally normal all of this is?" Alice cried aloud at last, just before collapsing in a heap. The Beastie, whose nature was to comfort, tried to go to her, but Titania held it back.

"Now look what you've done," said her husband.

At first he was like her own sort of Beastie, a creature who followed her around and was pleasant to cuddle with. It didn't take long before he stopped his agitated weeping, before he stopped crying for the mortal parents whom he'd hardly known, and then he smiled for everyone, even for Oberon, who barely noticed him for months. He was delightful, and she was fond of him in the way she was always fond of the changelings, and yet she had dresses and shoes of which she was just as fond. She liked to dress him and feed him, and took him to bed every night, even when Oberon complained that he did not like to have pets in the bed. He might get lost under the covers and migrate by morning to some remote corner, and she would half wake in the early afternoon, feel around for him, and not sleep again until she had gathered him up.

He grew. This was unexpected—she had completely forgotten even this basic fact of human physiology since the last changeling—but quite exciting. He wouldn't fit anymore in the footed pajamas in which he'd been stolen, and then she kept him naked. Many evenings she would stare at him, hoping to *see* him get bigger. She liked to feed him, initially just milk and dew and a little honey on her finger, but then she woke one morning to find him attached to her breast, and she wondered why she hadn't fed any of the other changelings this way. It was easy enough to make food come out of her nipple: not-quite-ordinary milk at first, but then less usual substances: weak wine and chocolate and peanut butter and yogurt.

It wasn't long before Oberon regretted his gift and started to hide the child somewhere on the hill, attended by faeries, so he could have his wife to himself. She tolerated that for weeks, but within a few months she couldn't stand to be apart from the boy, though she couldn't really say why. Perhaps it was because he smiled at everything she said and never argued with her; for months and months he never even said a word, but only babbled. It was different from talking to her husband, who could turn any conversation into an argument, or from talking to the members of her court, who always seemed to be listening for ways to curry her favor.

The boy grew, and changed, and became ever more delightful to her, and she imagined that they could go on forever like that, that he would always be her favorite thing. It would have been perfect, and maybe it would have been better if he had stayed her favorite thing—a toy and not a son—because now he would just be a broken toy. She ought to have had the foresight to make him dumb, or Oberon ought to have, since the boy was his terrible gift to her. But one evening the boy ran back to her, and climbed upon her throne, and giggled at the dancing faerie bodies leaping and jumping all around them, and put his face to her breast, and sighed a word at her, *molly* or *moony* or *middlebury*—she still didn't know what it was exactly. But it was close enough to *mommy* to ruin everything.

They poisoned the boy exquisitely. Beadle and Blork had reviewed it all with them, the names and the actions and the toxicities of the variety of agents they were going to use to cure him, but of that whole long conversation only a single phrase of Blork's had really stuck. "We'll poison him well again," he'd said, rather too cheerily, and he had explained that the chemotherapy was harder on the cancer than on the healthy boy parts, but that it was still hard, and that for the next many months he would act like a boy who had been poisoned. "Sometimes we'll poison him a little," he said, while Beadle frowned more and more vigorously at him, "and sometimes we'll poison him a lot." And indeed in that first week it seemed to Titania that they were poisoning him as vigorously and enthusiastically as anyone ever poisoned anybody, for or against their own good. The chemotherapy came in colors—straw yellow and a red somewhere between the flesh of a watermelon and a cherry—but did not fume or smoke the way some of her own most dramatic poisons had. There was nothing in them she could comprehend, though she peered at the bags and sniffed at the tubes, since there was no magic in them. She was only reluctantly interested in the particulars of the medications, but Oberon wanted to know all about them and talked incessantly about what he learned, parroting what Beadle and Blork said or reading aloud from the packets of information the nurses gave them. He proclaimed that he would taste the red liquid himself, to share the experience with the boy, but in the end he made a much lesser faerie do it, a little brownie named Doorknob, who smacked his lips and proclaimed that it tasted rusty in the same way that blood smelled rusty, and went on to say he thought he liked the taste of it and was about to sample it again when he went suddenly mad, tearing at his hair and clawing at his face and telling everyone his bowels had become wild voles, and perhaps they had, since there was an obvious churning in his hairy little belly. Oberon knocked him over the head with his fist, which brought him sleep if not peace, and though he had previously been one of the meekest spirits over the hill, every day after that he was angry and abrasive, and more than anything else he liked to pick a fight.

The boy had a very different response. Right away the poisons settled him down in a way that even the morphine did not. That put him to sleep, but in between doses he woke and cried again, saying that a gator had his leg or a bear was hugging him to death or a snake had wound itself around the long part of his arm and was crushing it. Within a few days the poisons had made him peaceful again. Titania could not conceive of the way they were made except as distillations of sadness and heartbreak and despair, since that was how she made her own poisons, shaking drops of terror out of a wren captured in her fist or sucking with a silver straw at the tears of a dog. Oberon had voiced a fear that the boy was sick for human things, that the cancer in his blood was only a symptom of a greater ill, that he was homesick unto death. So she imagined they were putting into him a sort of liquid mortal sadness, a corrective against a dangerous abundance of faerie joy.

Then he seemed to thrive on it. If she hadn't been so distracted by relief it might have saddened her, or brought to mind how different in kind he was from her, that a decoction of grief should restore him. His whole body seemed to suck it up, bag after bag, and then his fever broke, and the spots on his skin began to fade like ordinary bruises, and the pain in his bones went away. She watched him for hours, finally restored to untroubled sleep, and when he woke he said, "I want a cheese sandwich," and the dozen little faeries hidden around the room gave a cheer.

"You heard him," she said, and ordered them with a sweep of her arm out the door and the windows. The laziest went only to the hospital cafeteria, but the more industrious ventured out to the fancy cheese shops of Cole Valley and the Castro and even the Marina and returned with loaves under their arms and wheels and blocks of stolen cheeses balanced on their heads and stuffed down their pants, Manchego and Nisa and Tomme Vaudoise, proclaiming the names to the boy as if they were announcing the names of visiting kings and queens. The room filled rapidly with cheese and then with sandwiches, as the bread and cheese was cut and assembled. The boy chose something from the cafeteria, a plastic-looking cheese on toast. Oberon, asleep on the narrow couch beneath the window, was awakened by the variety of odors and started to thank the faeries for his breakfast, until a pixie named Radish pointed and said in her thin high voice, "He mounches! He mounches!" Oberon began to cry, of course. He was always crying these days, and it seemed rather showy to Titania, who thought she suffered more deeply in her silence than he did in his sobs. He gathered the boy in his arms, and the boy said, "Papa, you are getting my sandwich wet," which caused some tittering among the faeries, some of whom were crying too now, or laughing, or kissing one another with mouths full of rare cheese. Titania sat down on the bed and put a hand on the boy and another on her husband, and forgave Oberon his showy tears and the boy the scare he'd given her.

Just then Dr. Blork entered the room, giving the barest hint of a knock on the door before he barged in. The faeries vanished before his eye could even register them, but the cheeses stayed behind, stacked in sandwiches on the dresser and the windowsill, wedged in the light fixtures and stuck to the bulletin board with pins, piled in the sink and scattered on the floor. He stared all around the room and then at the three of them, looking so pale and panicked that Titania had to wonder if he was afraid of cheese.

"He was hungry," Titania said, though the glamour would obviate any need for an excuse. "He's hungry. He's eating."

"You have poisoned him masterfully!" said Oberon, and Titania asked if they could take him home now.

He was never a very useful changeling. Previously Oberon had trained them as pages or attendants for her, and they learned, even as young children, to brush her hair just in the way she liked. Or they were instructed to sing to her, or dance a masque, or wrestle young wolves in a ring for the entertainment of the host. But the boy only hit her when she presented him with the brush, and instead she found herself brushing *his* hair.

And she sang for him, ancient dirges at first, and eldritch hymns to the moon, but he didn't like those, and Oberon suggested that she learn some music more familiar to him. So she sent Doorknob into the Haight to fetch a human musician, but he brought her back an album instead, because it had a beautiful woman on it, a lovely human mama. She looked at the woman on the cover of *Carly Simon's Greatest Hits,* golden-skinned and honey-haired with a fetching gap in her smile, and put on her aspect, and spun the record on her finger while Radish sat upon it, the stinger in her bottom protruding to scratch in the grooves, and Titania leaned close to listen to the songs. Then she sang to the boy about his own vanity and felt a peaceful pleasure.

Oberon said she was spoiling him, she had ruined him, and he had no hope of ever becoming a functional changeling, and in a fit of enthusiastic discipline he scolded the boy, ordered him to pick up some toys he had left scattered in the hall, and threatened to feed him to a bear if he did not. Weepingly, the boy complied, but he had gathered up only a few blocks before he came to a little blue bucket on the floor. "I'm a puppy!" he said, and bent down to take the handle in his mouth. Then he began to prance around the hall with his head high, the bucket slapping against his chest.

"That's not what you're supposed to be doing at all!" Oberon shouted at him, but by the time Titania entered the room, warned by Radish that Oberon was about to beat the changeling, Oberon had joined him in the game with a toy shovel in his teeth. Titania laughed, and it seemed to her in that moment that she had two hearts in her, each pouring out an equivalent feeling toward the prancing figures, and she thought, *My men.*

They were not allowed to go home. It was hardly time for that, Dr. Beadle told them. The boy was barely better at all. This was going to be a three-year journey, and they were not even a week into it. They were going to have to learn patience if they were going to get through this. They were going to have to learn to take things one day at a time.

"I like to take the long view of things," Titania said in response, which had been true as a rule all through her long, long life. But lately her long view had contracted, and yet it was no comfort to take things, as Dr. Beadle suggested, as they came. Even without looking ahead into the uncertain future, there was always something to worry about. Oberon suggested she look to the boy and model her behavior after his, which was what he was doing, to which she replied that a child in crisis needed parents, not playmates, to which he said that wasn't what he meant at all, and they proceeded to quarrel about it, very softly, since the boy was sleeping.

Still, she gave it a try, proceeding with the boy on one of his daily migrations through the ward. Ever since he had been feeling better he went for multiple daily promenades, sometimes walking and sometimes in a little red buggy that he drove by making skibbling motions against the ground. He had to wear a mask, and his IV pole usually accompanied him, but these seemed not to bother him at all, so Titania tried not to let them bother her either, though she was pushing the pole and had to stoop now and then to adjust his mask when it slid over his chin.

The ward was almost the ugliest place she had ever seen, and certainly the ugliest place she had ever lived. Someone had tried, some time ago, to make it pretty, so there were big photographs in the hall of children at various sorts of play, and some of these were diverting, she supposed. But the pictures were few. In other places on the wall, someone had thought to put up bas-relief cartoon faces, about the size of a child's face, but the faces looked deformed to her eye—goblin faces—and they seemed uniformly to be in pain.

The boy was not allowed to wander beyond the filtered confines of the ward, so they went around and around, passing the posse of doctors on their rounds and the nurses at their stations and the other parents and children making their own circumnavigations. The boy called out hello and beeped his horn at everyone they met. They called back "Hello, Brad!" or "Hello, Brian!" or "Hello Billy!" since he answered to all those names. Everyone heard something different when they asked his name and Titania replied, "Boy."

She walked, step by step, not thinking of anything but the ugliness of the hall or the homeliness of Dr. Blork or the coarseness of Dr. Beadle's hair or the redness of the buggy. *There is no past and no future,* she told herself. *We have been here forever, and we will be here forever.* These thoughts were not exactly a comfort. She considered the other parents, staring at them as she passed, remembering to smile at them only when they smiled at her. It seemed a marvel to her that any mortal should suffer for lack of love, and yet she had never known a mortal who didn't feel unloved. There was enough love just in this ugly hallway, she thought, that no one should ever feel the lack of it again. She peered at the parents, imagining their hearts like machines, manufacturing surfeit upon surfeit of love for their children, and then wondered how something could be so awesome and so utterly powerless. A feeling like that ought to be able to move mountains, she thought, and then she wondered how she had come to such a sad place in her thoughts, when she meant to live entirely in the blank present. They went back to the room where Oberon was playing a video game with a brownie perched on his head.

"I hate this place," she told him.

They always called the good news good news, but for the bad news they always found another name. Dr. Blork would say they had taken a little detour on the way to recovery or had encountered a minor disappointment. Occasionally, when things really took a turn for the worse, he'd admit that something was, if not bad news, not very good news. It was an unusual experience, to wait anxiously every morning for the day's news and to read it—in the slips of paper they gave her that detailed the results of the previous day's tests and in the faces of the people who brought the news, in the pitch of their voices and in the absences they embraced, the words they did not use, and the things they did not say.

Oberon said the way that good news followed bad news, which followed good news on the tail of bad news, made him feel as if he were sailing in a ship on dangerous swells or riding an angry pony. Titania was the only one among them ever to have ridden on a roller coaster, but she didn't offer up the experience as an analogy, because it seemed insufficient to describe a process that to her felt less like a violent unpredictable ride and more like someone ripping out your heart on one day and then stuffing it back in your chest on the next. There was very little about it that she found unpredictable, and it was as much a comfort to know that the bad news would be followed by good as it was a slumping misery to know that the good news was not final. She was starting to believe that, more than anything, they had only lucky days and unlucky, that some cruel arbiter, mightier than either she or her husband, was presiding over this illness, and she wasn't always convinced, when Beadle or Blork told them something was working, that something they did was making the boy better.

His leukemia went away, which was good news, but not very quickly, which was bad news. His white blood cells would not grow back, which was bad news, and yet it would have been worse news if he had had too many of them. He had no fever, which was good news, until he got one, and that was very bad, though Blork seemed to intimate, in his stuttering way, that there were worse things that might happen. It meant they could not go home, though Beadle and Blork were always promising that a trip home was just around the corner. On the third week the fever went away and the white blood cells began to come back, but then Dr. Blork came to them with a droopy slip of paper documenting that the white blood cells were the evil, cancerous sort, and Titania could tell that there was not much worse he could think of to be telling them. They shuffled the boy's poisons, and brought him shots of thick white liquid that they shoved into his thighs. The shots made him scream like nothing else had, and she could not bear to be in the room when it happened, because she could not bear the look the boy gave her, which asked so clearly, *Shouldn't you kill them for hurting me like this?* The new poison turned him around again; the evil cells began to retire from his blood and his bones. But then his innards became irritated, and they decided, though he was always ravenous, that he couldn't eat.

"It's a crime," Oberon said. "Damn the *triglycerides,* the boy is hungry!" The nurses had hung up a bag of food for him, honey-colored liquid that went directly into his veins. Oberon slapped at the bag, and said it didn't look very satisfying. He fed the boy a bun, and a steak, and a crumpled cream puff, pulling each piece of food from his pocket with a flourish. Titania protested and threatened to get the nurse and even held the call button in her hand, almost pressing it while Oberon laughed and the boy shoved steak in his face. He threw it all up in an hour, the steak looking practically unchanged when it came back up, and became listless and squash-colored for three days. When they were asked if the boy had eaten anything, Oberon only shrugged.

But as soon as he had recovered, he was crying again for food, pleading with them all the time no matter how the nurses fiddled with the bag that was supposed to keep him sated. One morning the whole team showed up: Beadle and Blork and the junior-junior doctors whose names Titania could never remember and Alice and the nurse and another two or three mortals whose function, if it was something besides just skulking about, she never did discover. When Dr. Blork asked him how he was doing, he pleaded with them, too.

"Can't I have one tiny little feast?" he asked, and they laughed at him. They chucked his chin and tousled the place where his hair had been, and then they went out, leaving her with this dissatisfied, suffering creature. "Mama, please," he said all day, "just one little feast. I won't ask again, I promise." Oberon was silent and left the room eventually, once again crying his useless tears, and Titania told the boy he would only become sick if he ate, that even one feast might mean another week before he could eat again. "Don't think of eating," she said, "think of this bird, instead." And she pulled a parrot out from within the folds of her robe. But the boy only asked if he could eat it.

He wore her down toward evening. Oberon had still not returned, and when she sent Radish to fetch him she said only, "He's still weeping. See?" And she held a thimble up, brimming with tears. Titania sighed, wanting to run from the boy and his anxious, unhappy hunger, which had seemed to her as the day dragged on to represent, and then to become, a hunger for something else besides food. He didn't want food. He wanted to be well, to run on the hill under the starlight, to ride on the paths in the park in a little cart pulled by six raccoons. He wanted to spend a day not immersed in hope and hopelessness. She could not give him any of that right now.

"All right, love," she said, "just one bite." And she brought out a chocolate from her bag, but before she could give it to him Oberon returned, calling for her to stop because he had something better. He cleared a space on the bed and put down a little sack there, and very delicately, pinching with his thumb and his forefinger, removed all the ingredients of a tiny feast and laid them on the bed.

"It will be faster if you help," he told her, as he squinted to chop up a mote-sized carrot. So she picked up a bag the size of her thumb, emptied out the beans from them, and began to snap. The boy kept trying to eat things raw at first, but Oberon slapped his hand away and told him to be patient, and eventually he helped as well, twisting the heads off the little chickens when Oberon handed them to him, and laughing when they danced a few seconds in his palm. It took a long time to prepare the feast, though they had more and more help, as more faeries popped up in the room, some of whom were sized better for the work. Still more of them gathered round in an audience, stuck to the walls, crowding the shelves, perched on the lintel, all of them muttering opinions as the preparation went on, that they would have baked the fish, not seared it, and salted the cabbage but not the asparagus, and chosen caramel over fudge for the cake.

When it was done the boy ate the whole thing and did not share a morsel, which was exactly as it was supposed to be. Aside from the size of it, there was nothing magical about the food. It shouldn't have sated him any more than half a dozen peanuts, but even the aroma calmed him down as they were cooking, and by the time he had finished off the last tack-sized pastry and dime-sized cake, he was very quiet again. He looked around the bed and around the room, as if for more food, so when he opened his mouth wide Titania thought he was going to shout or cry. But he burped instead, a tiny little noise, commensurate with what he had eaten.

She had lost him once, just for a little while. He liked to hide but didn't do it very well, too giggly ever to make his location a secret. But she woke one morning to find him gone from his customary place underneath her arm, and she couldn't find him in the usual places, in a lump under the covers at the foot of the bed, or on the floor next to the bed, or even under the bed. "Is this a game?" she asked her husband, shaking him awake, and she demanded, "Where have you hidden the boy?"

He had not hidden him anywhere, and no faerie had made off with him or used his parts in a spell or put him in a pie to eat. But all through the early part of the evening he was nowhere to be found, though she commanded the whole host to search for him under the hill. She began to suspect that his mortal mother had stolen him back and not even done her the courtesy of returning the little hobgoblin that had been left in his place. Oberon could not convince her of how extremely unlikely this would be, so she strapped on her armor, greave by greave. For a while Oberon was able to get it off her as fast as she could put it on, nuzzling her and speaking ever so soothingly about how the boy would be found, but eventually she outstripped him. She placed her helm on her head and called the host to war, and all the peace-loving faeries of Buena Vista Park reluctantly put on their silver mail and took up their ruby-tipped spears and made ready to stream out into the Mission to slay the woman who had stolen their Mistress's child. But Doorknob found him before they could march out of the woods. He was under a cupboard, sound asleep, and one had only to sniff at him to understand that he had wandered thirsty from bed to the kitchen, drunk at length from the wine bowl instead of the water bowl, and perhaps had had a solitary toddling drunken party all his own before hiding himself away to sleep. Titania wanted to kiss him and hold him, of course, but it occurred to her that there were other things she could do right then as well, shrink him down enough to carry him around in her mouth, or make him a hump on her back, or chain him to her, foot to foot. He woke as she was considering these things, and blinked at her and then at the faeries all attired for war, and turned on his side, and went back to sleep.

"What a terrible gift you have given me," she said to her husband. They were sitting at the boy's bedside, not holding hands, but their knees were touching. There had been bad news, and then worse news, and then the worst news yet. The bad cells were back in his blood, and he had a fever, and there was an infection in the bones of his face. Dr. Blork said a fungus was growing there and had admitted that this news was in fact bad, and he had looked both awkward and grave as he sat with them, twisting his stethoscope around in his hands and apologizing for the turn of events, though not exactly accepting responsibility for the failures of the treatment. Oberon had said that mushrooms were some of the friendliest creatures he knew, and he could not understand how they could possibly represent a threat to anyone, but Dr. Blork shook his head, and said that this fungus was nobody's friend, and further explained that the presence of the new infection compromised the doctors' ability to poison him anymore, and that for that reason the leukemia cells were having a sort of holiday.

The boy was sleeping. They had brought back the morphine for his pain, so he was rarely awake and not very happy when he was. Titania moved from her chair to the bed and took his hand. Even asleep he pulled it away. "A terrible gift," she said.

"Don't say such things," Oberon said.

"Terrible," she said. "Terrible, terrible." She sat on the bed, taking the boy's hand over and over again as he pulled it away, and told her husband she was afraid that when the boy died he would take away with him not just all the love she felt for him but all the love she felt for Oberon too, and all the love she had felt for anything or anyone in the world. He would draw it after him, as if by decree of some natural law that magic could not violate, and then she would be left with nothing.

"Do not speak of such things, my love," her husband said, and he kissed her. She let him do that. And she let him put his hands inside her dress, and let him draw her over to the narrow little couch where they were supposed to sleep at night. She tried to pretend that it was any other night under the hill, when they would roll and wrestle with each other while the boy slept next to them oblivious. They were walked in upon a number of times. But everyone who walked in saw something different, and no one remembered what they had seen after they turned and fled the room. The night nurse, coming in to change some IV fluids, saw two blankets striking and grappling with each other on the couch.

A nursing assistant saw a mass of snakes and cats twisting over one another, sighing and hissing. Dr. Beadle actually managed to perceive Oberon's mighty thrusting bottom and went stumbling back out into the hall, temporarily blinded.

One evening Dr. Beadle came in alone, Blorkless, and sat down on the bed, where the boy was sweating and sleeping, dreaming, Titania could tell, of something unpleasant. "I think it's time to talk about our goals for Brad," he said, and put a hand on the Beastie over the boy's foot, and wiggled the foot back and forth as he talked, asking them whether they were really doing the best thing for the boy, whether they should continue with a treatment that was not making him better.

"What else would we do?" Titania asked him, not understanding what he was saying but suddenly not wanting him in the room, or on the bed, or touching the boy.

"We would make him comfortable," he said.

"Isn't he comfortable?" Titania asked. "Isn't he sleeping?"

"Not...finally," Dr. Beadle said. "We could be doing more and less. We could stop doing what isn't helping, and not do anything that would prolong...the suffering." Then Oberon, who had been eyeing the man warily from the couch, leaped up, shouting, "Smotherer! Smother-doctor! Get back to Hell!"

"You don't understand," Dr. Beadle said. "I don't mean that at all. Not at *all!*" He looked at Titania with an odd combination of pleading and pity. "Do you understand?" he asked her. In reply she drew herself up, and shook off every drop of the disguising glamour, and stood there entirely revealed to him. He seemed to shrink and fell off the bed, and while he was not kneeling purposefully in front of her, he happened to end up on his knees. She leaned over him and spoke very slowly.

"You will do everything mortally possible to save him," she said.

The night the boy died there were a number of miraculous recoveries on the ward. They were nothing that Titania did on purpose. She did not care about the other pale bald-headed children in their little red wagons and masks, did not care about the mothers whose grief and worry seemed to elevate their countenances to resemble Titania's own. Indifference was the key to her magic; she and her husband could do nothing for someone they loved. So all the desperate hope she directed at the boy was made manifest around her in rising blood counts and broken fevers and unlikely remissions. It made for a different sort of day, with so much good news around it seemed hardly anyone noticed that the boy had died.

Oberon sat on the floor in a corner of the room, trying to quiet the brokenhearted wailing of the Beastie but not making a sound himself. Titania sat on the bed with the boy. A nurse had been in to strip him of his tubes and wires and had drawn a sheet up to just under his chin. His eyes were closed, and his face looked oddly less pale than it had in life and illness. The glamour was in tatters; Oberon was supposed to be maintaining it, and now Titania found she didn't really care enough to take up the work. No nurse had been in for hours, and the last to come had lain down upon the clover-covered floor and giggled obtrusively until some thoughtful faerie had put an egg in her mouth to shut her up. Before she had gone drunk, the nurse had mentioned something about funeral arrangements, and Titania was thinking of those now. "We should take him home," she said aloud, and no one stirred, but she said it again every few minutes, and by twos and threes the faeries crowding the room began to say it too, and then they started to build a bier for him, tearing out the cabinets and bending the IV pole and ripping the sheets and blankets. When they were done the walls were stripped and the furniture was wrecked. Twelve faeries of more or less equal size bore the bier, and they waited while another dozen brownies hammered at the doorway to widen the exit. When they were ready they all looked to Titania, who nodded her permission. Oberon was the last to leave, standing only when Doorknob tugged at his arm after the room had emptied.

There was no disguise left to cover them. People saw them for what they were, a hundred and two faeries and a dead boy proceeding down the hall with harps and flutes, crowded in the service elevator with fiddles and lutes, marching out of the hospital with drums. Mortals gaped. Dogs barked. Cats danced on their hind feet, and birds followed them by the dozen, hopping along and cocking their heads from side to side. It was early afternoon. The fog was breaking against the side of the hill and Buena Vista Park was brilliantly sunny. They passed through the ordinary trees of the park, and then into the extraordinary trees of their own realm, and came to the door in the hill and passed through that as well.

They marched into the great hall and put down the bier. The music played on for a while, then faltered little by little, and the players came to feel unsure of why they were playing. Then the hall was quiet, because they didn't know what to do next. They had never celebrated or mourned a death before. They were all looking to Titania to speak, but it was Oberon who finally broke the silence, announcing from the back of the room that the Beastie had died of its grief.

EVERYTHING IS BEAUTIFUL

BL Pawelek

THE REST OF the house is asleep. No one moves on the streets, no noises, no moon above.

I turn on the red lamp with brilliant white light, directed immediately to the red couch. I whisper into my son's room, hold him in my arms, bring him to the light and begin.

Tonight, I start just above his right ear and down to the nape of the neck, over both cowlicks with the mess they cause, and finally to the longer, sun-bleached hairs which lounge across the top. The rest was completed last night.

My son has 89,812 hairs on his angel head. This is the lowest count this month. The result is possibly due to:

- ocean swimming
- multiple sessions in a rough-and-tumble jumpie
- summer heat in Southern California
- he took a pretty good pop to the head today

Sometimes I rest from the count and watch him sleep, look out the windows, or listen for sounds. This week, it took nine hours, and thankfully no start-overs. When he was younger, it was so much easier with less hair. Thankfully, he has brown hair. Brown-haired people have less hair.

I remember 100 (actually hit that count twice after losing some hair as an infant) and 1,000. When he turned five and counted more than 80,000 it became more difficult.

I turn off the light and all goes dark. I pat my boy's brown hair, bring him back to his bed, and cover him. I slide into mine and smile thinking of the number, whispering it out loud. The boy is growing, and everything is normal, everything is beautiful.

MASHA'ALLAH

Mariah K. Young

IT WILL PROBABLY snow on the pass to Reno, Sullivan Gibbs thinks as he pulls the black Lincoln town car against the curb. If he and Suze and Cherise leave tomorrow night, maybe they'll miss the storm, let it pass them, and they'll be in the casinos after the storm has cleared. Suze is probably packing her casino-wear right now, and he imagines his wife in her gold and black lamé smock, shimmering tights, and her silver slippers, the lucky flats she always wears when they go to San Pablo or Reno or any of the Indian casinos between. "Silver and gold, Sully baby," she will coo at him on the drive through the Sierra, fluffing her dyed-black hair every now and then. When they were first married, she would prop her right foot (sans silver shoe) in the crook of the passenger side mirror and lay her long arm along the ridge of the seat, her fingers grazing the hair on his neck. He wants to turn to the empty passenger seat as a reflex, as if to catch a glimpse of the twenty-three-year-old Suze reclining across the black leather. Of course she isn't there, and she isn't twenty-three anymore. He laughs a little at that, how far he and Suze are from twenty-three, and how they are only getting farther away.

The rain drives hard against the townie windows, slithering down the waxed exterior. Mr. Edward's flight is at 2:20 in the afternoon, and Sully has the executive at San Francisco International Airport at 12:55, allowing a healthy amount of time for check-in and security. Sully opens the back door with one hand and holds an umbrella out with the other to shield his passenger.

"Enjoy Cincinnati, sir," Sully says as Mr. Edwards takes his briefcase and then the umbrella from Sully, lifts himself from the seat, and strides toward the sliding glass doors without a word. Sully waits a beat until his regular is inside and then quickly jumps back into the townie, dusting away the water beads from his cap and wool coat. Pulling off his cap and looking in the rearview, his cheeks are ruddy, and the wet has made his gray temples black again. This is what he needs to stay young, he thinks: a fine, perpetual mist. While the clouds are patching across the bay, the rain hasn't let up over the city, and the wind bites cold.

The cell phone beeps beside him. Cherise. He checks his watch and answers.

"Salaam aleikum, Uncle Sully! Keef al-halak?" His niece's voice bubbles like Alka-Seltzer. Sully never quite knows how to respond to her Arabic. He feels like he should try to answer her like she wants to be answered but he always trips over the syllables, mangles the words. So he keeps it simple.

"I'm all right, sweetie. What's going on?"

"Nothing, I'm done with class and I'm getting on BART. I can't wait for Reno!" He pictures her on the train platform in West Oakland, her backpack slung low on one shoulder and her silver-hooped ear pressed into the phone, how the rain is letting up on that side of the bay and she can probably see the sun over the water, feel a breath of warmth. "I wanted to ask you, though..." Cherise's voice curls into a question. "Is it okay if Mouhamad comes to dinner tomorrow night, before we leave?"

Sully grimaces. One hungry eighteen-year-old in the house is enough, and the last thing he needs is a hungry boyfriend coming around. Another person at his dinner table chattering in a language he doesn't know. "All right." He nods a little. "But he's not staying too long—"

"Toyeb, toyeb, I know," Cherise says. Sully thinks this must be the tone that parents complain about. She says goodbye in Arabic and Sully says goodbye in English.

Sully rolls down the window and pulls a pack of Parliaments from the glove box, lights the last white stick in the pack. He's not supposed to smoke in the townie, as per the new company policy. The management firm that took over the car service a few months ago has been getting on all the drivers, especially the ones nearing retirement like Sully, about what they call "professionalism," as in the new black suit policy for drivers and annotating the logs for time spent between pick-ups. Sully and the other drivers have been doing their best to comply without really complying. On top of that, his next pick-up, Mr. Ferdinand, has a notoriously sensitive nose: if he detects smoke or food smells or even a heavy air freshener, he starts sneezing and sniffling and sniveling about his hyper-allergenic bronchial-esophageal tract. But Sully doesn't have to pick up Mr. Ferdinand until 3:30 p.m. at the Hilton on Embarcadero, leaving plenty of air-out time. So Sully smokes, sometimes blowing out the window, other times letting the blue smoke drift up against the windshield, its trails straight and undisturbed.

A little farther down the terminal, about a hundred yards away, a fresh batch of arrivals streams out of the glass doors. They look for awnings or run for the parking lot, bending their heads against the rain, with their luggage dawdling behind them. Sully looks at the clock, considers the time. He could pick up a fare easy, maybe even two if the traffic isn't too bad. Sometimes he trolls for cash fares, even though the yellow cabbies give him shit and threaten to call the airport cops when they see his townie in the cab pick-up line. He's a poacher, sure, but in the end, catching fares is all about right place and right time—at some point every driver has swooped in to scoop a fare from some other cabbie who wasn't willing to cut a red light or hit the gas a little. It beats heading back to the garage on Harrison Street and sleeping with his cap pulled over his eyes like the other old-timers, riding out the afternoon shifts until they retire. Besides, he could use the extra cash, what with Cherise in the house, and the trip to Reno. He always gives Suze the money from picking up fares, and he loves the look on her face when she finds the money tucked in her purse and asks him, "What poor bastard did you shake down so I could have a good time?" She takes care of the bills, never knows how Sully drums up the extra cash, and he likes it that way—Sully can kiss her forehead and never answer her, just do his best Don Corleone as they head into the casino.

The townie creeps at an easy fifteen along the arrival terminals, staying away from the intersections where airport cops stand around and the security level alerts are on display. Sully chucks the last of his cigarette into the falling rain. He looks for the arrivals that scream "business class" with their roll-away leather luggage and matching computer satchels. The ones with rumpled suits are the most likely to jump into the cab and bark a destination, and they're the least likely to ask why Sully doesn't have a meter or his license laminated and taped to the back window. They seem to prefer the townie—they will walk past the yellow cabs with their burgundy velour seats pocked with cigarette burns and make for Sully, just beyond the baggage terminal. Usually it's quick and clean. He gets the fare to the destination, gets his flat rate of forty dollars and sometimes a tip, and he's back in the city with time to spare in picking up Mr. So-and-So or Ms. Blah Blah Blah. On top of all that, the Associates of Hedrick, Polk, and Lardner catch the cost of gas.

On his third pass around the arrival terminals, Sully spots a woman holding a newspaper over her head at the far end of the American Airlines baggage claim. She's been there on each pass, almost ten minutes, and her coat is soaked through. Tucked beneath a sliver of concrete beside the sliding doors, the wind drives the rain at her. The wipers barely clear the windshield before it blurs with rain again. Normally Sully would pass up a fare like her—he sticks with the suits, always has. He can see one farther down the terminal with just a briefcase and an open umbrella. But the rain is coming down hard and he decides he'll pick her up; all she has is a newspaper that's warping in her hands. The townie sloshes up to the curb and it's then that he sees her pregnant belly, which is pulling her closed coat tight around her. Her pink sweater peeks out in little triangle openings between each stressed button. Sully tries to remember the last time he saw a woman that pregnant at the airport. They're few and far between, he's sure of that.

Sully stops, pops the trunk, taps his black hat over his thinning hair, and rolls down the window. "Need a ride, miss?"

The woman looks at Sully from under her sopping newspaper but says nothing. He gets out of the car and walks over, his steps avoiding the rain that runs quick through the gutter. He motions to the suitcase at her feet. "Can I take that?"

After a beat of silence, she steps toward the townie. Sully opens the rear door and gives his most courteous smile. She twists her torso as she gets in, pulling her body in first and her belly last. Sully picks up the suitcase, which is much heavier than it looked at her feet, pitches it in the trunk, and shuffles around the car into the driver's seat.

"Do you know how to get to the Skyline?" the woman asks in a throaty voice. Sully adjusts the rearview, taking a quick look at the fare. The woman rakes a wet lock of brown hair across her forehead. Her diamond earrings glimmer like the raindrops stuck on the windows. Her tan handbag matches her tan heels. Everything about her looks expensive.

"Off Redwood Road in the hills?" Sully and his friends used to drag their Fords on Redwood and Skyline when they were kids. They'd race up and down the road, dark with tall pines. Those country club pricks at the Skyline always called the cops on them before they could make any juicy bets or settle some real scores.

She looks directly at him in the rearview mirror. "Of course."

He feels a tiny twitch above his eyebrow press and then release. "Sixty dollars," Sully says and pulls away from the curb. He wonders why this woman doesn't have a ride. She looks like the type who would have a car service at her beck and call, or some eager husband to pick her up at the very least. But he dismisses the thought. You never can tell, he thinks, and merges into the left lane. With the rain and the afternoon traffic another two hours away, he figures he'll be across the bridge in thirty minutes, have her in the Oakland hills in another fifteen. All told, he should be at the Hilton on Embarcadero right on schedule. He might even have time to swing by the Thai joint off the 101 freeway for spring rolls.

They are more or less silent as they leave the city. The woman adjusts herself in her seat and shakes out her damp hair. The leather seat groans and squeaks under her. She asks him to turn off the sports radio, and he turns it down. She digs in her bag, the contents rustling with little clicks and clanks every time her arm dives deeper. She unbuttons her coat and wiggles out of it noisily. Sully waits for it, and sure enough, out comes the cell phone. She talks loud enough for him to hear: "Oh, Chella, Chicago was terrible. I couldn't come to any kind of agreement with him...There's simply no talking to him about any of it...Of course they didn't want me to fly...You wouldn't believe the paperwork just to board! On top of that the production was atrocious...You wouldn't believe. The theatre was so cramped my ankles swelled up in an hour... I'd rather deliver vaginally than sit through another Molière venture..."

From the mirror Sully sees that she's huge, big-as-a-house pregnant, as Suze would say. Lately Suze has been pointing out the pregnant ladies at the grocery store. She buys the gossip rags and reads about Hollywood actresses popping the munchkins out. It has been on her mind lately, Sully can tell, that they never had kids. Sully's buddy Chuck says it's "the change"—says his wife got a little funny once she hit fifty. Sully knows it's not that, it's Cherise. Suze's sisters had no problems in the baby department, and so it was assumed that Sully's soldiers weren't up to the task. Suze never says anything about it, doesn't blame him, at least not out loud. Just last week, Sully came home and saw Suze watching their niece asleep, curled up on the love seat with the TV still on. Suze took in breaths real slow, with her hand pressed tightly to the hallway frame, and she walked away from Sully when he came up behind her.

Off the bridge and onto land, the five-lane traffic slows and stops and slowly starts again. Inching into Oakland, Sully ignores the woman as best he can and thinks about dinner tonight—Suze always bakes chicken on Tuesdays—and how tomorrow night Cherise will bring that boyfriend over for dinner. He will eat three helpings of everything and scrape the platters clean, and he and Cherise will go on and on in Arabic while Suze grins and Sully chews. Sully's seen worse, been worse himself, but still, he feels like he's on watch. Since Cherise moved up from Reno, Sully has started thinking about her like a daughter, even though most times it feels like he's wearing a borrowed hat that's too snug around the brim. Cherise moved in at the beginning of fall when she was accepted at Cal Berkeley. She took up linguistics because of that boyfriend, something Sully's been meaning to have a talk with her about, how she shouldn't get too wrapped up in some guy.

She's a good kid, though: she found an office job at her campus, and she's always studying her textbooks. Cherise wants to be a translator, and she's forever rattling off some phrase or string of words, every English word followed with one in Arabic. Sometimes it sounds like a penny sliding and clinking around in a glass jar, the way she speaks: *good morning, Aunt; good evening, Uncle. Coffee, apple, car, record player,* and whenever he comes in from a smoke on the porch, *ashtray*. Suze laughs and laughs at this.

If Suze were here, she'd be ticking off questions about the pregnancy to the woman sitting rigidly and speaking coldly into her phone. She'd ask when she was due, was it a boy or girl, what the name would be. Her eyes would get real big and real small at the same time; her eyes become little slits when she can't stop smiling. She'd want to know all the things about the birth that were as far removed from Sully's life as Cherise's Arabic.

They are edging toward downtown on the overpass; the rain has slowed the movements of the whole freeway, with brake lights forming in bunches like a clot lodging and then dislodging down a narrow artery.

"Oh...Oh, Jesus."

Sully hears the woman, though her voice barely registers over the engine and the rain. He waits a beat, glances in the rearview. He only sees her hair.

"Everything okay back there?" Sully says.

"You have to get around this traffic." The woman readjusts in her seat. She slides to the other side of the cab, then moves back to her original position.

"What's wrong?"

"You have to drive faster," she commands in a hoarse voice. Sully turns back to see the woman's head hanging, her folds of brown hair bobbing slightly with the slow creep of the car.

"What, are you having it right now?" Sully says. And then he realizes that she is, she must be, what else could it be? A heat rises in Sully's chest and his body pushes against the seatbelt as if the townie were being slammed into from the left side. All lanes are crawling. The red lights stare back at him. He leans on the horn for lack of anything else to do. A chorus of horns responds from behind and in front and across five lanes.

"Turn around! Take me to UCSF!"

Sully motions to the wall of rain and red lights. He tries to think of a polite way of saying "Imfuckingpossible."

"I can't maneuver to the other side of the bridge."

She seems to have bigger things on her mind, because she doesn't respond for a while, what seems like hours. Traffic opens up intermittently, and Sully slams on and off the brake with each opportunity to move. He can hear the woman jostling in the backseat, and finally she shouts, "Lay off the lead-foot shit!"

He closes his eyes for a second, and he remembers his father's advice about the eggshell under the brake, how to gently push on the foot pedals or else an imaginary eggshell would crack. He wonders if she's in pain or just in shock. In the back he can hear her panting in that short-short-long, short-short long pattern he'd seen on TV. It all seems to be happening too quickly; he had assumed that birth was a slow process with time between stages to adjust, to prepare. He doesn't know anything about it personally, and he's acutely aware of it for the first time in his life.

"Hey, don't do that in here!" The words leave his mouth as he realizes that some things refuse to abide by plans or orders.

The woman looks at him in the mirror, her eyes wild and pale.

Sully's hands are slick on the steering wheel. "All right...here's what's gonna happen. Highland's the closest hospital. I'm taking you there."

The woman squeaks, a hiccup of protest. "Don't you dare take me to Highland! I'm not giving birth next to some junkie in the waiting room!" she bellows, her hand gripping the backseat, straining to pull the rest of herself closer to Sully's ear. The white hospital towers are almost in sight, just a few blocks from the highway. Sully accelerates towards the 14th Avenue off-ramp. He turns to the backseat for a second. The woman's face is red and flushed, and the windows around her have fogged into a strange halo around her head. Her hands are gnarled knots pressed together, as if she could keep the baby inside long enough to get out of the townie and anywhere but East Oakland. Sully's eyes dart between the red lights in front of him and the blue eyes behind him.

"Not up for discussion," he sputters. Traffic opens up in the right lane and Sully dives in and speeds until he's following the Cadillac in front of them by no more than a foot or so.

The woman rolls her head back against the headrest and mumbles. "I had three weeks, I had three more weeks..." She is either half laughing or half crying, Sully can't tell which. Her belly seems to be pushing farther and farther out, and Sully is sure if he turns to look he'll get damp pink cashmere and a protruding navel in his eye.

Christ, Sully thinks. I should have picked up the suit in the next terminal.

Her phone chirps. She shakes out her hair and answers, her voice strong and almost steady. "Elliot...Elliot. Shut up. It's starting...Yes, I know...Some cab...Stop your babbling and page Dr. Hennepin. You're a sack of shit, Elliot! No, he's taking me to Highland. Against my wishes." Her voice growls on the last phrase.

Sully gases it down the off-ramp and nails the brake hard at an intersection—the egg would have cracked.

"Stop praying and get it together, Elliot! Do what you have to do! Have the team on standby, and get someone over to Highland to get me!" She slaps the phone shut and reels in the backseat, her breaths heavy and loud.

Dammit, Sully thinks, his wheels squealing with the rain as he sails through a red light. Dammit dammit dammit. It becomes a mantra in his head as soon as the smell hits him. It's damp and hovers in his nostrils, and it smells like sex and sweat and mucous and something else that he can't quite name, a smell that he, as a man, isn't supposed to know anything about. The scent is faint but it sits heavy in the air. It reminds him of when he was younger and he could go with Suze all night, the sheets under their bodies damp. He thinks about the leather seats and the thick carpeting on the floor of the back. "God dammit," he finally says it aloud.

"Fuck you!" the woman howls.

Sully accelerates. "Just keep your knees together and fucking don't push!" he says more loudly than he means to. He turns a hard right onto East 31st and up the short hill to the ambulance bay. His hands are wrapped tight around the steering wheel, as tightly as he imagines the woman is holding onto her belly.

He maneuvers around the open doors of an ambulance and stops under the concrete enclosure near the entrance. The rain running off the beige stucco canopy makes Sully feel like he's under the ledge of a waterfall. He throws the car in park and scrambles out of the townie, runs into the waiting room and is almost too out of breath to shout, "Some lady is having a baby in my car!" He commandeers a wheelchair out of an orderly's gloved hands. When he gets back outside with the orderly in tow, the woman has already kicked the passenger door open and is trying to roll herself out. One of her heels has come off and is rocking on its side on the floor of the car. The seat leather is shiny wet, not in puddles but a trail.

The orderly and two security guards ease the woman onto a quickly produced gurney, and she begins barking at them as they wheel her through the emergency room entrance. "Get my bags from that son of a bitch cab driver!" is the last thing he hears before the glass doors slide shut. The orderly is still outside, and Sully opens the trunk and slumps her luggage into the wheelchair. He surveys the damage as the orderly rolls her bags into the hospital. Looking at the soggy interior and the tan heel that remain, Sully realizes he wasn't paid. If there were ever a time he'd earned his fare, this was it. He sniffs the back and detects that body smell, mixing with the humidity.

"Hey, you got any towels or anything?" Sully turns to the orderly, but he is already inside and the doors have closed.

Auto Bob's on Seminary doesn't have the dazzling array of leather cleaners Sully assumed they'd carry, and the only leather shop he can think of offhand, one on International Boulevard, is closed. At the 7-Eleven, he buys a pack of Parliaments and lets the engine idle in the lot, watching the rainclouds crack and drift across the puddles in the parking lot. He decides to call Chuck, who runs a dry cleaner shop on High Street. As he drives, his fists work the steering wheel until there are hot patches under his palms. He went through a package of paper towels wiping up the backseat before the ambulance drivers told him to move the townie out. He asked one of the EMTs what they did if a woman's water breaks in the ambulance, and the EMT just laughed and said she requisitions a new gurney.

That smell won't let up, even with all four windows rolled down. It's clinging to the upholstery, and the seat still feels sticky when he reaches back to touch it. There's a smudge where the woman sat, and Sully's not sure if there's really a slight discoloration on the material or if he's being paranoid. The damp patch of mottled black looks vaguely reddish, like a splotch of bleach that was allowed to sit on the leather too long. He checks his watch—he has seventy-five minutes to take care of the smell and the wet and be at the Hilton to take Mr. Ferdinand back to his condo in the Sunset. The only bright side is that the rain has let up.

As he parks in front, Sully can see Chuck arguing with his new cashier. Chuck drops the laundry tickets on the counter when he sees Sully through the window, his one gold tooth shining. It's been a few weeks—they haven't seen each other since they went to Cache Creek last payday. Sully relays the tale, points to the backseat. Chuck goes out to look in the back, rubs the stubble on his chin, and laughs hard before bringing out a handful of terrycloth towels and a solution in a spray bottle for Sully to try.

Sully goes at the floor first, giving the carpet a generous series of sprays and a thorough scrub. After ten minutes, three scrubs, and several of Chuck's towels, Sully sticks his nose an inch from the carpet, inhaling deep until he's almost dizzy. His back aches from hunching, and he decides to step out and stand up straight while considering how to go about cleaning the actual seat. He consults Chuck on the broader points of leather care. Chuck tells him to spray and wipe, all the while tossing the woman's high heel from hand to hand.

"Trolling the tarmac again?" Chuck sucks his teeth and taps a Kool out of the pack, points a filter toward Sully. "So where are you two heading? San Pab? Chumash?"

Sully leans against the trunk, takes the cigarette, and lights up. "Supposed to go to Reno this weekend. Suze and I are gonna drive up Friday afternoon. Cherise too." Sully makes a point of exhaling fully before turning back into the cab for another survey of the scene. It's almost time to go and fetch Mr. Ferdinand. He's not sure what will piss the old man off more, the smell of smoke or the smell of birth. The suit will probably make him take the car back, probably bitch to Mendoza, the new supervisor and the face of the new management firm. Mendoza has already been on Sully about the mileage on the odometer and the gas receipts he's turned in. Sully suddenly wishes he'd made a point of getting paid. It was the least the preggers could have done.

"You making a weekend of it?" Chuck asks and looks toward the clouds breaking in light and dark patches. He coughs a puff of smoke. He and Sully smoked their first cigarettes together at Oakland High.

"Well, we've been meaning to go up for a while, and Cherise wants to visit her folks. There's that new poker section at the Horseshoe, so that'll be good. And you know Suze is all over the machines. Regular family vacation," Sully says, and catches himself in the kind of chuckle that only comes when you say something that surprises yourself. He turns and sprays the solution again into the back. It smells vaguely like soap and overripe fruit.

Sully swirls the towel across the leather in figure eights. Suze loves Reno; Sully tries to take her every few months. Her sister, Cherise's mother, lives up there and they always visit, but really Suze loves the slots, can stay plugged into one for hours. "You remember that trip last spring? She played a quarter that got her six hundred dollars. She was jumping around like a kid, and I'll be damned if most of it didn't go straight back into that same machine." Sully works at the spot on the leather, watching the seat give slightly with every swipe of the towel. "She found a machine she thought liked her, and she stuck with it until her six hundred got whittled down to two. She didn't want to be far from the lucky machine that had paid out, so the rest went into the next slot over. We didn't make a dime that trip."

Sully inches out of the back, finds his cigarette balanced on the edge of the shop's window. He inhales and thinks that same logic is probably what keeps Suze with him—Sully was a good bet once, and she's too loyal or too stubborn to admit that he didn't pay out the way he was supposed to. No kids, a pissant pension, and they are still living in the same house on 26th Street, the house that they were supposed to move out of once he got a management job at the shipping yard and they had their first batch of rugrats. But Sully was let go from the warehouse during the last round of cuts, and he and Suze were too busy staying afloat themselves to think about adding a small squealing mouth to feed. He'd taken the job driving the townie as a quick fix, just like she took on extra hours at the dress shop, but the rough patch became the long stretch. The years slipped by like pulls on the handle, one after another until you looked at your empty quarter bucket and wondered if you really were at that same machine the whole time.

The cigarette is nothing but filter and Sully tosses it into the gutter.

Chuck cranes his neck into the cab. "When you think luck's on your side, you get superstitious," he says. He would know, Sully thinks—Chuck wears the same pair of black ribbed socks every time they go to Reno, or even just to the casino in San Pablo. Sully nods. He keeps his father's billfold in his back left pocket whenever he plays craps. Suze always wears her silver shoes, those flats he bought for her so many trips ago from an outlet store on the way back from Vegas. The heels are worn down and there are creases bent deep into the patent leather, but she still wears them every single time.

Sully takes off his black cap, scratches his head, and then pulls it back on snug. "You smell anything?"

"I think you're pretty fucked, my friend," Chuck laughs. When Sully doesn't join him, he straightens out, inhales loud and deep enough for Sully to hear, and then shakes his head. Nonetheless, he goes into his shop and comes out with another spray bottle.

"Fabric refresher. Maybe it'll work the same as it does on mothball smell."

When Cherise first moved in and Sully was still figuring out how to have an eighteen-year-old in the house after twenty-six years of just him and Suze, the easiest thing to talk about was school. They'd sit across from each other in the kitchen or the living room, him in his easy chair and her on the couch—regardless of where she was, her books were always spread out around her. He'd ask what she was studying, and she'd prattle on in Arabic a while, occasionally finding a clean piece of paper and writing in thick lines and abrupt curls. Sully would smile, nod, and then ask about what else she was learning. She talked about her psychology class and every morning her professor told the class to be quiet for a few minutes and visualize how they wanted things to happen that day. Sully had thought it sounded like horseshit, but Cherise looked so earnest, her eyes closed and her lips bent in a half smile as she talked about imagining Arabic words flying from her mouth in her voice. She said every morning she visualized the calligraphy flowing out of her pen as if it were a geyser spewing ink.

"Masha'allah," she had said and smoothed the curled edges of her notebook, and Sully felt like he should have understood her, that he'd heard her say the word so many times he should have picked it up by osmosis. But she saved him, didn't make him ask her again what it meant. "What God wills, Uncle Sully, what God wants," she had said, then turned back to her notebook and scribbled out the word for him to see.

"Masha'allah," he breathes as he rounds the corner onto Embarcadero, all the windows down, his neck cold. He says it like he remembers Cherise saying it, thick on the first syllable, his voice as sure as hers would be. He hopes he is saying it right.

He is thirteen minutes early to pick up Mr. Ferdinand. When he pulls up to the curb and throws the townie into park, he reluctantly takes another look in the backseat. The leather has been buffed and sprayed and buffed again, and he wonders if the woman's baby has already been born or if it is still laboring into the world, its lungs still content in water.

As the second hand ticks loudly from his watch he tries to visualize: the wetness will have dried completely, and there will be no trace of the smell, carried away by Chuck's miracle spray and the push of the bay winds. Mr. Ferdinand emerges from the revolving glass doors, his steps deliberate and his copy of the *Times* folded neatly under his arm. He will enter the back without comment, and perhaps halfway to the Sunset he will ask Sully who he's been banging on company time, and then he'll laugh and turn back to the paper. Sully will drop off the townie at the garage on Harrison, Mendoza will have gone home for the day, and there will be no traffic on the way back to 26th Street.

Suze and Cherise will just be serving the chicken legs, greens, and potatoes when Sully walks in the door. He will come home and they will eat and he will ask the girls if they are excited to go to Reno. What time should they leave on Friday, or should they drive up early Saturday? Sully won't mind doing the lion's share of the driving, and the highway through the mountains will be salted and clear of snow. When they get there, he'll have cash for them—tens and twenties to press into their palms like secrets—and he'll tell them to have fun, go shopping. Cherise will thank him in Arabic and he will understand her, say "Masha'allah," and Cherise will guffaw and be impressed. Suze will pinch his left earlobe, kiss his right cheek, and click her silver heels together for luck, as she always does before she heads to the slots.

HOME FOR THANKSGIVING

Rebecca K. O'Connor

I DREAMT OF PLACES other than Southern California this Thanksgiving, wild places where I could hunt with my falcon. I had a whole week off to do as I please, a week to loose my peregrine falcon to the sky while the dog and I ran beneath him, pushing ducks off the water so that he might catch a meal. It's the thing I love best, but there are not many places left for hunting here.

I wanted to go to Amoroso. I wanted to go to Amarillo. I wanted to go to New Mexico. Then I stood one morning on a reservoir in my desert near the Salton Sea, warming my hands. I imagined the snow to come on the jutting horizon and couldn't bring myself to leave home.

California is cruel to me, but I forgive her everything in her rare kindnesses. I know our relationship is waning. She leaves me a little every year and I understand she's ultimately going to leave nothing more than memories—dreams of open spaces and the flash of wild wings. I know this, but I can't let her go.

I can't seem to stop myself from wandering the desert, even though it gets harder to find a place worth flying every year. I'm drawn to the sod farm, its reservoir steaming in the surprising desert chill, a quick chat with a farmer. Like me, he counts these days as stolen. The land is leased and other plots have already been sold for housing tracts.

I'm in awe of the sparkling Salton Sea, a mirage of hope rising in the southern skyline of the Musashi's field. The Musashis have been farming this land for decades, a fertile place for artichokes and romaine, a place now more home than the Japanese land the family left. Finding me on their property on Thanksgiving, they insisted I couldn't leave without a cup of coffee and a slice of pumpkin pie. We tried not to talk of the price of water, the cost of last week's hard freeze.

And there's Artesian Acres, a duck club that's been quietly tucked near the accidental sea since before World War II. It's gingerly tended by men in their eighties, a water garden in the desert. The gentlemen kindly share the land with me, hoping that a young writer might sway hearts toward the protection of their strange desert wetlands. I do adore the amazingly busy stillness on an off day in the Acres. The duck club is beautiful if only for the striking smatter of pintail ducks, the regal arc of their necks bending to read my intentions. It is a place where I sometimes stop just to hear the crack of a shot, the splash of an eager Labrador. I can't allow the falcon to fly there on shooting days but I want to hear which ducks will be immortalized in careful handwriting, added to fifty years of records in the log book, a poem of named species, lines that already read like a eulogy.

These places I've made my own—paying in tears, sweat and blood. Hunting with a raptor is frightening, punctuated by a small peregrine's near death experiences, illuminated by surprise successes and heartbreaking in its losses. In short it is life. And these places belong to me because I have lived on them.

These are places that I do not get to keep. None of us get to keep them, really, and I think our sad acceptance makes us kin—us farmers, hunters and philosophers. I guess for Thanksgiving this year, I just really wanted to be with my family.

I didn't catch a single duck Thanksgiving week. Although Booth, my Brittany spaniel, found me a hawk-wounded coot, kindly bringing it to me and laying it at my feet while I searched the crowded sky of the duck club for my overwhelmed falcon. The coot was something for the larder and it was enough. It was enough to watch a good dog and a proven falcon work the land I love. I know I should leave. I know the love affair is ending, but I can't seem to let go. California is home.

MNEMONIC

Deborah A. Miranda

I WAS BORN ON the San Andreas Fault. I carry
that promise of violence and destruction down
the center of my body like a zig-zag of lightning.

My father was born there, my mother too,
all my brothers and sisters. Sometimes I think
that's the only thing we still have in common:

our emergence on the edge of a rippling continent
where the sun goes down over warm waters;
born in the desert's shadow, between

mountains and sea. Some of us got into cars,
drove north on long interstate freeways.
Some of us stayed not twenty miles

from our birthplace, bound by love or hate
or fear, unable to imagine a sunrise
without palm trees—or sun. Some of us

died, turned to dust inside incinerators
built for human flesh; our ashes tucked
in a niche at Inglewood or scattered by children

in the green ripples at Tuolumne. Some
of us no longer speak to one another, silent
as rusty knives; others learn old languages,

make new songs out of scraps. A few
souls have traveled too far, can never
come back. Others haven't fled far enough.

Some of us journey only in motes of dust
shining above the fractured chasms of earth.
And some of us return in solitary dreams

to sacred places we could not find
in this lifetime. Today, I wind
a string of shells around my wrist

four times, a bracelet strung so I can bear
the beauty of my homeland with me
wherever I go. The sharp edges bite

my skin, rattle soft as pebbles when I write
these words. Abalone hangs from my neck:
polished shards of oceanic memory.

I was born on the San Andreas Fault.
I carry that rattlesnake in my spine, feel
the plates of a restless continent grind

and shift from tailbone to skull, a tectonic
rosary that keeps coming unstrung, keeps
me tied to the plundered bones of this place.

PRISON CHRONICLES

J. Tony Serra

MISDEMEANANT

"AREN'T YOU *TONY SERRA*, the lawyer?" Yes, indeed, I respond. The same question, in different words, is asked over and over of me at Federal Correctional Institution Lompoc's "adjacent satellite prison camp that houses minimum security male inmates," fifty-five miles northwest of Santa Barbara.

"What are you doing in here?" goes the refrain.

I tell them I'm only a misdemeanant. I got ten months. This is my third conviction. I am a TAX resister. It's not a moral turpitude offense. It's willful failure to pay TAXES, not TAX evasion, which is a felony. I will have my law license when I get out; I even have a murder trial scheduled shortly after my release date.

"But why don't you pay taxes?" they ask. "Why didn't the IRS just seize some of your property?"

I try to tell them I am an aberration. I have odd, old-fashioned beliefs. I am an old MARXIST. I don't believe in owning anything. I have no property, no money in the bank, no stocks or bonds—NO ASSETS. I don't believe in TAXES. TAXES are the plunder of victory paid by the defeated. Only the working class pays TAXES. Corporations pass tax on to the consumer. TAX resistance is my little principle. I have been convicted three times, because I am loyal to my principle.

Most of my fellow inmates are convicted of crimes where they sought financial gain. They do not understand my "principle."

Down deep, I'm a bit ashamed of being a mere misdemeanant. I have defended against prosecution in every category of felony, from marijuana to murder. I know the secrets of the felons. I've represented the Hells Angels, the Norteños, the New World Liberation Front, the Symbionese Liberation Army, the Black Panther Party, the Earth Liberation Front, the Animal Liberation Front, EarthFirst. I've represented the Devil himself. My mind is shelter for all serious crimes. I am the consummate, culminating deposit for all felony mentalities. I am the greatest felon of them all, but in this camp I am recognized only as a misdemeanant.

CORN FOR ALL

Our camp occupies a bluff that overlooks a lush valley. Inmates sit on wooden benches behind a chain-link fence and stare out at the rolling hills but a few miles away. A tree-lined river winds its way along the perimeter of the valley. Hawks circle overhead. Eucalyptus trees scent the wind. All is pastoral. The area was once a thriving Native American domain. It's even near the sea.

The entire valley is now planted to corn. The corn feeds cattle. The cattle supply meat and dairy products to the federal prison system. Giant water sprinklers, six to eight feet high, feed the crop and keep it green and fecund. On a quiet night, it is said that you can hear the corn growing.

On one far side, near the river, where the tree and plant growth is thick, herds of deer still roam the valley. They leave their riverbed hideaways at dusk. First the does, then the fawns, and last some long-horned bucks. All feast undisturbed on the growing corn.

We like to fantasize that the Indians made a contract with the prison authorities: "You get the land of our ancient tribes. You can grow your corn and feed your cattle so long as you allow the deer to roam freely without harm and to fill themselves on your growing corn." It's a fiction, but that's what we see from our lawn chairs as the sun sets: bucks butting heads, mother and baby deer eating contentedly. There is corn for all in our prison camp.

I AM A RIVER

My work assignment is "groundskeeper." My team tends the grass, flowers, and gardens around the hub of the camp. We water, cut lawns, add plants, trim vegetation, trim lawns, repair the railed fences. My teammates are twenty to forty years old; I'm the oldest, seventy-two.

My specific responsibility is to water a limited share of the lawns and flowers, principally in the front areas of the dorms, administration buildings, chapel, dining room, and visiting area. I am the waterman. I boastfully call myself the "rainmaker" or the "river." I set sprinklers, turn on and off permanent sprinkler systems, and water by long hoses or by hand. At least half my area has to be watered by hand.

Most of the time, I stand in green uniform, white baseball cap, holding a maroon hose. I shoot streams of water on the grass. I also sprinkle it sometimes, by waving the hose gently back and forth. I use my right and left hands. By end of day, my feet, shoes, and socks are soaked.

The sun in the spring and summer beats down on me. I sweat. I wear sunscreen block. I sizzle in the heat. I stand very tall, like on stilts, sometimes. Other times, I curl over in the direction of the flow. I daydream through the spray. I smile at my reveries. I watch the giant eucalyptus, which surround the area.

I must appear a solitary figure, way out on a lawn, connected to the buildings like a deep-sea diver. I like to imagine that I provide the life force, that what I touch turns green and new and clean and pure. I romanticize my prison work. It makes things easier to accept: to give life when life is taken.

Maybe, in actuality, the lawns are really deserts, the flowers a mirage, and the trees a hallucination. Maybe I am really dead, and this is the afterlife. I will water forever; the flow of life is eternal.

If I am incarcerated, if one human being is incarcerated, everything is incarcerated—the loved ones, the friends, the trees, the birds, the flowers, and the grasses. The lonely waterer is the centerpiece of his captured, contained, and suppressed microcosm.

IT'S FOR MY FRIEND, HE SAID

Friday night, after a dinner of fried chicken strips, canned corn, faded green lettuce, and a banana, I walked the circle around the camp alone. The muscles around my two hip implants hurt a little, five days of unaccustomed physical work had stiffened them up. I walked slowly and stiff legged. The fog had come in early, the air was a bit chilled, and my spirits were elevated.

Toward the end of the circle, near the weekend visiting area, an inmate acquaintance—not a friend—greeted me. "I've been looking for you," he said. For me, sometimes solitude is precious. I resented the intrusion, but quickly quashed the resentment. He had to see me "privately." It was a matter of importance. I knew he needed legal advice. "I'm suspended," I thought, but I concluded "talk" is not "practicing." I said, "Sure." We walked to a secluded area, and sat on a fence. We turned toward each other. He was young, tall, athletic, with puzzled demeanor.

He told me, "You will never get to know me. I am leaving in two weeks, but I need a favor." I said "sure" again.

I am a lawyer; it's like a doctor. You cannot deny services to the needy.

"It's for my friend," he said. "He's truly innocent. He has a long sentence. His appeal is over; he lost. He needs a writ of habeas corpus."

I told him I was not an appellate lawyer and that I was suspended for six months, but I know appellate issues because trial lawyers must preserve appellate issues on the record for appeal purposes if the case is lost. I asked what are the issues that his friend appealed upon and lost?

He didn't know; all he knew was his friend was factually innocent; that a government material witness had perjured himself at trial against his friend. He was dismayed and puzzled. He strongly believed in his friend's innocence.

I outlined some of the areas where writs are valid: incompetency of his trial counsel; newly discovered exonerating evidence; attorney-client conflict of interest; provable perjury at the trial. The list was short. My acquaintance seemed unable to understand. "But he's innocent," he kept saying.

I told him that many innocent defendants are found guilty; that appeal or writ issues seldom address that situation. I said if it could be shown that someone else committed the crime that would be a viable writ issue. He responded that it was the lying informant who had committed the crime. I told him that was just one man's word against another. I asked if he could get some corroboration? He said he didn't know.

I thought the matter was hopeless. I didn't want to tell him that. He wanted so badly to clear his friend. We sat in silence a long time on the fence poles.

To give him some hope, I said, get me the appellate pleadings—the Appellant's Opening Brief, the Government's Reply, Appellant's Final Closing Brief. I will read them. Then I'll know the case and the appeal issues. After that, we can discuss it again. Maybe something good will emerge.

The muscles in his face loosened. He felt better. He could tell his friend there is some hope. There are hundreds of these scenarios in a prison camp.

WITHOUT MARIJUANA

It is well known that I am a marijuana activist. I have a doctor's recommendation to use medical marijuana, and I espouse its use for physical and mental ailments. I have smoked every day for forty years. To my knowledge, I have suffered no detriments, and my physical being and state of mind have certainly been enhanced. All my trial-lawyer role models have been alcoholics, so I am pleased that marijuana appears to me to mitigate stress without the ill effects of alcohol.

But in prison camp, I do not smoke. I terminated before entering, like turning the page of a book.

"How does it feel without it? Want a hit?" goes the refrain from inmates that know that I am a long-term user.

I always decline, saying "I will wait. I'm a short-timer. I don't want to be busted for a joint and do more time."

I tell everyone the following: Pretend that you have a garden of beautiful, multicolored flowers. When I smoke marijuana, I can see a gorgeous shimmering color that no one else can perceive. The beauty of this color gives me joy, pacifies my mind, provides stimulation to my imagination, and bestows upon me a feeling of well-being.

Marijuana is not an addictive drug; it does not enslave. It simply enhances awareness. It increases one's appreciation of beauty, and beauty is a component of truth and love.

And abstinence does not enfeeble or destroy any portion of mind or body; it merely eliminates one blissful dream within the reality of one's life.

Thus, I am able to survive without marijuana in prison, with the occasional idiot-savant smile of "flashback" memories.

NO EXEMPTION FOR AGE

In prison mentality, Judas exists in many roles. There's the informant that gets one arrested. There's the codefendant who turns government witness and gets one convicted. There's the convicted inmate who debriefs after arriving in prison and names criminal suspects in exchange for a reduced sentence. And, lastly, there is the jailhouse "rat" who snitches on the criminal behavior of fellow inmates—or their breaking of camp rules. All these types are ostracized and punished, stabbed, sliced, assaulted; clothes and bedding thrown out of the barracks, beds urinated on. Wherever a snitch appears, the cry "Rat-Rat" goes up.

The night before he was to be released, a seventy-two-year-old inmate was beaten while he was asleep in his lower bunk. The assailant got away. The victim was left with a swollen eye and cut cheek. He washed up, said not a word to the authorities about the beating, and was discharged the next day. The rumor was that he had filed a Cop Out, a grievance form submitted to the prison staff that told that some inmates had put a lock on a storage cabinet containing contraband food—or maybe locked a refrigerator. Because he himself couldn't use it anymore, he complained about it.

Does this kind of informing sound innocuous? Perhaps worthy of a verbal confrontation? Certainly not appropriate for an assault punishment? Well, not so; an old man beaten in the dark while he slept was the collective judgment of the inmates who had locked the container. Any kind of snitching in prison is reviled.

TRAPPING ANIMALS

Ground squirrels—or prairie dogs—abound on the outskirts of camp. Their burrows are everywhere. They come out, stand on their hind legs, look around like little sentinels. Their tunnels reach everywhere.

Brown weasels are the squirrels' predator. Their long tubular bodies fit into the tunnels; their razor teeth find the victims.

Twice, I have seen inmates with caged weasels. Somehow, there are animal traps here, presumably made by inmates for sport; they set the traps with food to entice the animals on the outskirts of camp. They parade their catch throughout the camp, putting the cage on the back of the electric carts that are used for inmate transportation. The driver stops here and there, and the other inmates watch the frenzied weasel scurry about the cage.

The same traps are used to catch the cats that flourish on the grounds. The cats are relocated, I believe; even the weasels are freed after being shown about.

The irony to me, unseen by the trappers and the admiring inmates, is the analogy between us, the prisoners, and the weasels and cats. We seem to pass on the cruelty perpetrated upon ourselves.

ARRESTED FOR A CIGARETTE

After thirty years, smoking has been banned at Lompoc. Signs for "No Smoking" areas, like in the law library, are still present, but only the guards can smoke legally.

Cartons, packs, and even individual cigarettes used to be the inmate currency of exchange, i.e., a pack of cigarettes for a haircut, three cigarettes for an apple, a carton for meal or laundry services. Now U.S. postage stamps and books of stamps have taken the place of the cigarette as the coin of the realm.

If an inmate is caught smoking, and inmates do smoke somewhat openly outside and in the rear of the camp, there are a number of possible sanctions. The usual are extra work assignments, washing camp vehicles, or sweeping the dorms, suspended phone and/or commissary privileges, thirty to ninety days. Inmates are willing to risk the punishment; hand-rolled contraband cigarettes are everywhere.

Recently, a popular young inmate was searched at his job, and a few cigarettes were found on his person. He was handcuffed at gunpoint by two guards and taken to the The Hole. Arrested at gunpoint for a few cigarettes, taken away to a barred cell—Inhuman, the inmates shudder.

THE PIANO IN THE CHAPEL

At the camp's hub, there is a chapel. A small building, nothing denoting religion on its outside; three or four small rooms and one medium-sized room with about sixty chairs facing a raised platform. A painting of a hawk floating over a river valley hangs behind the platform; a podium at its center and, to its side, a small piano.

The chapel is multidenominational. Islamic services on Friday, Jewish on Saturday, Catholic, Protestant, and Buddhist on Sunday. On weekdays, the chapel is also used as an educational facility for the small number of classes given at the camp, and as a TV room. During free time, inmates use the piano.

I frequently water the grasses around the chapel and listen dreamily to the imperfect melodies emanating from the piano. Even amateur playing gives delight to the untutored inmate ear.

Yesterday, an inmate friend of mine, a seventy-four-year-old medical doctor, confided to me, in disgust, that the Catholic priest "caught him" using the piano on a weekday. The priest had forbidden him to use it, because it was part of the Catholic Mass and therefore could only be used by them on Sundays.

Thus, even the Catholic priest punishes the inmate: no piano for the inmate until Sunday Mass for Catholics only!

A PEACH AS A SACRAMENT

"My kingdom for an orange," I used to remark to fellow inmates the first few months of incarceration when they asked if I needed anything. At camp, fresh fruit is a rare luxury. What is procured by food services goes underground and is distributed like drugs for appropriate consideration. I don't participate in the contraband food system, so an orange or pear or peach is a treat as well as needed nutrition. Everyone knows that I help as much as I can with inmate legal problems, so, on many occasions, I am the recipient of a gift of an orange, banana, or peach. Oranges are out of season now, so currently I receive from fellow inmates one or two peaches.

They come to me unripe and hard. I hide them in my locker under a spare white baseball cap. (Frequently, there is a locker search and contraband items removed.) It takes about four days for them to ripen. They are middle-sized peaches, rosy red and cream-colored. The flesh under the skin is orange. They are juicy and sensuous. In the afternoon, after standing four to five hours in the hot sun, I come in and devour a peach. The flavor impacts my taste buds with explosive force. The juices spill down from my lips. It is a lush stimulant to my physiology and psychology. I feel the vitamins buoying my health. For me, the peach is a sacrament. It connects me to the gracious lifestyle of the free outside.

THE "POSSIBLE" FOOD RIOT

Vandenberg Air Force Base is in our valley. Occasionally, at night, we see the trail of a rocket shot out to space. Frequently, huge cargo planes pass closely overhead as they go in for landing. Jets flash by all the time.

About twenty inmates are assigned to assist the clean up and maintenance of the base, which is an hour bus drive from the hub of our camp. The inmates take bag lunches. Recently, four or five base-assigned inmates filled out Cop Out forms complaining that their lunches were deficient.

When the complaints were received and considered by the administration, each complainant was "rolled up"—their bunks and possessions were seized, and they were placed in locked-down isolation in the main institute outside of camp. They remained in The Hole for nine weeks. Their infraction was designated *inciting possible food riot or food strike.*

I saw them when they were released. They looked wan, fearful, and agonized. They and all the others who know about their treatment will never again complain about the prison.

I SEE NO CATS

"Fuck the rat who snitched me off. Fuck his father. Fuck his mother," an inmate in a wheelchair screamed to a watchful gathering of fifty inmates and a dozen guards. He had just been taken into custody. An outlawed cell phone was found somewhere on his person or in the wheelchair he used. He had been paralyzed by a drive-by gunshot while on the street. He knew that a rat had tipped the authorities to the whereabouts of the phone. The guards circled him while he screamed, but did not touch him. The inmates froze in awe. He was thereupon wheeled away to The Hole.

The guards ordered all the inmates out of the sleeping barracks. They searched each of us, and then searched all our lockers. The phone incident became a dormitory "raid." Dogs were brought in to smell for drugs. It was a show of force; it was overkill for a simple mobile phone contraband arrest.

Later that afternoon, while I was watering, the camp administrator asked me if I had seen any cats around. (They wanted to trap and remove all the strays.) I knew where they were, but with "fuck the rat" still ringing in my ears, there was no way that I would inform on anything, not even on a cat!

ANOMALY

Anomaly is the general rule in prison camp, from the physical to the ideological. In the physical realm, I eat food that I would not consider outside—cheap hot dogs, sweet cereals, cold cuts, white rice, and endless canned vegetables and fruits. I go to bed at the same time every night. I get up at the same time every morning. I receive mail at mail call time. Outside, my life is irregular; inside, it conforms to prison schedule.

But the strangest abnormality for me is my choice of friends. Outside, my associates and intimates all share my general social values: pro-working class, antimaterialistic, egalitarian, antigovernment. But inside, I have gravitated to those who are semantically oriented, those who are knowledgeable of world events, those who have traveled; in essence, those who have been acculturated by education or experiences similar to my own. Oddly enough, the ones that I have found in this category are all committed capitalists: a doctor who owns a chain of diet clinics in the Los Angeles area; a New York mortgage banker multimillionaire; a tax lawyer with a huge second home on an estate in Idaho; a hard drinking land developer from Tahoe.

Money drives them all. Opulence characterizes their lifestyles. They are all victors in the capitalist world. But they are hip to the prison system fallacies and contradictions; they revel in ridicule of the guards and camp rules. They have the latest news on Iraq or Israel; they have read and traveled. Our discussions are animated. We share anecdotes and humor. We have bonded. We are known as the "gray power" clique. They know my social philosophy, but that doesn't seem to deter our friendship. I strongly believe that on the outside, we will revert to having "nothing in common," and never see each other again.

I feel bad that the inmates that constitute the class I've always represented—drug outlaws, for the most part, who are abundantly present here in camp, whom I still serve when called upon, with whom I'm friendly, but not close. I don't share my thoughts and ideas with them. It's because they are average-minded with average world experience, just not as interesting at a personal level as my friends, the capitalists!

SWALLOWS

Barn swallows or starlings, no one seems to know which, are ecstatic co-occupants of the camp. Their straw-and-mud nests line the perimeter of the dorm roof.

These birds are small, with black heads, brownish bodies. They fly in a frenzy, like bats, like bees swarming.

At dawn and dusk, they appear to feed on insects drawn by a high-poled light near the dorm. During the afternoon, the birds fly in and out of their nests. Perhaps they are feeding their babies.

The number of these birds seems to increase steadily. They swarm above our heads. Because they always fly so helter skelter, they are psychologically unsettling—no gliding, no grace, no peace instilled in us from them. Just their chaos added to our own mental chaos. I wish they would settle elsewhere.

GREAT MATTRESS FIASCO

Camp-issued mattresses for our bunk beds are spartan-sized—about six feet long and three and a half feet wide and four inches thick. They are hard, probably stuffed with synthetic cotton. They do not soften to accommodate body pressure. It's like sleeping on the floor.

But at some indefinite period in the past, the prison issued normal mattresses, much larger, eight inches high, seemingly with springs inside, certainly with bounce and softness. They did depress to fit the body's size and pressure. Only a handful of inmates had them by the time I arrived.

Recently, by top administrator's fiat, without notice, the old and comfortable mattresses were confiscated.

There was a hue and cry from the dispossessed. A wave of rumor and invective swept over the camp. There was no advance notice of the administration's intent to confiscate. There was therefore no due process. The seizure was arbitrary and punitive. No prison objective was accomplished. The mattresses had been legally issued. The charge was ex post facto.

The dispossessed appealed formally to higher camp authorities. The action taken by the Administrator was approved, however. The next level of appeal would take ninety days. The "price" would be no commissary privileges for ninety days. Obviously, there would be no justice.

Inmates get used to random cruelty perpetrated without logic. They are quick to protest small issues—a bad meal, being wakened at night for a random head count, working in the rain, not enough tools for a job, being castigated by a guard falsely. But on the big issues—punishment versus rehabilitation, penal retribution versus education, long incarceration versus parole—the inmates observe universal silence.

MY HANDS

Until I reached my sixtieth year, I had the hands of an El Greco priest: thin, elastic, sinewy, elongated, clean-fleshed with an almost religious hue.

I could write verbatim testimony of witnesses almost as fast as a shorthand reporter. My thumb and middle finger of my right hand were callused and tough, because I wrote incessantly. My hands flew along the paper like a piano virtuoso. I had the hands and fingers of a surgeon attached to the mind of a lawyer.

Today, I sit in the library of a Federal Prison Camp and examine my hands. Eight months of watering prison campgrounds have made them shriveled, withered, and cracked. The heat of sun has burned them. The intensity of freezing cold has made them brittle. They are mottled and peeling.

I have bumped and scraped so many plants and trees. I have picked up so much debris and hauled so many buckets and garbage cans that my hands are no longer art, they are function.

THE SWEAT

It's Sunday. We're allowed to sleep in, wear sweats, avoid the work "greens." It's a day of visits for many, laundry for most. We wash our issued clothes, sheets, and towels in machines unpleasantly next to the toilets. Sunday is also for chess, cards, writing letters, playing horseshoes, religious services.

The Native Americans have created a garden—a space on the bluff, one of the choicest plots in the camp. Eucalyptus hide it from the dormitories. Flowers in raised plots between logs glorify the area. Bushes, cut grass, logs for seats, and tree rounds form a sensuous environment. Upright limbs of trees carry ribbons and hawk feathers. Circular spirit nets hang from tree limbs, standing erect in the garden. A bold totem raises its heads. The centerpiece is a bent-limb structure, an igloolike half sphere about thirty feet in diameter. The floor is raw earth. This is a Native American sweat lodge: an altar, a temple, a holy spot for Native Americans, the "womb" of Mother Earth.

I rise at 6:30 a.m., a half hour later than usual. I wear camp-issued sweat shorts, a dirty T-shirt. I put on my work boots, without socks. I know that I'll have to strip to my shorts for the sweat. While dressing I have trepidations: Will I be able to squat adequately? (I have two total-hip replacements.) Will I be able to endure the intense heat? Will I humiliate myself? Am I qualified? I may look Indian, but I'm only a wannabe. My Indian friends tell me that I was an Indian in the last life. I have been asked before, but this time I go, but not without serious moral reservations.

The ceremony will start at 7. I get there at 6:45. Five men precede me. There is already a huge oak bonfire blazing. The wood is piled on one side of the garden, presumably from outside the camp. I don't see them, but later learn that the rocks that will be brought into the sweat lodge are embedded deep in the hot flames.

Someone brings a wheelbarrow piled high with old, green camp blankets, worn with many cuts and holes, but clean. I rise from a log and help. We throw all the blankets over the frame. Then, a canvas is stretched over the blankets. Only a small crawl-hole entrance is open. A thick blanket tied to a limb is placed over the hole.

We undress to our shorts. We form a circle around the lodge. We will enter clockwise. It is known that I have hip problems and that this is my first time, so I am allowed to enter third.

Just inside is an abalone shell filled with burning organic matter, some of which smells like burning sage. I get down on my hands and knees, place my face directly above the burning shell and with my hands fan the smoke to cover my face. I feel blessed. The smoke brings wetness to my eyes. At just this moment, I feel drops of rain on my head and back. This is an auspicious sign for me.

I crawl backward into the dark of the lodge. I turn and crawl clockwise to a place close to the opening. I sit with my legs pulled under me. I am the third from the entrance.

The rest crawl in. Most of us look European. I would learn later that all of us had strong ties to Native American culture, and the majority had Indian blood.

One remained outside. With a pitchfork, he pushed in searing red-hot rocks, twelve of them, in several trips; they were then pushed into the center dugout. Our feet were very close to the burning heat.

There were fourteen of us in the circle. The outsider came in and closed the entrance. It became pitch black, but for the glowing rocks. I sat as if hypnotized by their fiery emanations.

The ceremony begins. Colored ribbons, one by one, are hung from the limbs of the structure inside symbolizing the four directions, symbolizing the sky and the earth.

In the darkness, each man presents a prayer. Tobacco is passed from hand to hand, and, as the prayer is offered, a pinch is thrown on the rocks. This is all done by touch and sound; it is too dark to see. The leader, whom I had seen outside, is a large, powerful man, embellished with many tattoos. He prays and speaks to us. It is forbidden to repeat any words spoken in the lodge. Each of us spoke with heartfelt sincerity. All prayed for other than themselves.

Water is thrown by the leader on to the red-hot rocks from a plastic bucket. The steam rises and envelops us. Wave after wave of water crashes on the rocks. The heat is intense. My mind became mystic. Tears roll from my eyes.

Prayer chants begin; someone had brought a drum. The rhythm rises and falls, all sing out together, mouths open, steam being swallowed, singing with tears running down into open mouths. I join only the chorus at the decline of the song rhythms. I cry out the sounds sometimes softly, sometimes loudly.

Then there is an interval. The door is opened. More rocks are brought in. The same process is followed: prayer, chanting, water on rocks, steam rising. My mind melting: a great unity occurring. I am in an earth womb. I am merging spiritually with the other participants. I am in a state of alternative consciousness. I am elevated, disembodied. By song and thought, my mind connects with the others and in a unity we transcend the ceremony.

Five times the red-hot rocks are brought into the lodge. Five times we are steamed. Each time it is hotter and hotter. The fifth time I can barely breathe. The hot steam is smothering. I gasp silently for oxygen. I do not want to faint, and I do not.

After the fifth time, a long-handled pipe filled with tobacco is brought in. It is passed from person to person. We inhale deeply, blowing smoke, first upwardly, then onto our own shoulders, one shoulder at a time. I am throbbing. My heart is pounding. I am a mass of sweat. Thoughts fly from head to sky.

I crawl out. The rain has stopped. For the rest of the day, I remain in a mystical state of mind.

IN THE WATER OVER STONES

Stephen Meadows

for Isabel Meadows

YOUR VOICE ISABEL
is a quail's voice
as the sun's song ticks
in the brush

It is the hawk's voice
and the heart's heat
of the rabbit
in the parched summer grass

Nearby in the river
in the water over stones
it is a willow voice
it is a crayfish voice
in the hollows
in the darkening places

At first light
it is the wind's voice
the mouth of the river
tule voice the voice
of a hundred breezes

The sun marks out
the red madrone
and in the canyons

it is a redwood voice
a sycamore voice
sweet scented

In the spring
it is the lupine voice
a blue white and purple
coverlet voice
all over the hills
and the meadows

On the river banks
as the set fires burn
and the steelhead run
it is the hunter's voice
flinging the gleamers
silver on the sand

Though the houses
of rich men now cover these hills
it is your spirit voice
your evening voice
your voice of the western waters

The stars hang out
over the point of wolves
on the edge of the world
the sea lions call
the otters break open
abalone

It is the voice of the land
It is the voice of bright shells
It is the voice of the valley
And the mountain Isabel

It is the voice of the people too

It is the weaver's voice
It is the young girl's voice
The gatherer's and the singer's
and the farmer's voice
the wives' and the children's
and the old woman's voice
It is the Indian voice
and the whalerman's voice
and the voice of the servant
escaping

It is the voice of your face
across the years Isabel
in my grandfather's face
in my father's face
and in my face as well

It is the voice
of the ones on the edges Isabel
It is the voice
of those ones with no voices

Hawk and rabbit
Quail and brush
Water and willow and crayfish and stone
Wind in the canyons
Daylight through limbs
The lupine the steelhead
The cookfire's call
Beans and tortillas
Your memories Isabel talking
Talking to us all

PERMISSIONS

Adrian, Chris. Excerpt (chapter 3) from *The Great Night* by Chris Adrian, Farrar, Straus and Giroux, 2011. © 2011 by Chris Adrian. Reprinted by permission of Farrar, Straus and Giroux, LLC.

Asher, Don, and Lois Goodwill. Excerpt ("Contrasts," "The Ubiquitous Priest," and "Sarah's Journal") from *Entangled* by Don Asher and Lois Goodwill, Heyday, 2011. © 2011 by Don Asher and Lois Goodwill. Reprinted by permission of Heyday.

Bernard, Sean. "Torturers" by Sean Bernard, from *Santa Monica Review*, Spring 2010. © 2010 by Sean Bernard. Reprinted by permission of the author.

Block, Francesca Lia. "Wind Girl" from *Fairy Tales in Electri-City* by Francesca Lia Block, Midsummer Night's Press, 2011. © 2011 by Francesca Lia Block. Reprinted by permission of the author.

Boyle, T. Coraghessan. Excerpt (from "The Wreck of the *Winfield Scott*") from *When the Killing's Done* by T. Coraghessan Boyle, Viking, 2010. © 2010 by T. Coraghessan Boyle. Used by permission of Viking Penguin, a division of Penguin Group (USA) Inc.

Carroll, Jon. "In the Third Kind of Fog" by Jon Carroll, from *Bay Nature*, January–March 2011. © 2011 by Jon Carroll. Reprinted by permission of the author.

Chau, Angie. "Silver Girl" from *Quiet As They Come* by Angie Chau, Ig Publishing, 2010. © 2010 by Angie Chau. Used by permission of Ig Publishing Inc.

Day, Lucille Lang. "Journeys" by Lucille Lang Day, from *Redactions: Poetry and Poetics* 13, October 2010. © 2010 by Lucille Lang Day. Reprinted by permission of the author.

Dungy, Camille T. "The Blue" from *Smith Blue* by Camille T. Dungy, Southern Illinois University Press, 2011. First published in *The Rumpus*, April 16, 2010. © 2011 by Camille T. Dungy. Reprinted by permission of the publisher.

Flanagan, Caitlin. "The Madness of Cesar Chavez" by Caitlin Flanagan, from *The Atlantic Monthly*, July/August 2011. © 2011 The Atlantic Media Co., as first published in *The Atlantic Magazine*. Distributed by Tribune Media Services. Reprinted by permission of Tribune Media Services.

Gilligan, David Scott. Excerpt (from "Life on the Rise") from *Rise of the Ranges of Light* by David Scott Gilligan, Heyday, 2011. © 2011 by David Scott Gilligan. Reprinted by permission of Heyday.

Goodman, Allegra. Excerpt from *The Cookbook Collector* by Allegra Goodman, The Dial Press, 2010. © 2010 by Allegra Goodman. Used by permission of The Dial Press/Dell Publishing, a division of Random House, Inc.

Janigian, Aris. Excerpt from "The Splendors of Death" by Aris Janigian, from *The Nervous Breakdown*, June 29, 2011 (1–6), and July 26, 2011 (7–10). © 2011 by Aris Janigian. Reprinted by permission of the author.

Johnston, Hilda. "On the Day of the Dead" by Hilda Johnston, from *The Redwood Coast Review*, Fall 2010. © 2010 by Hilda Johnston. Reprinted by permission of the author.

Kingston, Maxine Hong. Excerpt from *I Love a Broad Margin to My Life* by Maxine Hong Kingston, Knopf, 2011. © 2011 by Maxine Hong Kingston. Used by permission of Alfred A. Knopf, a division of Random House, Inc.

Lummis, Suzanne. "Gone, Baby" by Suzanne Lummis, from *Connotation Press,* December 2010. © 2010 by Suzanne Lummis. Reprinted by permission of the author.

Meadows, Stephen. "In the Water over Stones" from *Releasing the Days* by Stephen Meadows, Heyday, 2011. © 2011 by Stephen Meadows. Reprinted by permission of Heyday.

Miller, Matt W. "Club Icarus" by Matt W. Miller, from *Harvard Review,* Fall/Winter 2010. © 2010 by Matt W. Miller. Reprinted by permission of the author.

Miranda, Deborah A. "Mnemonic" (revised version) from *When Turtles Fly* (weblog; whenturtlesfly.blogspot.com) by Deborah A. Miranda, April 4, 2011. © 2011 by Deborah A. Miranda. Reprinted by permission of the author.

Muñoz, Manuel. Excerpt from *What You See in the Dark* by Manuel Muñoz, Algonquin Books of Chapel Hill, 2011. © 2011 by Manuel Muñoz. Used by permission of Stuart Bernstein Representation for Artists, New York. All rights reserved.

Myers, Holly. "The Guest Room" by Holly Myers, from *ZYZZYVA*, Winter 2010. © 2010 by Holly Myers. Reprinted by permission of the author.

Nimura, Tamiko. "How It Feels to Inherit Camp" by Tamiko Nimura, from *Kartika Review*, Spring 2011. © 2011 by Tamiko Nimura. Reprinted by permission of the author.

O'Connor, Rebecca K. "Home for Thanksgiving" by Rebecca K. O'Connor, from *The Coachella Review*, Spring 2010. © 2010 by Rebecca K. O'Connor. Reprinted by permission of the author.

Oglesby, Briandaniel. "Off-Limits (In Which the Bitchy Virgin No One Can Get with Visits a Gay Bar)" by Briandaniel Oglesby, from *Arroyo Literary Review*, Spring 2011. © 2011 by Briandaniel Oglesby. Reprinted by permission of the author.

Olivas, Daniel. "How to Date a Flying Mexican" from *The Book of Want* by Daniel Olivas, University of Arizona Press, 2011. © 2011 by Daniel Olivas. Reprinted by permission of the University of Arizona Press.

Orozco, Daniel. "The Bridge" from *Orientation* by Daniel Orozco, Faber and Faber, Inc., 2011. © 2011 by Daniel Orozco. Reprinted by permission of Farrar, Straus and Giroux, LLC.

Pawelek, BL. "Everything Is Beautiful" by BL Pawelek, from *Monkeybicycle*, Summer 2010. © 2010 by BL Pawelek. Reprinted by permission of the author.

Pollan, Michael. "The 36-Hour Dinner Party" by Michael Pollan, from *The New York Times Magazine*, October 10, 2010. © 2010 by Michael Pollan. Reprinted by permission of the author.

Powell, D. A. "Goodbye My Fancy" by D. A. Powell, from *TriQuarterly,* Summer/Fall 2010. © 2010 by D. A. Powell. Reprinted by permission of the author.

Puchner, Eric. "Schemes of My Father" by Eric Puchner, from *GQ*, March 2011. © 2011 by Condé Nast. Reprinted by permission of Condé Nast.

Rader, Dean. "Ocean Beach at Twilight: 14" from *Works & Days* by Dean Rader, Truman State University Press, 2010. © 2010 by Dean Rader. Reprinted by permission of Truman State University Press.

Roberge, Rob. "Earthquake" from *Working Backwards from the Worst Moment of My Life* by Rob Roberge, Red Hen Press, 2010. © 2010 by Rob Roberge. Reprinted by permission of Red Hen Press.

Rowe, Jonathan. "Fellow Conservatives" by Jonathan Rowe, from *West Marin Review*, Fall 2010. © 2010 by the Estate of Jonathan Rowe. Reprinted by permission of *West Marin Review*.

Sarris, Greg. "Bluebelly" by Greg Sarris from *Bay Nature*, January–March 2011. © 2011 by Greg Sarris. Reprinted by permission of the author.

Satoda, Daisy Uyeda. "The Red Coat" by Daisy Uyeda Satoda, from *Making Home from War,* edited by Brian Komei Dempster, Heyday, 2011. © 2011 by Daisy Uyeda Satoda. Reprinted by permission of the author.

Serra, J. Tony. "Prison Chronicles" by J. Tony Serra, from *ZYZZYVA*, Fall 2010. © 2010 by J. Tony Serra. Reprinted by permission of the author.

Shapiro, Janice. "Predation" from *Bummer* by Janice Shapiro, Soft Skull, 2010. © 2010 by Janice Shapiro. Reprinted by permission of Soft Skull Press.

Stillman, Deanne. "The Tortoise Quadrille: A Few Thoughts on Skipperdee, Mojave Max, and My Father" (originally titled "We All Live on Turtle Island") by Deanne Stillman, first published on Truthdig, July 23, 2010. © 2010 by *www.truthdig.com*. Reprinted by permission of the author.

Teague, Alexandra. "Four Games Played While Riding the Bus" from *Mortal Geography* by Alexandra Teague, Persea Books, 2010. © 2010 by Alexandra Teague. Reprinted by permission of Persea Books, Inc., New York.

Tintocalis, Stacy. "Honeymoon in Beirut" from *The Tiki King* by Stacy Tintocalis, Swallow Press, 2010. First published in *Post Road*, 2010. © 2010 by Stacy Tintocalis. Reprinted with the permission of Ohio University Press/Swallow Press, Athens, Ohio, www.ohioswallow.com.

Vang, Soul Choj. "Approaching San Francisco" from *Bridge~Owner* (weblog; hmong poet.blogspot.com) by Soul Choj Vang, July 18, 2011. © 2011 by Soul Choj Vang. Reprinted by permission of the author.

Willen, Stef. "Paranormal Activity" by Stef Willen, from *McSweeney's Internet Tendency*, February 17, 2011. © 2011 by Stef Willen. Reprinted by permission of the author.

Young, Mariah K. "Masha'allah" by Mariah K. Young, forthcoming in *Masha'allah and Other Stories*, Heyday, 2012. © 2012 by Mariah K. Young. Reprinted by permission of Heyday.

AUTHOR BIOGRAPHIES

CHRIS ADRIAN is the author of three novels, most recently *The Great Night* (Farrar, Straus and Giroux, 2011), and a collection of short stories, *A Better Angel* (Farrar, Straus and Giroux, 2008).

DON ASHER was a jazz pianist and author of nine books, including two memoirs, *Notes from a Battered Grand* (Harcourt, 1992) and *Entangled* (Heyday, 2011; coauthored with Lois Goodwill), as well as a biography of musician Hampton Hawes, *Raise Up Off Me* (Da Capo, 2001).

SEAN BERNARD's fiction has appeared in *Copper Nickel*, the *Santa Monica Review, Storyglossia,* and *West Branch*. In 2010 he won the *Poets and Writers* California Writers Exchange Award.

FRANCESCA LIA BLOCK is best known for her young adult contemporary fairy tales, including the Weetzie Bat series (HarperCollins, 1989–2005). Her website is www.francescaliablock.com.

T. CORAGHESSAN BOYLE's twenty-two novels include the PEN/Faulkner Award–winning *World's End* (Viking, 1987) and the recent *When the Killing's Done* (Penguin, 2011). His website is www.tcboyle.com.

JON CARROLL has been a popular columnist at the *San Francisco Chronicle* since 1982.

ANGIE CHAU's debut story collection is *Quiet As They Come* (Ig Publishing, 2010). Her writing has appeared in the *Indiana Review, Night Train Magazine,* the *Santa Clara Review,* and *Slant*. Her website is www.angiechau.com.

LUCILLE LANG DAY is the author of eight poetry collections, most recently *The Curvature of Blue* (Červená Barva Press, 2009); a textbook, *How To Encourage Girls in Math and Science* (Prentice Hall, 1982); and a forthcoming memoir, *Married at Fourteen* (Heyday, 2012). She is also the publisher of Scarlet Tanager Books. Her website is lucillelangday.com.

CAMILLE T. DUNGY is most recently the author of the award-winning poetry collections *Smith Blue* (Southern Illinois University Press, 2011) and *Suck on the Marrow* (Red Hen Press, 2010). She is also the editor of *Black Nature: Four Centuries of African American Nature Poetry* (University of George Press, 2009). Her website is www.camilledungy.com.

CAITLIN FLANAGAN is the author of *To Hell with All That: Loving and Loathing Our Inner Housewife* (Little, Brown and Company, 2006). She was a staff writer for *The New Yorker* and is now a contributing editor of *The Atlantic Monthly.*

DAVID SCOTT GILLIGAN is a naturalist and author of *Rise of the Ranges of Light: Landscapes and Change in the Mountains of California* (Heyday, 2011); *In the Years of the Mountains: Exploring the World's High Ranges in Search of Their Culture, Geology, and Ecology* (Thunder's Mouth Press, 2006); and *The Secret Sierra: The Alpine World Above the Trees* (Spotted Dog Press, 2000).

ALLEGRA GOODMAN's recent novels include *The Cookbook Collector* (The Dial Press, 2010), *Intuition* (The Dial Press, 2006), and *Paradise Park* (The Dial Press, 2011). Her website is www.allegragoodman.com.

LOIS GOODWILL is a retired clinical psychologist and coauthor, with Don Asher, of the memoir *Entangled* (Heyday, 2011).

ARIS JANIGIAN's novels include *Riverbig* (Heyday, 2008) and *Bloodvine* (Heyday, 2003).

HILDA JOHNSTON is a Bay Area teacher whose writing has appeared in *The Redwood Coast Review.*

MAXINE HONG KINGSTON is the author of the National Book Critics Circle Award winner *The Woman Warrior* (Knopf, 1976); the National Book Award winner *China Men* (Knopf, 1980); and, most recently, *I Love a Broad Margin to My Life* (Knopf, 2011).

SUZANNE LUMMIS is a widely anthologized poet and the cofounder and present director of the Los Angeles Poetry Festival. Her work has appeared in *The Antioch Review, The Hudson Review, Ploughshares, Poetry International,* and *Pool.* Her website is suzannelummis.com.

STEPHEN MEADOWS's first poetry collection is *Releasing the Days* (Heyday, 2011). He is a longtime folk music DJ on KFOK.

Stegner Fellow **MATT W. MILLER**'s poems have appeared in the *Harvard Review*, *Slate*, and his collection *Cameo Diner* (Loom Press, 2005).

DEBORAH A. MIRANDA is the author of poetry collections *The Zen of La Llorona* (Salt Publishing, 2005) and *Indian Cartography* (Greenfield Review Press, 1999). Her memoir *Bad Indians* is forthcoming (Heyday, 2012). Her weblog is *When Turtles Fly*, whenturtlesfly.blogspot.com.

MANUEL MUÑOZ is the author of the novels *What You See in the Dark* (Algonquin, 2011) and *The Faith Healer of Olive Avenue* (Algonquin, 2007), and the short story collection *Zigzagger* (Northwestern University Press, 2003). His website is www.manuel-munoz.com.

HOLLY MYERS's story in *ZYZZYVA* is her first published work.

TAMIKO NIMURA's writing has appeared in the *San Francisco Chronicle*, *Kartika Review*, *Seattlest.com*, *International Examiner*, and *Rafu Shimpo*. Her blog, *Kikugirl*, is at www.kikugirl.net.

REBECCA K. O'CONNOR is the author of a memoir, *Lift* (Red Hen Press, 2009); a novel, *Falcon's Return* (Avalon, 2002); and several pet and reference books. Her website is rebeccakoconnor.com.

BRIANDANIEL OGLESBY's fiction has appeared in the *Arroyo Literary Review*, the *Indiana Review*, *Mosaic*, *The Literary Review*, and *ZYZZYVA*. His website is sites.google.com/site/briandanieloglesby.

DANIEL OLIVAS's first novel is *The Book of Want* (University of Arizona Press, 2011). Himself widely published and anthologized, he is also the editor of *Latinos in Lotusland: An Anthology of Contemporary Southern California Literature* (Bilingual Press, 2008). His website is www.danielolivas.com.

DANIEL OROZCO's short stories have appeared widely in magazines—among them *Harper's* and *Zoetrope*—and anthologies, including editions of the annual *Best American Short Stories* and Pushcart Prize anthologies. He is the author of the short story collection *Orientation* (Faber and Faber, 2011).

Artist and writer **BL PAWELEK** blogs at blpawelek.wordpress.com.

MICHAEL POLLAN's books include *The Botany of Desire: A Plant's-Eye View of the World* (Random House, 2001), *The Omnivore's Dilemma: A Natural History of Four Meals* (Penguin, 2006), and his recent *Food Rules: An Eater's Manual* (Penguin, 2009). He can be found online at michaelpollan.com.

D. A. POWELL's fourth and most recent poetry collection, *Chronic* (Graywolf, 2009), is the winner of the Kingsley Tufts Poetry Award.

ERIC PUCHNER's debut novel, *Model Home* (Scribner, 2010), won a silver medal in the California Book Award fiction category and was a finalist for the PEN/Faulkner Award. His website is www.ericpuchner.com.

DEAN RADER's debut collection of poems, *Works & Days* (Truman State University Press, 2010), won the T. S. Eliot Poetry Prize. He is also the author of the recent *Engaged Resistance: American Indian Art, Literature, and Film from Alcatraz to the NMAI* (University of Texas Press, 2011). His website is www.deanrader.com.

ROB ROBERGE is the author of a short-story collection, *Working Backwards from the Worst Moment of My Life* (Red Hen Press, 2010), and two novels, *Drive* (Hollyridge Press, 2006) and *More Than They Could Chew* (HarperCollins, 2005). His website is www.robroberge.com.

JONATHAN ROWE was an editor at the *Washington Monthly* magazine and a staff writer at the *Christian Science Monitor.* His writing has appeared in *Harper's, The Atlantic Monthly, Reader's Digest, The Washington Post,* and numerous other publications. Many of his articles are archived on jonathanrowe.org.

GREG SARRIS is the chairman of the Federated Indians of Graton Rancheria. His short story collection, *Grand Avenue* (Hyperion, 1994), was made into an HBO movie. His other publications include *Watermelon Nights* (Hyperion, 1998) and *Mabel McKay: Weaving the Dream* (University of California Press, 1994).

DAISY UYEDA SATODA is a contributor to *Making Home from War: Stories of Japanese American Exile and Resettlement* (Heyday, 2010) and *From Our Side of the Fence: Growing Up in America's Concentration Camps* (Kearny Street Workshop, 2003).

J. TONY SERRA is a civil rights and criminal lawyer and activist, famous for his defense of Black Panther leader Huey Newton. "Prison Chronicles," published in *ZYZZYVA*'s Fall 2010 issue, is his first published literary piece.

JANICE SHAPIRO's first book is *Bummer* (Soft Skull, 2010). Her website is www.janiceshapiro.com.

DEANNE STILLMAN is the author of *Mustang: The Saga of the Wild Horse in the American West* (Houghton Mifflin, 2008); *Twentynine Palms: A True Story of Murder, Marines, and the Mojave* (William Morrow and Company, 2001;

new, updated edition Angel City Press, 2008); and the forthcoming *Desert Reckoning: A Town Sheriff, a Mojave Hermit, and the Biggest Manhunt in Modern California History* (Nation Books, 2012). Her website is www.deanne stillman.com.

ALEXANDRA TEAGUE's first book of poetry, *Mortal Geography* (Persea Books, 2010), won the California Book Award for Poetry. Her website is www.alexandra teague.com.

STACY TINTOCALIS is the author of *The Tiki King* (Swallow Press, 2010). Her website is stacytintocalis.weebly.com.

SOUL CHOJ VANG is a widely anthologized poet and a contributor to *How Do I Begin?: A Hmong American Literary Anthology* (Heyday, 2011). His weblog, *Bridge~Owner,* is at hmongpoet.blogspot.com.

STEF WILLEN is the author of "Total Loss: A Column about Inventorying Other People's Tragedies" on *McSweeney's Internet Tendency*. Her weblog, *Eagles on My Face,* is at eaglesonmyface.blogspot.com.

MARIAH K. YOUNG won the James D. Houston Award for her forthcoming *Masha'allah and Other Stories* (Heyday, 2012).

ABOUT THE EDITOR

GAYLE WATTAWA is thoroughly addicted to contemporary literature and is always maxing out her allowable holds at the Berkeley Public Library. (Even so, she sometimes suspects that she reads more book reviews, literary journals, and lit news blogs than actual books.) She is the founding editor of the New California Writing series and editor of *Inlandia: A Literary Journey through California's Inland Empire*. She has supervised the assemblage of many literary anthologies as Heyday's acquisitions and editorial director.

ABOUT THE SERIES

NEW CALIFORNIA WRITING is an annual literary anthology that collects fresh and thought-provoking writing about California that has been published in the previous year, with a special emphasis on Californian writers, publications, and publishers.

Heyday welcomes and encourages your suggestions. For more information about what we are looking for and how to submit material, please visit http://www.heydaybooks.com/newcaliforniawriting.html.

HEYDAY
into California

About Heyday

Heyday is an independent, nonprofit publisher and unique cultural institution. We promote widespread awareness and celebration of California's many cultures, landscapes, and boundary-breaking ideas. Through our well-crafted books, public events, and innovative outreach programs we are building a vibrant community of readers, writers, and thinkers.

Thank You

It takes the collective effort of many to create a thriving literary culture. We are thankful to all the thoughtful people we have the privilege to engage with. Cheers to our writers, artists, editors, storytellers, designers, printers, bookstores, critics, cultural organizations, readers, and book lovers everywhere!

We are especially grateful for the generous funding we've received for our publications and programs during the past year from foundations and hundreds of individual donors. Major supporters include:

Anonymous; Evenor Armington Fund; James Baechle; Bay Tree Fund; S. D. Bechtel, Jr. Foundation; Barbara Jean and Fred Berensmeier; Berkeley Civic Arts Program and Civic Arts Commission; Joan Berman; Peter and Mimi Buckley; Lewis and Sheana Butler; California Council for the Humanities; California Indian Heritage Center Foundation; California State Library; Keith Campbell Foundation; Candelaria Foundation; John and Nancy Cassidy Family Foundation, through Silicon Valley Community Foundation; Center for California Studies; Compton Foundation; Nik Dehejia; Frances Dinkelspiel and Gary Wayne; George and Kathleen Diskant; Donald and Janice Elliott, in honor of David Elliott, through Silicon Valley Community Foundation; Euclid Fund at the East Bay Community Foundation; Eustace-Kwan Charitable Fund; Federated Indians of Graton Rancheria; Mark and Tracy Ferron; Judith Flanders; Furthur Foundation; The Fred Gellert Family Foundation; Wallace Alexander

Gerbode Foundation; Wanda Lee Graves and Stephen Duscha; Alice Guild; Coke and James Hallowell; Carla Hills; Sandra and Charles Hobson; G. Scott Hong Charitable Trust; James Irvine Foundation; Kendeda Fund; Marty and Pamela Krasney; Guy Lampard and Suzanne Badenhoop; LEF Foundation; Judy McAfee; Michael McCone; Joyce Milligan; National Endowment for the Arts; National Park Service; Steven Nightingale; Theresa Park; Patagonia, Inc.; Pease Family Fund, in honor of Bruce Kelley; The Philanthropic Collaborative; PhotoWings; Alan Rosenus; The San Francisco Foundation; San Manuel Band of Mission Indians; Savory Thymes; Hans Schoepflin; Contee and Maggie Seely; Sandy Shapero; William Somerville; Martha Stanley; Stanley Smith Horticultural Trust; Stone Soup Fresno; Roselyn Chroman Swig; James B. Swinerton; Swinerton Family Fund; Thendara Foundation; Tides Foundation; Lisa Van Cleef and Mark Gunson; Marion Weber; Whole Systems Foundation; John Wiley and Sons; Peter Booth Wiley and Valerie Barth; Dean Witter Foundation; and Yocha Dehe Wintun Nation.

Getting Involved
To learn more about our publications, events, membership club, and other ways you can participate, please visit www.heydaybooks.com.

green press INITIATIVE

Heyday is committed to preserving ancient forests and natural resources. We elected to print this title on 30% post consumer recycled paper, processed chlorine free. As a result, for this printing, we have saved:

14 Trees (40' tall and 6-8" diameter)
6 Million BTUs of Total Energy
1,473 Pounds of Greenhouse Gases
6,641 Gallons of Wastewater
421 Pounds of Solid Waste

Heyday made this paper choice because our printer, Thomson-Shore, Inc., is a member of Green Press Initiative, a nonprofit program dedicated to supporting authors, publishers, and suppliers in their efforts to reduce their use of fiber obtained from endangered forests.

For more information, visit www.greenpressinitiative.org

Environmental impact estimates were made using the Environmental Defense Paper Calculator. For more information visit: www.papercalculator.org.